Water and Light

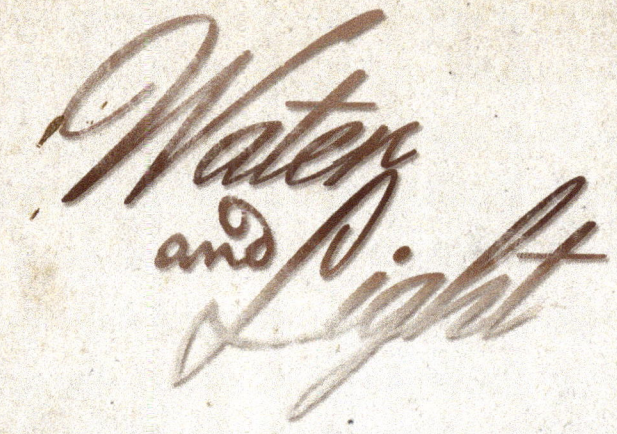

Water and Light

TRAVEL JOURNAL OF THE
Cambodian Mekong

George GROSLIER

Foreword by
Henri COPIN

Edited by
Kent DAVIS

Translated by
Pedro RODRÍGUEZ

Including supplemental appendices
and the complete original French text
of the 1931 edition, *Eaux et Lumières*.

DatAsia Press
MMXVI

About the cover and artistic enhancements:

George Groslier by his boat on the Mekong River in February 1929. Cover designer Rebecca Klein flipped the restored and colorized image for the cover layout. The original photo from the Groslier family archive appears on page x.

Endpapers feature a handwoven Cambodian silk, courtesy Gillian Green. Culs–de–lampe and frame images in the text are based on original sketches by George Groslier.

Acknowledgements

With gratitude to **Nicole Groslier Rea** for her guidance and inspiration in reissuing her father's works.

With the editor's special thanks to the Groslier family, to Joel Montague for access to his antique photo archive, and to Sophaphan Davis, Jon Dobbs, Lia Genovese, Tom Kramer and Duffy Rutledge for their special contributions.

A **Translation Fellowship** from the **National Endowment for the Arts** (**NEA**) awarded to Pedro Rodríguez subsidized this effort. To join the discussion on how art works visit the NEA at **www.arts.gov**

Production Credits

Edited by **Kent Davis**

Translated by: **Pedro Rodríguez**

Cover and design: **Rebecca Klein**

Text design: **Daria Lacy & Kent Davis**

French proofreader: **Sandra Bourgi**

Antique photo restoration & colorization: **Artsiom Yatsevich**

Archival assistance: **Darryl Collins, François Doré** and **Meng Dy**

DatASIA Press — www.DatASIA.us

© Copyright 2016. DatASIA, Inc. Holmes Beach, Florida

All rights reserved. No part of this book may be reproduced, stored in a retrieval system, or transmitted, in any form, without prior permission in writing from the publisher.

First Edition
ISBN 978-1-934431-87-0

Library of Congress Pre-Assigned Control Number: 2015942994

Printed simultaneously in the United States of America and Great Britain.

Table of Contents

Dedication. vii
Map of Cambodia ix
Foreword by Henri COPIN xi

Water and Light

Author Preface. 3
Part One – High Water 5
Part Two – Low Water 91
A Visit to Pailin 155

Appendices

George Groslier – Profile by Paul E. BOUDET 171
The Works of George GROSLIER 177
George Groslier Awards by Kent DAVIS 183
Sakrava – The Moon Songs by Kent DAVIS 195
Sakrava Songs in *Saramani* by Kent DAVIS 199
Model Sakrava Lyrics by Solang UK 209
The Lunar Origins of the Khmer People by Paul CRAVATH 222
The Game of Thirty-six Beasts by Kent DAVIS 229

Eaux et Lumières (1931)

Complete original French text .241
Préface. 242
Premier Partie — Hautes Eaux. 245
Deuxième Partie — Basses Eaux. 282

VI *Water and Light*

George and Nicole at the front gate of their Phnom Penh home in 1923.
Their historic residence still stands behind the National Museum of Cambodia at the corner of Preah Ang Makhak (St. 178) and Preah Ang Yukanthor (St. 19).

Dedicated to

Nicole Groslier Rea
June 15, 1918 - February 12, 2015

*Loving daughter of George Groslier
who inspired and witnessed
the publication of her father's literary works
twice in her lifetime.*

Water and Light

Map of Cambodia — 1928

❖ *Map of Cambodia - 1928*

In ancient times the Mekong cut Cambodia into quarters, as if rendering a coat of arms. Its main branch comes in from China. A second doubles back to the Great Lake, to pick up Angkor's reflection. The two others flow down to the sea. Phnom Penh knots them together. This was an enterprise undertaken with scale and pageantry. There is a bit of pomp to it, a bland magnificence

The upper and southeast branches meet obliquely. Noting the fact, the Father of Waters[1] thought to close it off and create a triangle. He thus laid down a new branch, to start in Kampong Cham and flow to Banam. This is the Tonlé Touch, or "little river," which divides the euphoniously named and exceptionally rich provinces of Srei Santhor and Sithor Kandal. Within this triangle the Mekong has enclosed the heart of Cambodia.

The great river is too great. Civilization spreads upstream too easily. Too many merchants have set up shop along that avenue, and too much sun blazes down upon it. In every season the current runs too fast, gnaws away at its channel, builds up islands where none are needed, and makes foreign lands of the two banks that it keeps apart.

But the Tonlé Touch, flowing near the giant that gives it life and absorbs it in death, is a river without headwaters or estuary. There is nothing at the end of its course that was not already there at the beginning. It waddles along, slowly, in no hurry to rejoin the tumultuous trunk from which it has diverged. The Tonlé Touch plays the fop, putting on airs between banks never too far apart for a child's voice to carry across.

George GROSLIER
September 28, 1929

---

1 Groslier here inverts the literal meaning of Mekong (mother of waters), perhaps to suggest a prior, creative force — a sort of Adam (namer, if not creator, of creatures) to the river's Eve.

x *Water and Light*

"Le grand garçon qui fait joujou avec le petit bateau."
"The big boy who plays with the little boat."
Suzanne Groslier's caption (top) for this photo of George
on the Mekong at low water, February 1930.

Foreword

"I find myself writing at water level..."

George Groslier opens his singular account of drifting through the shimmers and eddies of Cambodia's great Mekong River with this phrase.

Let us for a moment picture the scene: the author as figure on the prow, watchman of a launch gliding through muddy waters. With these words—the inaugural pact, as it were, of *Water and Light*—Groslier sets out his point of view: a man at water level writes. Nothing more.

His pretext is seemingly simple but in truth is far richer than it appears. We do not yet know the man behind the "I", or the nature of the water before him, or, of course, what it means for him to write from that place. For it is the blend of all these ingredients, dosed like the spices of an exotic Asian dish, that produces an inimitable flavor.

The figure on the prow

Let us begin with the "I": George Groslier. The keen-eyed observer addressing his readers was forty-two years of age when, in 1929, he recorded his two Mekong trips. His account was first published as *Eaux et Lumières* (*Water and Light*) in 1931 to coincide with the International Exposition in Paris. Unlike most colonial authors writing about French Indochina George had actually been born there in 1887, the son of Antoine Groslier, a civil servant working in the French protectorate of Cambodia since 1885.

At age two, however, George's mother Angélina decided that France was a far safer place for her son to grow up. They returned to their family home in

Marseille with George going on to study art at the School of Fine Arts in Paris[1] under French master painter Albert Maignan. His goal was to become a painter but through a twist of fate George instead found himself returning to Cambodia in 1910 on a mission for Albert Sarraut, then the Minister of Public Education.[2]

It was therefore at the age of 23 that George truly came to know his Cambodian birthplace. Dazzled by his first astounding glimpse of Angkor, and of the former splendor of the civilization that built it, he determined to explore the vast Khmer culture. This vision of the grand Angkorean past was the wellspring of his love for Cambodia and its culture. From that moment he spent his life sharing the knowledge of its prestigious past, its ruins, its enduring arts, and its endearing people.

One of his first fascinations was with the ritual dancers of the king's court; an elite group of women cloistered within the palace walls that practiced an art of sacred dance stretching back to Angkorean times. With the blessing of King Sisowath, and guidance from long-time resident Charles Gravelle, George studied the art in depth. In 1912, he returned to France to publish his first book, and the first academic look at this ancient tradition: *Danseuses Cambodgiennes – Anciennes et Modernes*.[3]

In 1913 George was again bound for Cambodia on Sarraut's behalf, this time for an adventure traveling deep into the jungles to document the kingdom's most remote Khmer temples. On his lonely journey (only accompanied by native porters) he wrote extensively about the structures, their architecture and history. Even more engaging are his personal observations of the indigenous arts, cultural traditions, village life and the people themselves.

At the outbreak of the First World War in 1914 George quickly returned to military service in the defense of France, with two important outcomes to follow in 1916. First, the book about his jungle trek was finally published as *À l'Ombre d'Angkor*.[4] Most significant, he met his future wife, Suzanne Poujade, and they were married in Paris on May 27.

---

1 The prestigious school was established in the mid-seventeenth century and is now known as L'école nationale supérieure des beaux-arts de Paris (ENSBA).
2 Albert Sarraut (1872–1962) played a major role in shaping George's career, especially while serving as Governor General of Indochina in 1911–1914 and 1916–1919. Returning to France he served as Minister of the Colonies in 1920–1924 and 1932. Sarraut went on to become Prime Minister for two terms during the Third Republic and continued his high-level political career until retiring in 1958.
3 Available in English as *Cambodian Dancers – Ancient & Modern*. DatAsia Press, 2012.
4 Available in English as *In the Shadow of Angkor – The Unknown Temples of Ancient Cambodia*. DatAsia Press, 2014.

With the war in Europe still raging, Governor General Sarraut gave George a new mission: to return to the Far East to assemble a French Air Force team. Though officially forbidden from joining him, George's bride Suzanne accompanied him on his return to Cambodia. In the passage below, Groslier biographer Kent Davis observes the man taking this life-changing voyage:

By his 29th year George had proven himself as a son, student, artist, author, civil servant and soldier....

> Close to midlife, as the ship carried him from West to East, his life also began to transform. The son had now become a husband and, in the coming year, he would be a father. The soldier would become a scholar, the student would become a teacher, and the loyal follower would be given the power to lead, allowing him to become an idealistic proponent of the Cambodian arts. It was all to unfold, as if by design, but of course George never saw his future as he lived it. None of us do.[5]

Reviving the arts of Cambodia

George (and Suzanne) arrived in Phnom Penh in May 1917. Sarraut quickly ended his military duties for another role that had, perhaps, been prearranged. As French historian Maxime Prodromidès describes, Groslier's new assignment

> was to spark a renaissance, in the very midst of the French colonists and their latent hostility. Henri Marchal had already had a world of trouble convincing the officers and administrators of his own country of the value of Cambodian decorative arts. They had laughed in his face. George Groslier went over their heads and made a convert of the governor general, Albert Sarraut.[6]

The governor charged him with founding a new school for the preservation and restoration of Cambodia's traditional arts, so the artist at the launch's prow began growing as both a scholar and teacher. With Sarraut's political support, Groslier proved himself to be a skilled organizer devoted to his passion for Khmer heritage. He proposed an ambitious plan that, in addition to the school, would create a museum and ultimately an Arts Service to create and distribute new works of Khmer art through a global network.

With the Cambodian sovereign's accord, and support and confidence of the governor and résidents, Groslier set about his tasks. His explicit objective: not only to

---

5 "Le Khmérophile: The Art and Life of George Groslier" by Kent Davis, from *Cambodian Dancers – Ancient & Modern*, p. 208. DatAsia Press, 2012.
6 Prodromidès, Maxime. 1997. *Angkor: chronique d'une renaissance*. Paris: Kailash. Pp. 120-121.

revive the traditional arts but also to insulate them from Western influence. This was in direct contrast to the School of Fine Arts of Indochina that would later seek to train Asian students with Western styles.[7] Groslier proceeded to organize his school, devising and regulating its artistic curriculum. Simultaneously, he founded the Albert Sarraut Museum, drafting the blueprints himself and overseeing construction before taking the reins as its first curator to collect and expand the collections. Today, it still operates as the National Museum of Cambodia.

The Arts Service became the heart of Cambodia's artistic production and distribution. Under its auspices casts, photographs, and brochures made their way to the public and the products of the artist's guilds appeared in such fairs as the Paris Colonial Exposition of 1931 and even the later exposition in San Francisco.[8] The program certainly served the interests of France, celebrating the colonial power for its protection of Cambodian culture. However, it also served the interests of Cambodia, spotlighting the kingdom as a unique entity within the landscape of Indochina, and fostering an assemblage of a national cultural heritage that is today fundamental to Khmer identity.

It was actually as museum director that Groslier played a leading role in one of Indochina's most sensational criminal affairs. In 1923 Groslier engineered the highly publicized arrest of one overeager "lover" of Khmer antiquities, a man who planned to loot exquisite statues from the remote temple of Bantéay Srey. The perpetrator, however, was not just an ordinary man who found himself on the wrong side of the law. He was André Malraux, who would later become a recognized writer and political activist, and the future French Minister of Culture under Charles de Gaulle.

Though the arrest was a success, and the statues returned, the controversial court cases that ensued shook the colonial administration from Indochina to Paris. During the trial Malraux became a vocal and highly visible opponent of the colonial administration, calling many of their practices into question. But after his final return to France in January 1926 Malraux never looked back to the people or politics of French Indochina. His actions there seem to have just been another rung in the ladder of his own career. Groslier, on the other hand, remained steadfast. He devoted the rest of his life to Cambodia and its people. Indeed, he did so up to his dying breath.

---

7 The school opened in Hanoi in 1925 as the École Supérieure des Beaux-Arts de l'Indochine.
8 For more details, see Gabrielle Abbe's 2008 paper, "La « rénovation des arts cambodgiens» George Groslier et le Service des arts, 1917-1945". *Bulletin De L'Institut Pierre Renouvin*. 27 (1): 61-76.

In addition to his academic publications, Groslier began crafting remarkable fiction in the mid-1920s. His first novel, *The Road of the Strong* (1925) was soon followed by *Return to Clay* (1928), which won the 1929 Grand Prize for Colonial Literature in France. Both books intimately dealt with the clash of Western values and Asian cultures.

Discover, explore, meditate, dig deeper, write: this was Groslier's way, as is abundantly evident in *Water and Light*. This is the literary style of the passenger observing the river flowing under the prow of the launch. He is at once sensitive artist, acknowledged scholar, and top institutional administrator. He has vision; he is a fervent protector of Cambodian arts and heritage; and he is himself, we must recall, a child of Cambodia, who speaks the language, knows the customs, and savors every quotidian detail that he discovers and rediscovers of Khmer life.

The water, the river...

We come now to the water flowing before our eyes. This is, of course, the Cambodian Mekong of the title, charging down from the heights of the Himalayas to cross China, delimit Laos, and irrigate Cambodia before spreading its delta in Vietnam. It is a giant, Asia's fourth-largest river. The Chinese call it "the turbulent river." In Khmer its name means "Mother of Rivers" or "Mother of Waters" (though Groslier once characterizes it as the "Father of Waters"). In Vietnam it is called "River of the Nine Dragons." This force of nature, this myth, is feted every year in the great Festival of Waters, with pirogue races, offerings, libations, and revelry. "The river flows on into the sky," in Groslier's striking image, a cosmogonic vision of the alliance of two elements, river and sky, the land seeming to vanish at high water.

Naturally, the river figures on every page of the travelogue, for it is the focus of life, for human being, beast, fish, village, and pagoda alike. The capital city, Phnom Penh, sits at the Four Branches, the confluence of the Bassac and the Tonlé Sap. "The Mekong cut Cambodia into quarters, as if rendering a coat of arms," writes Grolier, underscoring once more the country's fluvial identity. The Tonlé Sap, which designates both the great lake and fluvial branch that leads to it, has a peculiarity: it flows in one direction part of the year, swelled by the melting snows of Tibet and filling its immense basin, then reverses course for the rest of the year, when its flow diminishes and the lake gradually empties. In this flat, low country the river invades land, forests, and pile-mounted villages. The lake's area can expand from three hundred to ten thousand square kilometers. Treetops break the surface like vertical plumes, and one travels by boat from one to the next. At low water the land, now laden and nourished with silt, reemerges.

The river, then, is the beating heart in the center of the country, irrigating the land with its vital flow. Systole, diastole—low water, high water—twice yearly. This was the rhythm, also, of Groslier's mission and bipartite diary. The latter, moreover, is split also between the symbolic dimension of nature and anecdotes of daily life, gleaned from the shifting glimmers of watery reflection.

Also living off the river was a kingdom, with its history and institutions, all under the French Protectorate since 1863, to stave off powerful Annamite and Siamese neighbors with a thirst for conquest.[9] In 1887 the kingdom joined Tonkin, Annam, and Cochin China in the Union Indochinoise, and in 1897 a French résident supérieur began governing the country, presiding over the Council of Ministers, and countersigning royal decrees, as per the constitution granted by the king. In the 1930s the country had a population of about two and a half million. The society was essentially rural and organized around villages and pagodas. France launched infrastructure projects, building canals, ports, and hospitals, but the economy was initially directed toward present-day Vietnam, which was much more populous and socially and culturally different. Viets, in fact, held a great many administrative posts—too many, some believed. This is the country in the background of *Water and Light*, a Cambodia as yet untouched by the great crises of Indochina in the 1930s and beyond.

"Was I writing for myself?"

The term travel diary usually refers to a chronological account of events occurring over the course of a physical displacement. Groslier's travel diary meets this definition; most chapter headings are calendar dates and one can usually follow his progress on a map, finding the places he goes and the pagodas he visits. The purpose of such a travel diary is to set up signposts to frame the reported information.

However, the author takes the trouble to lay out ulterior intentions in a few prefatory pages. In these it appears that the travel-diary structure is only superficial. He has written his text after the fact, and then reworked, pruned, condensed it, thinking especially of the reader who knows nothing of Cambodia. To him Groslier wishes to show how singularly picturesque the country is, wishes to seduce as well

---

[9] It was thanks to the Protectorate that, in 1907, Cambodia reclaimed provinces that had been annexed by Siam in the 15th century. Among these was Siem Reap, where Angkor is to be found.

as instruct. Moreover, adds Groslier, "During this voyage...my pen was swayed by my fifteen years of Cambodian life." We are thus far from the objectivity of a text composed in the moment with an eye toward documentary accuracy. It is, on the contrary, subjectivity that Groslier invokes—in composing the text, in making the author central, in filtering everything through his own experience, in choosing purposely to seduce a well-defined type of reader. The book is more work of art than documentary account.

Indeed, Groslier employs certain literary procedures that push his travel diary toward literature, and away from documentary account. The first of these is his reworking of the text to avoid the humdrum repetition of sights seen day to day. As a result, each chapter brings a surprise, and there is a ceaseless change of subject, theme, and point of view, as in the notebook of a painter producing a new sketch daily.

The first chapter is the Mekong of color and infinite shades. The next is the Mekong of sound, with an extraordinary aural "landscape" perceived at night, and thus partly reconstructed by ear. There follows the actual landscape revealed at daylight, rediscovered by the eyes. Elsewhere the landscape is seen as a series of juxtaposed vignettes, which the painter runs through, evaluates, and recomposes. The reader follows along through hesitations and selections, invited, as it were, to become a painter himself. Later come dialogues with fishermen, children, and a bonze, the portrait of a shrimp, an explanation of how fish is harvested and put to use. There are comedic scenes with a sailor of the government launch, whom Groslier christens Eh!, after the interjection he ends up using to summon him.[10] And so on. The rich palette allows us to see and hear places, beings, celebrations, rituals, and pagodas in narration of constant renewal, surprise, and delight.

But the continual shifts of perspective and theme have a purpose: they serve to compose an impressionistic tableau of the land of the Khmer. This overview borrows from history (the origins of Phnom Penh, the feats of explorers), economics (the

---

[10] Groslier has in fact been reproached for not giving Eh! a proper name, and thereby treating him as an object, a nonentity unworthy of interest. Some have seen in this a hint of the conquering colonial ideology, with its attendant denial of the "*indigènes*" (literally "indigenous peoples," but the term *indigène* is practically a slur in present-day French). Groslier's position with respect to that ideology is certainly complex and ambiguous, as illustrated in his novels where the author takes opposing points of view on these matters. In the case of Eh!, however, it must be noted that the character evolves along with his mission. From uncouth, unrefined, inconstant beginnings he develops for the author into an endearing figure—the attentive parent of a child whom he brings along aboard the launch and bathes in the Mekong—and eventually becomes a sailor of rank and responsibility. It is hard to see how the empathy he evidently felt for the Khmer could lead Groslier to regard his fellow Cambodian so negatively as to draw a caricature.

fishing industry), sociology (status and role of the Chinese in Khmer society), religion (the purpose of pagodas, the role of the bonzes, the rituals of the Buddhism of the Smaller Vehicle in Cambodia), the observation of daily life (encounters, feasts, negotiations), archeology (pagodas again), and ethnography (ethnicities present in Cambodia). Atop this overview Groslier lays a visceral sense of encroaching and threatening Western modernity, of the ugliness that "we Europeans sell to these artists," of cast concrete set next to wooden architectural treasures. At times, in fact, he can even take the Khmer to task for being so languid, for smiling so much, for mediocrity in the face of what is coming.

Diverse as they are, these pages have a unity that extends beyond the plan. This is due to Groslier's gaze, and thus to his writing, which is first that of a painter, whose rich, thick, concrete, precious vocabulary generates sumptuous images, like that aural night on the river, with the "propeller grinding up moonlight," or the "altars of bloody crimson, gleaming with gold and alight with flames," among many others. Images employed for their aesthetic quality, to render the unutterable beauty of the country, to translate Groslier's emotions, the beating of his Khmer heart. It is through images, too, that he endeavors to plumb the sense of his emotions.

Like a long-sought image blooming in Proust[11] after long analyses prompted by irresistible emotions, like a net dragging aboard a catch, Groslier seeks to give form to the buried secrets he can sense within beings, and within places. It is emotion stirred by the moist land that spurts between his toes, gorged with Cambodian sunshine—the land, that is, of the earth's original life, the clay of creation that provides a title for one of his novels. He writes: "all of Cambodia is made of this traveling mud."

The same inquiry, before the spectacle of women at their bath, possessed the natural, immaterial animal beauty of eternity. "Crude and perfect" is his description, for he sees in them the innocent, timeless beauty of the stone statues of Angkor. Elsewhere he speaks of "adolescent populations," but adds that "the child [the Khmer as a people]...bears the burden of an old man." In this story, Groslier strives to share a secret: his own attachment to a country, a culture, a way of being and an art of living.

---

11 French novelist, essayist and critic Marcel Proust (1871–1922) is regarded as one of the greatest authors of all time. His best known novel, À la recherche du temps perdu, explores the relationship of experience, memory, art and morality, and is available in English as In Search of Lost Time.

The "Ailleurs" of George Groslier

These few dozen pages carry exceptional weight in the literary depiction of Cambodia. No other writer has concentrated so many disparate and complementary qualities, all in the service of the gaze and prose of a poet. For Groslier, expression through poetic writing is not a matter of ornament; rather, it serves to elucidate truths perceptible at first only through the emotions. It is his emotional life as a Cambodian—as someone who is both external to Cambodia, in the manner of a Frenchman, and yet a child of the country—that Groslier conveys, without ever relinquishing the learning that he possesses in addition.

The genre of the *récit de mission*, or travelogue of a government assignment, was in fact evolving in Groslier's day to incorporate the subjective point of view into documentary text. Roland Dorgelès led the way with *On the Mandarin Road* (1925), exceptional coverage of a changing Indochina based on eye-catching current events. Later, Michel Leiris's *L'Afrique fantôme* (1934), an account of a great expedition to Dakar-Djibouti, in which Leiris keeps simultaneous diaries for the African crossing proper and for his intimate thoughts. It is the beginning of "reflexive anthropology," which destroys the belief in the social sciences in absolute scientific objectivity, and begins to recognize knowledge that includes the emotions.

We might therefore consider George Groslier as precursor to a genre of travel-writer that flourishes today. He was a man whose pen could stroke that singular balance between things he saw, encountered, and felt, within his own dreams embodied by the foreign land he explored. For Groslier, painting Cambodia in words was an act of sharing his innermost feelings, his ideals and his aspirations about a foreign country. In French, we call this "l'Ailleurs"—ideas of places and realities that are simultaneously far away, and yet held close in our hearts. As Groslier painted Cambodia he painted himself and his ideal dream... his *Ailleurs*, his feeling of Elsewhere if you will.

For such reasons as these we should take a fresh look at Groslier, who so deftly depicted the colors and forms of the ties that, at times, bind him to Cambodia, and attach us to Asia.

Henri COPIN
Nantes – July 2015

The author extends his special thanks to Florence Tison for her help with this foreword.

Henri COPIN

Henri Copin is internationally recognized as a leading specialist in French colonial literature for his lectures, critiques, works and analyses that help these historical masterpieces live again.

Copin first traveled to French Indochina in his mother's arms after his birth in Paris in 1945. There, he spent his first 16 years in Vietnam and Cambodia witnessing the Indochina War, the waning of French presence in the Indochinese Peninsula, and the early years of Cambodian, Laotian and Vietnamese independence.

Photo by Laurence Copin

A century of shared history between France and Indochina drew him to devote his professional life to the culturally rich literature of the region. In 1994 he received his degree at the Sorbonne, with Harmattan publishing his thesis in 1996: *L'Indochine dans la littérature française des années vingt à 1954, Exotisme et altérité* [*Indochina in French Literature from 1920-1954, Exoticism and Otherness*]. He was appointed Professor of Humanities at Saint Louis, Senegal and taught at the Center for Applied Linguistics in Dakar before returning to France where he is now a permanent professor and lecturer at the University of Nantes.

Water and Light

TRAVEL JOURNAL OF THE
Cambodian Mekong

Author Preface

The reader will probably find it useful to know how this book came about.

Duty called me to conduct an inspection of the pagodas of Cambodia, and I began with those that stand along the Mekong. I knew that I would find the greatest number there, along the river's almost two thousand kilometers, for in Cambodia, as in most countries of the world, the population is densest and life most picturesque on riverbanks.

Sailing for nearly two months in all, I made two journeys: in September–October, when the waters flood entire provinces in their fury, and in February–March, when in certain spots the same waters drop so low as to bar passage to all craft but pirogues.[1] I thus saw the river in its two most striking states. So great a shift in the waters must quite obviously transform the life and look of the banks. If I have managed here and there to capture something of these shifting seasons, then I will have dodged the monotony into which notes on a single subject tend to fall.

No complete work has yet been published on the Cambodian Mekong. Indeed, I do not think that any European has hitherto explored it as systematically, as gradually, or under such favorable conditions as I have just done, stopping and disembarking as many as thirty times on certain days. I could even claim that a tour like this, made by an observer with the writing mood upon him, will perhaps not be undertaken again anytime soon, if ever again. Launch travel is in steady decline, roads are gradually covering the land, and the automobile has become the chief mode of transport. Moreover, the old Cambodia has been so thoroughly upset by Western influence that soon any voyage, even at a rower's pace, will be thoroughly disappointing.

---

1   Small, flat-bottom boats commonly seen on Cambodian waterways.

Travelogue writers are usually tourists on their first trip through a country. I should therefore apologize for writing these notebooks so late in my sojourn, for I have already traveled all over Cambodia and lived in it for more than fifteen years.

This first admission leads me to a second. Contrary to custom, these notes have not been published as written, or in the order of composition. They therefore do not relate precisely what I saw during my voyage. In fact, I have allowed myself to add a few things that did not exist at the time or at the place described.

During this voyage of several weeks my pen was swayed by my fifteen years of Cambodian life. If some lively memory was called forth by the present moment and knocked on my mind's door, I let it in. The impulse was irresistible. However, despite this mixture of old impressions and things seen in the moment, I have been able — out of respect for the reader — to select and rearrange my notes, whittling more than six hundred pages down to about two hundred.

Yes, I proceeded out of respect for the reader. Was I writing for myself? No. I therefore had to fashion an account that would be comprehensible to a man who had never seen Cambodia: a man, in fact, who would never see it. In selecting and filtering, I could not draw on the innocence of a traveler disembarking for the first time — that is, on the mere ignorance of the reader, who stays home — so I thought it necessary to give my tableaux, however strange, the sort of contour and color that anyone snug in his armchair could easily understand. Hence the selection and rearrangement of notes.

I have tried my best to approach my readers, and I hope that in certain passages they will take a few steps themselves and meet me halfway. I hope they will make the effort to understand me when tempted to pass a harsh judgment. After all, could we not agree that, in more than one instance, it is not my clumsiness but the very subject of the book that keeps us apart?

George Groslier

Part One
High Water

21 September – 20 October 1929

"The sacred ground is an islet taken up almost entirely by the sanctuary."
[Groslier]

21 September

Phnom Penh — Ansrei Sat

I find myself writing at water level. Just to the side of my page the water whooshes and coils, conch-like. The top of the page seems to extend beyond the paper's edge to the high prow of my launch. The anchor, which I view from below, seems to grapple the clouds.

The river flows on into the sky and is filled with it. In spots the water lies flat and still and glacial. Farther on the current stops cold at a sand bar and briefly doubles back in a whirl of short waves. The wind whips these into a froth, raises them, flattens them, like a hand running whimsically through a coat of hair. Only when we notice the transparency of this steel and mother-of-pearl river do we notice the muddy waters rolling through it, thick with ochre and lees.

Spread out under the rising sun, fading fast into the distance, Phnom-Penh looked like a narrow scarf, waving, a bit limply, for my departure. The green and yellow roof tiles of the Royal Palace and the Silver Pagoda's spire sparkled like sequins.

As the hours passed the weather changed, and we met with a different sky at every bend in the river. We lowered the canvas to blot out the sun. In the distance the rain was a drapery fringe on tin-colored clouds. Rainy season. The water had gone as high as it would go. In rhythmic gusts, like a serene and prodigious breathing, the monsoon glides in unobstructed from the Indian Ocean along the Mekong, and the river spreads to welcome it.

No more banks. The river has scaled the five meters to reach the once-dry lowlands. Now it spreads to every horizon, up to the very floorboards of the

"Only pirogues ply the waters between houses." [Groslier]

huts. The banana trees have lost their trunks, and other trees are afloat. Only pirogues ply the waters between houses, where, for lack of land to stand on, chickens, dogs, and snakes have sought refuge along with the inhabitants. Of the useless, drowned carts I can see only the tips of the draft shafts, which break the surface like breathing tubes. Trapped on raised platforms, the oxen stand there like pitiable statues. They are brought aquatic plants to eat. A sow and her piglets sleep on a raft fashioned from three banana trunks. The raft is moored to a hut and covered with a small thatch roof. When we stop the launch drags a meter-long wake into the gardens, through sapodillas and lemon trees. Squatting low, we tie up to tree trunks at the height where they fork off into boughs and birds start to nest.

The pagoda is less than a hundred meters off. Between it and me lies water. Past the spot where I have disembarked children up to their shoulders in water are pushing along a pirogue. Little grey fish flee from the steps of a perron[2] erected five meters above the river's mean level.

---

2 Staircase.

"The sala swarms and hums with encamped bonzes." [Groslier]

The sacred ground is an islet taken up almost entirely by the sanctuary. Livestock has found refuge on what little dry land remains around the peristyle.[3] I cross the ox stall. Inside the temple I seek out the altar amid piled sacks of corn. The god has pride of place among the vermillion ears that have spilled from the sacks. A warm odor of manure wafts in through the windows, and the water whispers plaintively.

The bonze cells are so many sampans tied up amid the trees. Spanning the gaps between them are rickety footbridges, bamboo poles rigged on easels. A coconut farm whets its palms against a tin-colored sky and plunges its colonnade into black, viscous waters. To the left the *sala*[4] swarms and hums with encamped bonzes, sitting before their meal in yellow robes, reminding me of the ears of corn in the sanctuary. Pirogues grouped flank to flank in "banana

---

3   A series of columns surrounding a building or courtyard. Buddhist temples generally have many columns around their perimeter.

4   A common, Southeast-Asian open-air structure devoid of walls and consisting of a roof supported by pillars. They can be simple thatched shelters or massive structures like the Hall of Dance at the Grand Palace in Phnom Penh. The architectural concept is the same in both cases.

bunches" yank at their ropes. They rock the liquid reflections brimming between their gunwales, and disturb the reflections on which they float.

❧❀☙

The next pagoda to seek out was Ansrei Sat, opposite the preceding one, nestled among the trees on the river's invisible far bank. Indeed, when we got there we found that it stood *between* the trees and the waters.

At first we saw only its reflection at our feet, in the river. A water snake shot past, tearing through the reflection with its upright head. I climbed down from the launch into a pirogue. Looking from a lower angle between dark branches, I spied the façade and the frayed roof above their blurry doubles in the water. Into airy reality they rose, less concrete, less heavy, less shimmery. In front of these two pagodas, joined at the base and looking for all the world like the queen of spades, was a row of milkweed plants, their branches parallel like the lines of a musical staff.

Sheltered on a patch of dry ground in the shade of a long courtyard was a wonderful thing. It was long, lacquered in black, inlaid with gold ornaments. It lay belly up, curved like a bow that was slack but still quivering from an arrow it had loosed. It was a racing pirogue, aground, fat at the flanks like a fruit quarter, protected from sun and rain — beyond the reach of the vast stretches of water awaiting it. As I passed I could not resist caressing this lovely thoroughbred, kept immobile under fresh caulking, preserved against fatigue and wear, ready for the following month's great Water Festival.

Night of 21–22 September

I paid no heed to the site when we stopped, and now night has fallen, the sort of night whose cloud-lined sky absorbs all moonlight. I have placed my lamp at the fore of the launch, near the anchor, as far away from me as possible, because of the insects. The lamp casts its light onto the tree to which we have hitched our craft. I see whitish tamarind branches and a peppering of little leaves. Beyond this, no matter how hard I squint, I see nothing, a dark void. But there is, in fact, a village.

Behind me lies the river. I can hear it. I can hear that liquid night, and nothing else. I know damn well where it starts. Right there, at my feet. But where does it end? Ah! Over there, at that lonely fire burning on the opposite bank, which my map tells me is two kilometers off. How high it is! How the golden point shines, so far off! That, then, is where the two nights meet, the one trying to escape the earth, the other leaning on it for support. And I sit between them, suspended.

I turn to look at the bank, the invisible bank, that keeps me so close to the water's edge, that floats on the water's sound. Little by little I come to know this sound, sort out its components, and locate them in space. To the northeast, that halting rustle on water-logged fabric must surely be the sound of banana leaves as they beat the flowing water. Yes, there is a banana tree there, its trunks submerged. To my right, the nasal blasts and squishing mud must mean buffalo. So the bank must lead off to their corral, and the water must promptly run aground. I follow the bank on three separate planes until human voices, momentarily roused, sketch out the first hut of the village. Shortly thereafter a tam-tam[5] marks the hour: time for the day's last prayer.

---

5 A percussion instrument similar to a small gong.

This instantly situates the pagoda, in a swath of darkness where I had been feeling around in vain, for the waters had grown too distant and silent and left me to my own devices. Now, bringing to a close the semi-horizon that I have just conjured from the void, we come to the sound of a backwash, whose peculiar splash could only occur between tied-up pirogues. Indeed, from time to time I can hear their flanks bump together.

I see it as plain as day: the village, which the river has restored, molding it with its murmurs. The all but imperceptible plop of the sapodilla, the cleaner plop of the harder guava, the water-spurting splash of the weighty grapefruit — do you really believe that if one of those fruits falls I wouldn't recognize it? Oh, the village is there, all right — invisible, sonorous, concrete — just as I sense it. I began with nothing. I can still see nothing. The puzzle has come together tree by tree, plot by plot, flowing in with the current, assembling itself around my cabin as the little waves deliver the pieces. The whole has gotten clearer and clearer, forming in my mind behind my blinded eyes, my ears seizing on each piece in turn.

The rain has arrived and crackles on the leaves. I have hitherto estimated only distances, in a strictly horizontal advance. Now the rain sings of heights, tracing the contour of fronds. I listen as it models the leaf canopy. I had missed the big trees, just to the left of the buffalo. Where previously I had suspected nothing the prickling at water level has revealed grasses: floating weeds that a river-turned-smuggler transports in secret.

22 September

Kâs Kèo – Tuk Khléang – Kâs Noréa

At dawn I checked the nocturnal picture sketched by my ears. Everything was where they'd said it would be. My eyes took in the shape of the trees that the rain had described. Except for natives emerging from their sleep, a loom on a veranda, the shiny violet of some eggplants, and a plow hanging from a bush, I had heard everything that now reappeared before me. What the daylight now contributed seemed fraudulent and gratuitous. Everything that the storm, the river, and the night had selected, simplified, and presented to me and me alone the insouciant day now revealed indiscriminately.

The pagoda of Kâs Kèo looks as if it had been torn from the flood by a gigantic hand, with muddy roots and clods of earth trailing behind. Here, rather than encumber the sanctuary, the sacks of corn fill granaries. These are scattered around the monastery and erected on stilts. Every pagoda has a great mast proclaiming its presence far and wide, with Hamsa[6] the bird riding at the summit under a quintuple parasol. Here, undermined by water, the mast stands crooked. It might very well topple, but the bonzes do not care. Mango trees, arecas, and coconut palms too remain standing as if by miracle in this viscous mud, where one sinks in past the ankle. The dogs are famished, mere skeletons, too weak to bark. They drag themselves through mud that sucks at their legs. They stagger over, pause to relieve themselves, and stagger off again, gloomier than before, dragging their rumps on the ground.

---

6 Sanskrit name for the mythical swan or goose that served as the sacred vehicle of Sarawati and figures in many other Hindu legends.

It is morning. Pirogues laden with victuals and propelled by beautifully dressed women glide all the way in to the temple's perron, but the islet retains an air of fragile deliverance, as if threatened by some ignoble force that I cannot identify.

We arrive at the pagoda of Tuk Khléang, modest and harmonious. The fine pediment shows Vishnu[7] astride Garuda[8] the bird within a decor of flames. The reliefs rise in old gold against a background of flashy emerald-green, suggesting the opulence of this art as it was before Western influence. Neither partition nor high wall beneath this roof. Curves and slippery forms provide a certain lightness, and help keep the roof aloft like the columns on which the structure rests. The pupils of the pagoda's school recite the letters of the alphabet in acerbic, perfunctory tones. They are feigning work to ignore, or perhaps to acknowledge, the great event: the arrival of a Frenchman. Have no fear, boys! I am not the school inspector.

The head of the monastery suggests that we go see another pagoda nearby, over there. Accurate to perhaps a quarter-degree, his finger points somewhere over the liquid plain, to a place where I can see nothing but trees without trunks, like heads of cauliflower. Off we go, whither the clairvoyant finger commands.

Donning his toga once more, the bonze barks out vigorous, monosyllabic orders, casting seeds that instantly sprout: "A pirogue! A screen! A mat! Schoolchildren to row!" And the pirogue glides to my feet. I take a seat at the center. Ahead of me nine boys aged ten to twelve, their torsos naked, leap in two by two, settling by instinct into rows ranged by height. The smallest boy boards the farthest forward and squats, alone, upon the boat's neck. How many settle in behind me? I dare not turn around, for despite its eight-meter length the pirogue is less than fifty centimeters wide. My Western rump occupies it port to starboard, with two fingers' worth of flesh bulging over each side. "Go!" says the bonze, and nine backs bend to it.

Soon the water calms down. We seem to have struck bottom, but what do I know? The little rowers cry out all of a sudden, and I realize that what I have taken to be still water is in fact quivering with a current. To cross these

---

7 The supreme god of the Vaishnavite tradition of Hinduism. Depicted in numerous avatars and referred to by innumerable names.
8 Mythical bird-like creature in Hindu theology. Mount of Vishnu.

dangerous eddies, the boys make the efforts of men. They dip into the water with their short paddles, plunge them like daggers into the great, treacherous body, and have soon got the better of it by dint of wily youth. Their cries reveal cruel teeth, and their laughter suggests nothing so much as an imminent bite. When they reach open water, after launching the pirogue into that peaked hollow between the two liquid festoons raised by our speed, they stop and place their paddles on their laps. I can hear them panting in the silence. They turn to observe me. Where a moment earlier I had seen thick-haired napes bobbing along with our swift clip I now see quizzical faces.

The pirogue flexes and slackens like a bow. Fastened to the floodwaters by its paddle-daggers, it expands at the flanks. As it breathes I watch water leak in through ill-caulked seams. My feet are bathing in it. It is warm, and it comes and goes. The bailing pail is afloat, a tiny pirogue sailing within the big one.

Our passage flushes water birds from the archipelago of trees. They emerge alternately, displaying their various modes of flight: the slow flap of waders, the hurried flap of teals. Two ruby-headed sarus cranes[9] come right at us, their heads snug against their backs, their legs stiff and clamped to their bellies. And from this Japanese engraving fall into my hand a few drops of the water the birds have carried aloft in their feathers at take-off.

The sought-after pagoda lies ahead, behind huge trees covered with cormorant nests, dome nests each with a black tail protruding. I leave behind the dazzling water and enter the darkness of the temple. Laid out on the slabs, to keep cool, are about ten bonzes, sleeping so soundly that my footsteps do not rouse them. And, indeed, what is there to rouse them? They have not yet finished their nap, the day nap that follows the night nap, every day's following every night's.

No matter. Let us leave this place. The pagoda is ridiculous, built of concrete. I had been warned at the very entrance, by the two French soldiers painted in green, one to either side of the gate. In a cell I had seen a Buddha lying on its side since the previous year, distempered with Ripolin paint,[10] a doorknob of cut crystal set in his belly.

---

9   Standing nearly six feet tall, with wingspan of up to a hundred inches, the majestic saurus crane (*Grus antigone*) is the largest flying bird native to Australia, South and Southeast Asia.
10 A fast-drying commercial enamel paint available since 1887. The products were so well known that "ripolin" became synonymous with enamel paints in general and French dictionaries have included the word since 1907.

We tie up the launch for the night to a dead tree near the pagoda of Kâs Noréa. The propeller stops turning in a river of silver, but between us and the bank, under corn leaves and little cones of foam, the water shades from ochre to hues of asphalt. Oxen trapped on their platforms for the past eight days observe the tricolor flag draped over our poop.[11]

I ask the village chief whether we might buy some provisions.

"Ah, Sir, we have nothing here."

"No eggs?"

"It is not the season, and the flood has upset the chickens. They will not lay any." (The chickens have turned chicken!)

"Cucumbers?"

"There are none."

"What? Not even a lemon or a sapodilla? On those trees over there..."

"Those are not ripe, Sir."

"Fish, at least. Do you mean to tell me there is no water?"

"No fish either. As for water, there is too much."

Is the man mocking me? No. With too much water around (you have to be ready for anything when a Cambodian gives an explanation), there is not a clod of earth to be found where one might dig up worms to bait the creels with.

"What about the catch with the casting net, the one I see drying over there?"

"A very small fish, Sir. And that was this morning. It has since been eaten."

So I have nothing fresh to dine on this evening, but I am told of a celebration to take place at the pagoda tomorrow.

The chief of the pagoda appears. The usual protocol. I hand him my official letter, written in French and Khmer. It is signed by His Royal Highness the Prince, Minister of the Interior and of Religious Cults, and bears his purple seal, big and round like the face of a girl.

---

11 An enclosed structure at the stern of a boat.

22 September ❖ *Kâs Kèo – Tuk Khléang – Kâs Noréa*

The old man takes the missive and looks it over for a long time. He hands it back, and I assume that he has read it, but then he says that his eyes are bad. We call over a secretary bonze, who normally ought to be able to read it, but he has forgotten his glasses. A novice goes off to fetch the glasses. The glasses arrive at last, but night has fallen. So off we go to the monastery, nice and slow... Who in Cambodia is in a hurry?

The letter is read aloud. At last they understand my task and that they are to help me in every way to complete it. The chief of the monastery shakes my hand, offers me a chair, and confirms the lack of eggs and earthworms — whence the lack of chickens, the lack of fish, the misery of the people. He also confirms the news of tomorrow's celebrations. Goodnight. I return to my launch for a canned meal of sauerkraut and meat. I will attend the celebrations.

23 September

Village Ceremony

The pagoda emerges from the waters and the morning as if from a crystal globe. A tam-tam beckons. In the temple, along the central nave, old devotees are unrolling carpets and mats. Pirogues big and small, heaped with the faithful, glide in toward us from the cardinal points, like needles in brocade. Women, of all ages, predominate. They handle the rowing and carry their paddles as they enter the sanctuary. Inside, they set the paddles down along the wall of an aisle, lest the wicked abscond with their pirogues while they — the women, not the pirogues — tend to their devotions.

Offerings on great copper platters covered with cones of red fabric now begin to accumulate on the mats. At first I see only the many colors, the ornamentation, of this opulent still-life: candles and incense sticks being lit; natural flowers and flowers made of fabric; ingenious little decorative motifs, made of rolled and braided flowers of cut paper. Finally I turn my attention to the offerings themselves.

Ah! Inhospitable Buddha! Pyramids of bananas! No lemons in the land, eh? Here they are by the dozen, skewered on fine bamboo like billiard marks, and stuck into rice balls. "The sapodillas are not ripe, Sir!" No indeed. The ripe ones, as I can now see, are in those baskets. Two eggs here, five there. The chickens of the land have laid a few since yesterday evening. I had thought only ducks would lay at dawn. Now that I mention it, there are duck eggs too.

At my feet I count eighteen platters, arranged in platoon columns. They hold more than a hundred cups and basins; bowls brimming with fish soup, curries, lemongrass pork stews, chicken soups, rice soups, soups thick with everything that I could not buy yesterday evening, soups prepared from the misery of the wretched people, on whom the bonzes took pity. The center of the pagoda is a restaurant display, a fruit market, an illuminated banquet table. The air smells of incense, candles, hot rice, tobacco, betel, oil, cooked fish. A three-meter, cement Buddha dominates this veritable cornucopia, his size betokening a formidable stomach. With him are eighteen bonzes come to bow and pray as if sitting down to dinner. To judge by the spread before them, he and they could indulge in a three-day debauch without once coming up for air.

Everyone, clergyman or layman, chats away. Non-bonzes come and go, light candles and incense sticks, smoke, or, if idle, laugh. They make themselves at home. Children play. The tardy arrive without haste. Tam-tams resound. And suddenly I understand why lemons and eggs have appeared, why hopelessly elusive fish have been found, despite the flooded land, the seasonal fall from grace, and the general poverty.

Women on one side and men on the other have piously brought their hands together, fingers splayed. A single deep, bleating voice, so soft and fragile, so fraught with age and wear as to be pathetic, rises in the advancing silence. This voice, this ghost of a voice, chants a psalm stanza, which all the men repeat. The voice rises again, and the rumbling choir answers.

For a long time I search in vain for the source of the voice. At last I spy a far-off figure, separated from the double file of bonzes and crouching on a mattress of amaranth silk. It is the old, nearly blind chief of the pagoda, immobile as a mummy, his face hidden by a fan of feathers, his ancient, scrawny head held aloft on the folds of a new toga, whose silk is more golden than gold. No longer a living man, he is a sculpture. There is nothing inspired about his static, centenary pose. He is simply there, with his face hidden, existing in an objective majesty that one can sense is void. Neither he nor his followers understand the words of Pali[12] that they are reciting. He has been set there at the very heart of an infinitely wretched humanity. This

---

12 The liturgical language of Theravada Buddhism, originally of India. Groslier observes that, as with Church Latin in the West, few Cambodian commoners understand the language of their clergy.

"And it has thus become the pulverous flesh of the river, rendering the waters bronze..." [Groslier]

humanity believes in his form, reveres his mere presence. It knows without understanding, and consents before feeling any desire to consent, that its every precious appurtenance belongs first, and unconditionally, to its clergy. And thus wood cut, broken, and dried burns in a monastic flame.

24 September

Alluvial Mud — Dach

The receding waters leave behind a thick alluvial muck, very fine and pure, three-quarters clay. It gives way under my bare feet, squirts between my toes, and is all but unbearable to tread upon, so thoroughly has it imbibed the sun. It is earth of the earth that has flowed with the water, polishing its grain.

24 September ❖ Alluvial Mud – Dach

*"From morning to night I go from launch to pirogue,
from pirogue into water, from water into mud,
and from mud into sanctuary."* [Montague]

And it has thus become the pulverous flesh of the river, rendering the waters bronze and transparent when they carry it along. Now it is blackish, like the liver of a beast. Walking on it, I feel a powerful sensation of truly treading upon the country, of sinking to my calves into its essence, where rock commingles with spring water. All of Cambodia is made of this travelling mud, stripped from other lands.

In the morning, at certain unpolluted spots on the wildest banks, this potter's clay bears the imprint of the receding river's final caress. The soft contours, these undulations of tremulous skin, are crisscrossed in myriad ways by a network of narrow furrows: the paths of earthworms.

In just a few days, under a penetrating sun, this soft matter, this brown brain-flesh ripped from space, made of sprouts and rot, of creeping and aquatic life, of fish spawn, ground-up stones, bird feathers, amphibian spit, rotted leaves, and gold — this universal magma will rise into the sunlight, and the wind will

"...a saber-edged roof, where cooing pigeons pass the time with wind chimes." [Groslier]

carry it off. O great fronds of coconut palms, O broad, lustrous, festooned leaves of breadfruit, the river shall be with you shortly, carried over to you as dust. You shall bear my footprints!

Meanwhile, I am filthy. The mud is caked up to my knees. It dries there as I write, and I will plunge back into it presently, for we have another pagoda in sight. A little cure in the spas of Dax[13] to go along with my pilgrimage. And what sport it is! From morning to night I go from launch to pirogue, from pirogue into water, from water into mud, and from mud into sanctuary.

The oarsman brings us in to shore, under vegetation. The place appears deserted. We call out.

Who are we?

"A pirogue to reach the pagoda!"

---

13   A commune in the southwestern French region of Aquitaine. Known since Roman times for the curative mineral waters of its spa.

There is always a human ear listening in the brush, but nobody stirs. There is a village here, a monastery that doesn't give a hoot about appeals from the river; they will only to disturb the peace. After all, has the ear not heard the noise of a steam engine?

We repeat our calls, the pilot adding: "Government."

From the branches, the grasses, the mud, the water — I can never guess where they will pop out — a black snake head finally appears, upright, the body following: it is a pirogue, a man and his ears, a government subject, who can no longer feign deafness and who, having heard, can no longer not obey.

Sometimes the pirogue is minuscule. How am I supposed to fit in that thing? It's a damned a balancing act! My bellyaching goes on and on. Then comes my crew's turn. Sometimes the pirogue is immense, and one rides in it comfortably, but in that case it has more of a belly and will stop a meter and half short of dry land. This, as I have had occasion to note, is just far enough to keep me from bounding clean over the muck.

The grasses hurt my now-tender feet. Sunburn on my insteps. Scrapes on my calves, thanks to yesterday's corn thatch. My lower back hurts from balancing on rocking pirogues. Smooth sailing indeed, but the trip back awaits us. Our boat, half filled with water, has remained in the sun all day long. Bailing it out would fatigue the oarsman, so my sunburned, scratched up-feet are bathed and scalded, as if in a mustard bath. They emerge a lovely, shrimp-like shade of pink. Launch ahead.

Upsy-daisy! We clamber back aboard. The boiler sends oil-scented air at 40° C into my cabin, but I am in the shade! Weigh anchor! A blast of air to paste my icy shirt to my chest. We start over again in half an hour. On the far bank one group of trees dominates another. It must surely contain a saber-edged roof, where cooing pigeons pass the time with wind chimes.

But today we see the last of the flooded regions and pillory-pirogues. We cross paths with more and more of them, laden with coconuts, sacks of potatoes, gourds, or carefree travelers. The rise in the land becomes ever gentler, like a belly inhaling. We are penetrating the river's great northern branch. There the waters have risen to within a meter of the banks' summits but have been unable to submerge them. The river remains in its bed.

Oxen walk the land and graze on living grass. Pigs no longer ride rafts. Up at the island of Dach[14] I see a cart — that lovely, strictly Cambodian, three-bodied beast: two bodies of wild oxen and a third with a swan's neck, a sleigh's flanks, and squeaking wheels.

In these regions, which do not suffer from any of the Mekong's excesses, there is fish despite the water and because of the land, in keeping with the explanation given above. In fact, the population here — more industrious — even engages in fishing!

For the first time in three days, there is an entire bank bristling with iron bars, gleaming swords straining against one another. The sun shifts to and fro behind fans. There is, in other words, a bank covered with coconut and sugar palms. I have even spotted a road running along it under grapefruit trees, and on that road — God be praised! — a native on a bicycle.

My feet can dry out at last.

---

14 In Kandal Province, about fifteen kilometers north of Phnom Penh. About thirty kilometers square, the island is now a popular tourist destination known for silk-weaving, dying, wood carving, and pottery.

25 September ❖ *Alluvial Mud – Dach* 25

*"I spy a little island...
and find a marvelous thing burrowed in there."* [Groslier]

25 September

Prèk Pol

Among the crew is an astonishing sailor. He has been in my service for four days, has participated in shipboard maneuvers, and has carried my supplies every time we have disembarked. I feel as if throughout the voyage I had seen nobody but him, from every angle, in every position, and still I have not dreamt of asking his name.

Whenever I need him I call out "Eh!" and he responds. The mug of a Chinese smuggler. A sparse half-dome of a moustache over lips like two bits of cinnamon husk. Bloodshot eyes. Skin like boiled leather. Which way his hair lies on his scalp I am still unable to say. He is a Cambodian in a shirt with blue and white stripes, for he is also a sailor in the Protectorate's flotilla. The lovely brute incarnate, man just as God made him.

His foot appears suddenly over the roof's edge. The lower leg and thigh follow, the latter bearing the imprint of the roof's tin. Then come a rag covering his privates and, finally, his government-issue shirt. The whole man descends, lands in a crouch, stands, casts the cable into the water, and goes in after it, so as to tie up. Not long ago he was to be found fetching wood in the hold. Now he has removed his shirt, laid it out to dry by the engine, and set out to follow me, carrying the 18 × 24 view camera and its stand.[15] We return. The shirt is dry but so hot that he flaps it in the air before putting it back on. "Eh!" I call, five minutes later. "Bat!" he replies, setting aside the cold rice he has been

---

[15] A possible photo of the actual camera, now held by the National Museum of Cambodia, is in "Banteay Chhmar: First Automobile Visit by Groslier in 1924" by Darryl Collins, in *Return to Clay*, DatAsia Press, 2014 (pp. 139-147).

eating, and lowers the canvas. Then the pilot whistles to him from the roof. He climbs up. A moment later I see him plucking a chicken handed to him by my cook.

So as not to cross my cabin, which divides the launch fore and aft, Eh! goes around by the roof or the flanks. He is a will-o'-the-wisp, that man. From morning to night, in the air or in the water, amid the firewood or by the engine, in the recess where the stove is or on the white-hot roof (his feet must smell of burnt calluses when he treads on it), shirted or bare-chested, hair flattened like a fashionable coquette's or on end like a spray of palm fronds, Eh! serves the government.

You should see him set a table, for he is also a *maître d'hôtel*. What workmanship! What care! He fills the two egg-cups onboard with salt and pepper, for we forgot the shakers and he is clever. He never stores an object where I expect. As a civilized man, I know where each thing should go. But for Eh! taking up a fork entails a moment's reflection, aim, a decision. As soon as he has set the fork down he regrets it, wondering whether he has made a mistake. And so he returns to perfect his labor, shifting the fork two centimeters to the left. Whenever I speak to him I see two expressions struggling for supremacy on his face: that of a cow looking at its calf and that of a lion smelling fresh meat.

☙❀❧

We enter the pagoda of Prèk Pol around 1:00 p.m. Beyond a vast, torrid, just about empty courtyard stands a monster of reinforced concrete, decked out in the liveliest colors: the new pagoda. With the art of a cake, of a carrousel with wooden horses, it imitates the old pagoda, now too old, out of use, visible there to the north, under its wooden double roof, and pedigreed like a fine mare under saddle.

I know what awaits me in that newfangled carcass, with its traces of formwork. I am about to leave when I spy a little island of shadow about as wide as my hand. I go to it and find a marvelous thing burrowed in there.

In my fifteen years of travel in Cambodia I have seen a few bonze cells. I have seen cells of every size and shape. I have seen the always dirty and the never clean. I have seen them dilapidated, and I have seen them brand spanking new, with louvers, espagnolettes,[16] and alarm clocks. I have seen rabbit-hutch monasteries, fairground hermitages, cells supposedly reserved for the monastery chief yet vast as hangars and filled with bric-a-brac. But this one...

A meaty frangipani blots out one of the corners. Up front, a bush whose leaves are green on top and wine-red beneath. To the right of the ladder, a large, heavy, venerable earthenware jar shaped like an olive and filled with rainwater. Two twin roofs, very pointy, of impeccable proportions, and covered with thatch. A sculpted pediment.

The hardwood partition has a door and a sliding window, all of it sculpted like the pediment. An excellent piece of work, refined yet broad. Two stylized birds, face to face, surrounded by *rinceaux*.[17] The window set under a little, curved lintel. The whole enhanced by old illumination, bright enough to bring the reliefs to life, faded enough to render that life chimerical.

What lies within this unique shrine, partitioned with floral panels and so small that I can see the whole of it reflected in the water of the jar when I peer inside? Is this tabernacle supposed to honor a virgin? Did an artist carve this box sixty years ago to the dimensions of a princess? Protruding thatch rings it with a fringe of shadow, lit in turn by the sun-reflecting floor. The pediment's violet, sculpted border hangs there like a triangular necklace around a doe's neck.

I am told that the monastery chief, Sim, lodges there. They hail him. A sleepy voice replies from inside the reliquary. They proclaim once again that a Frenchman has come. "Government!" The poor old man has been sleeping. He appears. The virgin, the princess, is eighty years old! Mother-of-pearl eyelids drooping over discolored cheekbones. Dressed entirely in yellow silk, the old man climbs down the stairs. I see the hoary feet that have been polishing the rungs for half a century. He is big and solid. How can he stand being in that tabernacle?

I find out right away, for he takes me by the hand and pulls me up with him. I enter — and sit. First he shows me the certificate for his knighthood in the

---

16 A swinging hasp used to secure French doors and the like. A modern version is used to lock rear doors on semi-trailer trucks.

17 An ornamental design of intertwined branches and leaves.

Royal Order of Cambodia, well framed and hung between Japanese advertising pictures. Cigarette. We bake. He goes back out, still pulling me along, his eighty years guiding my forty.

He is a tireless talker, has the bearing of an astronomer, and walks around like a dandy, clamping a silver-knobbed cane under his arm and holding his cigarette like a young fop. He wants to take me to his pagoda. The new one! Thank you, but no. I am quite happy to see it from a distance. I lie to the saintly old man, telling him it is very nice and looks like a French train station.

Joy in his heart, he takes my hand again and drags me across the village, wanting to escort me all the way to the launch. He stops me in front of a stall, a sort of Chinese restaurant hung round with garlands of sausage, and bids me to enter. Is the singular fellow going to offer me a drink? An old woman approaches. His sister. He insists on introducing me to her, just as he had introduced me to his cell. She is married to a Chinese man who... I force myself to count to a hundred and then rise. This time he follows me, all the way to the boat. He climbs aboard and inspects my cabin. Ah! If only it had his cell's history and illumination! We exchange names on sheets of paper, and he leaves, mine in hand.

Back to that tabernacle of his, which clothes him in the eternal youth of all beauty. May the old man die long after I do!

27 September

River Life — Tortoise Island

My cabin window cuts the bank into successive tableaus framed in varnished wood — or rather into one tableau that endures in its overall lines but swarms with shifting detail. I erase and scratch things out, remove a patch of land, substitute one village for another, try arecas to see whether they do better than milkweed. I put people in, or take them out. I try a couple of pelicans, heavy, shaped like caravels,[17] but a bit grotesque. The only good thing about them is the way the wind pushes them along, ruffling their feathers. I quickly remove the pelicans, before they've even pierced their own sides to feed their young.[18]

Of course, I let the water take up the bottom of the frame. It flows away ever more slowly, its gleam growing ever brighter. The field plowed by the current becomes a mirror at just the right distance to reflect the bank. In the successive stages of its retreat the water has cut the gingerbread-ruddy land into more or less regular steps. The land and the water — these form the unchanging foundation of my picture.

To compensate, I have many boats to choose from. Chinese junks, under sails of woven straw, their poops upturned like chicken rumps, their noses sharp, low to the water, and painted with crossed eyes. What full bellies they have, even when unladen! The men upon them resemble mere gnats on heavy beasts, but it is they who bring their oars to bear in a flagging wind. A junk grows legs when sails lose their utility.

---

17 Small, maneuverable ships developed by the Portuguese in the fifteenth century.
18 In medieval Europe, perhaps because of the way they hang their heads when regurgitating, pelicans were believed to feed their young with blood from self-inflicted wounds. They thus became symbols of the Christian Eucharist.

For my picture of the most modest sampan I retain the rudder, with its plowshare profile, setting it under the semi-circular cabin. Between it and the back of the poop is a crescent of light, where floating weeds catch and form a tail. Standing rowers push the boat along, each using one leg as a counterweight. The last man holds the tiller between his toes.

Pirogues, meanwhile, I arrange as I like. No need for me to climb down into any of *these* pirogues. I use them exclusively for the pleasure of my eye. Even when dry, suspended along the bank, while the river waters recede; even as small-scale models, ex-votos[19] set on the altars of certain riverside pagodas, pirogues remain aquatic. When dragged through the mud they float. Their raised and distended bellies never cut the water. They shift it aside and rise up onto it, so as to shift as little as possible. They show the same obeisance to women, small children, and the old, because they can just as easily evoke a garment as a crib or a coffin. They become a sharp weapon under the impulse of a strong fellow.

Me, I am an inexperienced oaf, seventy kilos of flaccid flesh. Every time I have boarded a pirogue over the previous ten days, feeling it undulate underfoot, I have all but flipped the thing. I dare not sit anywhere but at the exact center. If I sit anywhere else the pirogue will not keep me aboard. I can feel it. But I see pirogues pass with whole families comfortably seated, with casting nets and casters, with plaice[20] fishermen, with provisions by the heap. They seem so stable as they float by, full of children at play. At the sight of them I am like the proverbial hen finding a fork: flummoxed. The pirogues' sensitivity to my touch adds another layer to their prestige. They are inaccessible beauties, too svelte, too sensitive, surrendering themselves only to those whom they know, and who know them. I can do no better than compare them with their sisters, the daughters of Cambodia. One sees them pass by, grave, stern lipped, hard faced, and wishing only to hide. But then you politely speak words that they understand and find pleasing, and they respond confidently with childish, utterly charming smiles. I dream of a time when I will find the right words for the pirogues, words that they will find comprehensible and pleasing.

---

19 From the Latin *ex voto suscepto* ("from the vow made"). Offerings to a saint or divinity in fulfillment of a vow made in exchange for a boon. Western churches and Eastern pagodas alike display a variety of goods donated by grateful worshipers whose prayers have been answered.
20 Any of various flatfishes, like flounder.

"Villages crown the steps of the bank, as if seated in the last row for a circus." [Groslier]

Villages crown the steps of the bank, as if seated in the last row for a circus. They are but one house deep and have but one road: the river. They stretch along and join together in a hundred-kilometer rosary of thatch-roof huts on bamboo trellises and piles. Here and there a heavy tile roof spreads over the top. Each door is a black hole. From it issue naked children the color of the earth; or a man hurrying to secure his pirogue, which the wake of our launch has threatened to rip from its post; or a woman carrying on her head a jug of a bread-like gold, which she fills at the river and carries back, heavy and gleaming, on her hip — two urns side by side.

Elsewhere the woman, the children, the man — always the same, always different — bathe, their black heads protruding from the water, their spirits troubled by the mysterious underwater force of our propeller. The man emerges revived, his torso muscular, the child in his arms. The woman, a scintillating loincloth clinging to her body, her belly parting the bubbly water, flees to the bank. Back on land, as if perched on a plinth, she collects the dry sarong that she had left there. Modest, bolt upright within that protective cylinder, she wriggles out of the streaming-wet veil like a molting snake, and it falls to her feet.

☙✺❧

Little by little one's sense of the landscape's grandeur diminishes. One has to see an ox and compare its size with that of the surroundings to realize that the topmost spray of the bamboo tufts overhead could easily fall onto a five-story house.

Suppose you were close to a bank and facing the river. The other bank would lie on the horizon, too thin and lacy to provide the slightest landmark. You might see what looked like an immobile leaf, but only when you realized that it was a sampan hurtling along with the current would the landscape's immensity dawn on you and take on its proper dimensions. But in being brought back into line like this I have never felt that I was correcting my focus. It is not as if I had been strangling the river, shrinking the banks, or lowering the sky unawares in my mind. Instead, I see a sudden positive shift. The horizon enlarges its circle, and the river reclaims the grandeur that I had begrudged it.

We cross the river ten times a day. The pagodas rise like milestones on both banks, and we zigzag between them, from golden roof to golden roof, as if lacing up the river. Whenever we find ourselves in the middle of the river, in its noblest flow, the two banks, equidistant and at comparable grandeur and value, confer on us a grandiose sense of equilibrium. They join together up ahead, with matching slopes, and form a liquid, airy triangle sitting up on its base. As we approach one of the banks the triangle leans, curving one of its sides into a semicircle. As we advance a little farther the land rises and takes on color. Trees take on the traits of their species, showing trunks, branches, spiny cormorant nests. I hear two peals of the bell from the pilot, the signal to cut the engine. Three peals: reverse propeller, to cut the launch's momentum. The bank falls upon us with its shadow. We sink into the muck, our stem[21] cleaving the clay like a butcher's blade cleaves meat.

Here stands a new, hidden pagoda, invisible as yet, but intimated by a tuft of trees taller and denser than their surrounding brethren.

There is a murmur of childish voices, the voices of young pupils chanting their alphabet somewhere behind those leafy walls, at the open-air school near the lean-to for racing pirogues — the voices of youth exhaling monastic peace.

This afternoon we round Tortoise Island[22] — not Tortuga,[23] that bastion of buccaneers, but an alluvial island, with three pagodas and a circumference of some ten kilometers.

Difficult navigation to the south. I hear the pilot's uneasy voice thunder down from the heavens: that is, from the little hut atop the launch's roof. From up there, alone, under a tent roof sixty centimeters to a side, he looks out over our route and bakes in the sun.

He hails pirogues crossing our path, his voice carrying over the river across distances that always leave me stupefied. The voice catches the oarsman, perks him up, and elicits a reply that I cannot hear. I see the man make a darting gesture at something. What is he pointing to? Clearer waters, a fold in the

---

21 The bow or prow of a boat, as opposed to the stern.
22 Cồn Quy Island is in Châu Thành, Bến Tre Province, Vietnam, about 58 miles northwest of the Mekong delta.
23 Tortuga Island, the seventeenth-century Caribbean pirate base off the northwest coast of Hispaniola, has the same name in French: Île de la Tortue.

27 September ❖ River Life – Tortoise Island

"Here stands a new, hidden pagoda..." [Groslier]

bank, a rustle in the grass? I can see nothing, but the old helmsman topside, with his anchor-decorated cap and gummy eyes, with his twenty-five years of life on the river, grasps the mysterious bit of information. I feel an adjustment at the helm. Dangerous spots in sandy passes. The voices and arms of anonymous passers-by show us the way.

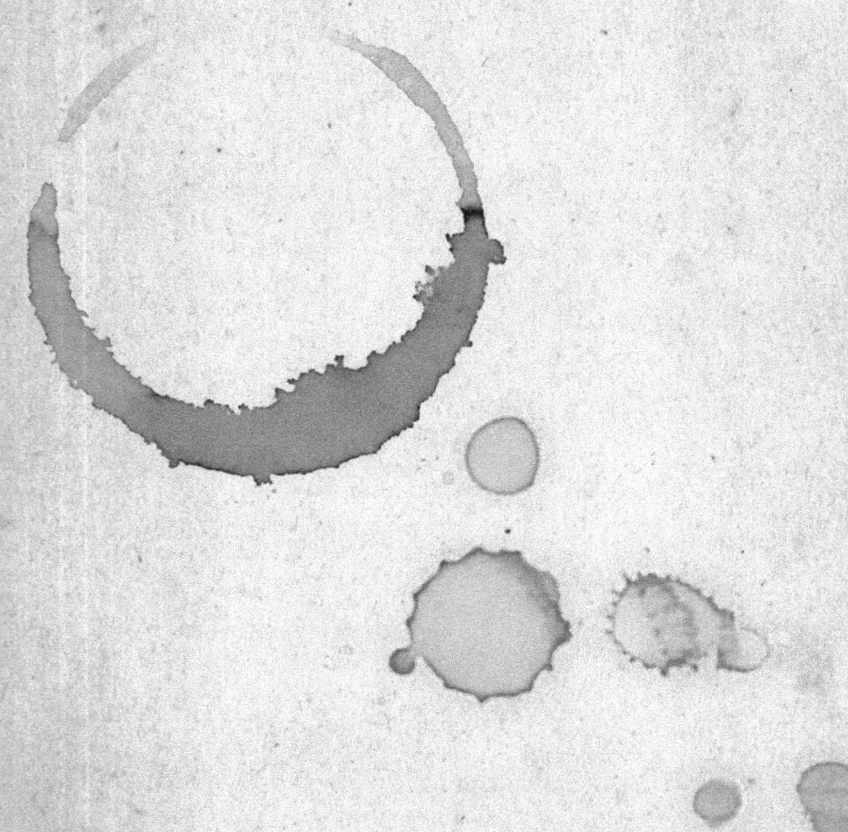

28 September

Tonlé Touch River

"Eh!"

"Bat!"

My man bursts from the water, wringing his mustache by sucking on it with his lower lip. We have just replenished our supply of wood. He plunged in afterwards and took my shoes with him, to wash himself and them off, right there, mid-river. He has broken my shoes in to such treatment, but they are so muddy today that even all that water from Tibet barely cleans them off.

I returned from the last pagoda with my pants sticky up to the knees. They are drying on the engine. My two pairs of shoes are there, too, but up front, hung next to the cooling bottles. Once again I set off barefoot and in my pajamas. None of my straight-laced friends are going to run into me in these ill-famed places.

The operator of the photographic equipment, a canny, considerate young Annamite[24] who insists on pointing out the way for me, rides up front. Lightweight that he is, he can do it. Me, I would have sunk us. Eh! follows with our gear. A godforsaken field of harvested sugar cane yawns ahead. It is one in the afternoon. The scalding mud and dry leaves inflict their wounds on me. We stop.

Eh! comes along with some bamboo and makes me a moveable bridge. Whenever I reach the end of my tether I settle onto a clod of earth, with the

---

[24] Archaic term for a native of what is now central Vietnam. In French Indochina, Annam lay between Tonkin, to the north, and Cochin China, to the south.

La Fileuse (*The Spinner*) by William Adolphe Bouguereau (1873) holding a distaff in her left hand, which Groslier compared to bird's nests he saw.

grace of a wading bird, and Eh! pushes the bamboo across. We make five hundred meters per hour. I am no acrobat. Worse, the bamboo rolls under my feet. But Eh! walks alongside me, up to his waist in the muck and holding his hand aloft with unction, like a loyal squire helping a horsewoman descend from her proud steed. We arrive. The materials used by sapper/bridge-builder Eh! will not follow along by themselves, so he sets off to fetch them, then rejoins us.

An hour from now, once we are back on board, Eh! will have made the trip six times. For the moment, since he cannot wash my shoes, he is washing my feet, scrubbing and rinsing with care, as if panning for gold.

Meanwhile, as we set out once more, never to return again, I survey the wood merchant's house. Overhanging the river is a terrace extending out from a miniscule balcony, where little Chinese pots are kept. The house is hemmed in by milkweed and a tamarind tree, from which dangle nests shaped like distaffs.[25] There are naked children, one holding a cat. A mixed-race Sino-Cambodian woman leans forward, and her nape blooms in consequence with a gleaming triple orchid: her chignon. Beneath her are three pirogues, moored to the same post and spread like a fan.

Children, woman, and fan recede into the distance, blurred into the most far-reaching undulations of our wake. I watch the roof descend all the way to the river. Behind it rises a spray of bamboo, bristling every which way with dry stems wrapped in a bark that tears off in triangles of black paper. Other bamboo stalks curve back down under their foliage and form arches over the roof. And then the roof slips into the water, and bamboo mingles with other bamboo, and there is nothing but the steady thump of the engine.

ଦ⚘ଓ

In ancient times the Mekong cut Cambodia into quarters, as if rendering a coat of arms. Its main branch comes in from China. A second doubles back to the Great Lake, to pick up Angkor's reflection. The two others flow down to the sea. Phnom Penh knots them together. This was an enterprise

---

25 In the spinning of thread, staff around which unspun fiber is wrapped. The mass of fiber held aloft by the spinner can resemble a bird's nest.

La Seine à la Grande-Jatte by Georges Seurat (1888).

undertaken with scale and pageantry. There is a bit of pomp to it, a bland magnificence

The upper and southeast branches meet obliquely. Noting the fact, the Father of Waters[26] thought to close it off and create a triangle. He thus laid down a new branch, to start in Kampong Cham and flow to Banam. This is the Tonlé Touch, or "little river," which divides the euphoniously named and exceptionally rich provinces of Srei Santhor and Sithor Kandál. Within this triangle the Mekong has enclosed the heart of Cambodia.

The great river is too great. Civilization spreads upstream too easily. Too many merchants have set up shop along that avenue, and too much sun blazes down upon it. In every season the current runs too fast, gnaws away at its channel, builds up islands where none are needed, and makes foreign lands of the two banks that it keeps apart.

---

26 Groslier here inverts the literal meaning of *Mekong* (mother of waters), perhaps to suggest a prior, creative force — a sort of Adam (namer, if not creator, of creatures) to the river's Eve.

But the Tonlé Touch, flowing near the giant that gives it life and absorbs it in death, is a river without headwaters or estuary. There is nothing at the end of its course that was not already there at the beginning. It waddles along, slowly, in no hurry to rejoin the tumultuous trunk from which it has diverged. The Tonlé Touch plays the fop, putting on airs between banks never too far apart for a child's voice to carry across.

Meandering thus, it has struck a balance, settled into tasteful proportions, leaving just enough room on its waters for a glimmer of sky between the reflected trees of opposite banks. This illumined furrow looks for all the world like the riverbed itself, as if the river flowed in the sky. The celestial blue never spoils the liquid green. The river piles bend on bend, doubling back to observe its own flow. It catches its breath after a throttling pinch and flattens out its anxious ripples. It is careful never to show one bank without the other, never to advance without its two concubines, never to keep them from their gossip, lest they drag it into the conversation. At every bend the river sets them side by side, for comparison, and chooses between them before pushing them apart once more. And so the river flows, gently, its current disturbed time and again. It pretends to be a series of little lakes, each ringed with trees, orchards, and villages, and each seemingly separate from the next. Like the pearls in a necklace, however, they are strung together by an almost invisible link.

We entered the river yesterday at about four o'clock. In this season the sun is already low at that hour and retires with the chickens. It sinks askew in the river's capricious bends. By five o'clock it was moving horizontally. I do not know how it accomplishes this feat or whether there is some malice on the part of the Tonlé Touch. The sun barely grazes the land or the water, and the shadows, finding no reflection, turn opaque. People and objects are embedded within, like luminous seeds in an olive-colored pulp.

The bank, backlit, forms a screen, combing the sunlight with leafy slits, so that only bits and bobs reach the far bank. Flashes dance on the water. Against this pebbledash landscape, against this Pointillist painting,[27] the light hangs like lanterns beneath the tawny ox bellies. Illuminated houses seem made of other stuff than houses in shadow. The impenetrable, night-like

---

[27] A style of painting in which small dabs of paint of contrasting, unmixed color are juxtaposed to create a picture. See illustration (left), *La Seine à la Grande-Jatte* by Georges Seurat (1859–1891), the French draftsman and painter credited with introducing the technique in 1886.

undersides of trees are crowned with flaming cupolas — for the sun soon begins tinting its projections.

Now the mango trees take on the color of their fruit. Garden balustrades lay down ladders of sunlight. Naked children run into this shower of gold, vanish, and reappear farther on. The small, acid-green underpants of one child slip down. He collects them off the ground and continues running, a big emerald under his arm. Marching geese, icy white under the bamboo, trundle along; they turn suddenly into egg yolks, then back into snowballs. I see a pirogue filled with violets, a single scale gleaming on its snake head. A fisherman raises his net, void of fish but full of pomegranate seeds. I see... I have never seen the like, never seen so shifting a landscape in God's fingers. It is, finally, more scintillating than the body of a fish, more sumptuous than the tail of a peacock.

Of course, a dense, curious crowd hangs from the houses' ladders like grapes on a vine, ogling us as we pass. Bathers emerging from the water stand and freeze into statues beneath the peristyle of arecas. Clustered chatterboxes break ranks for a moment under a tree speckled with a hundred bright little points: oranges. We pass an old man riding a bamboo raft downstream. He is sitting on a little roof, an anchorite atop a floating hermitage. How shall I forget the man lying in the sampan, one leg propped up to form a triangle? He is playing a guitar and never deigns to turn and look at us.

I look from bank to bank. At times, with the play of light, one side seems to me a photographic negative, the other a positive. I look away from the sunset, and already the meandering river will hold only cold colors, the colors of twilight. Our vessel slices through the pulp of a fruit, its propeller grinding up moonlight.

29 September

The Lovely Duchess of Moha Léap

I have just taken leave of the lovely duchess of Moha Léap. Unremittingly tasteful in her inner opulence, she was welcoming and dignified. At fifty years, she is rather old for a Cambodian lady, but she was born hale and strong, to rich parents who bequeathed to their only child their nobility and heritage. Though secluded in a monastery of modernizing tendencies, she has sacrificed nothing to the present day or to the West. I am speaking of a pagoda.

We may look upon her as one of the flowers of nineteenth-century Cambodian art. A few little details have a Chinese air, but the Chinese have been in Cambodia for so long, and Cambodia owes them so much, that it would be unseemly to bar their way into the temple — especially when they bring along their dragon, brother to the Khmer serpent, and some gold leaves to hang inside.

The pagoda of Moha Léap is surrounded by solid partitions. These are varnished with vermillion on the inside and rest on a plinth of openwork ceramic. Sixty columns undergird her roof, which shelters a double aisle. Twelve of those columns are ten meters tall and thirty-five centimeters in circumference. They are made of precious, carefully turned sokram[28] wood, as hard and heavy as marble. They are lacquered in black. Thirty years ago, on this doubly precious canvas, a master gilder went to work, decorating the sixty columns top to bottom. As always in Khmer architecture, the columns occur and serve their function in pairs. Accordingly, the lacy gilding changes motifs

---

28 A perennial flowering tree (*Xylia xylocarpa*) found in South and Southeast Asia, reaching heights of twenty to forty meters, and known for its excellent dark-brown wood. The seeds are edible, and the leaves are still used to treat wounds in elephants.

"Spirals, foliage, little animals, and nymphs of gold drift in the void..." [Groslier]

from pair to pair. Each stencil was thus used only twice — like a voice and its echo, swallowed up by the space and never to be heard again.

I enter the nave. The only light filters in through the openwork plinth and grazes the floor. The black lacquer of the sixty columns melts away and vanishes into the gloom, leaving only the ornaments visible. Spirals, foliage, little animals, and nymphs of gold drift in the void, like the filigree of openwork tubes. No longer rising to meet and support a roof, they hang there, regular garlands sinking into the gleam of a slab floor. I enter a sweet, gentle, golden night, under Indra's sky, held aloft by a floating, incorruptible foliage, where goddesses receive and nourish the blessed. The red of the partitions enlivens the night, strips all metallic sheen from the gold's luster, invigorates it, and gives it what I imagine is the color of the gods' blood.

29 September ❖ *The Lovely Duchess of Moha Léap* 45

"The roof reveals itself to be entirely painted,
covered with heroes and legendary animals."

[Groslier]

I am loath to dispel the atmosphere: Open a window and I take an axe to this austere fairyland, this palace of gold and black crystal. Let in a sliver of light and a whole new equilibrium, beyond my reckoning or judgment, will rise up.

The shutters creak on their hinges, and a vessel that has hitherto bared only its soul takes on flesh. An icy, gleaming, mother-of-pearl band hits every column. The illuminations regain their metallic sheen. The roof reveals itself to be entirely painted, covered with heroes and legendary animals.

Ah! I am delighted to have found on the banks of the Tonlé Touch the most beautiful pagoda known to me. From within a vermillion enclosure held aloft by sixty flawless giants and wrapped in gold lace she raises her horned head to the morning, and morning bathes her divine night. Insouciant, the lady allows the train of her dress to catch in the loveliest of rivers.

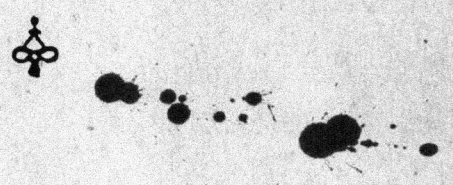

A Concrete Pagoda

A few kilometers farther down we draw up to the foot of another pagoda, one that to me seems a blatant affront. This one I know all too well, having fled thirty others just like her. But to find her here after breathing such pure air! To run smack into her, to smash my nose, so near to the old patrician! After so careful, so truly sacred an encounter — each word tumbling from such proud lips, spoken in so pure a language, and ringing sonorously as if in a conch shell — to find this upstart, this half-breed who feeds at every trough, this blemish on the landscape who makes imbeciles of her children!

She is whitewashed, and every part of her, from entrance to bells, is made of reinforced concrete. The cement, crammed into dulled molds, imitates everything that was once executed in sculpted, gilded wood. Imitates? How charitable of me. How can one expect a mold to digest finely wrought wood and spit it out intact? How could it render up wood that is alive, with gods jutting in *ronde bosse*[29] from flaming *rinceaux*? Here the unheard-of colors of a hideous whitewash substitute for gold leaf. There the decoration has all the vigor of a sponge — a mass of interlaced staffs, overcooked noodles, and other such tripe. Three piastres[30] of raw-color powder brushed on with a broom to replace three hundred piastres of tarnish-resistant

---
29 I.e., rendered as three-dimensional figures that emerge from the background.
30 To stabilize currency in the region, the French introduced a silver *piastre de commerce* in 1885. In 1930 its value was pegged at 1 piastre to 10 French francs.

"She is whitewashed, and every part of her,
from entrance to bells, is made of reinforced concrete."

[Groslier]

metal, hammered so thin that the gilder could apply it with his breath. Three piastres of daubing that three storms will wash off instead of three hundred piastres of illumination that thirty years of servitude deepen, adding a patina that serves as further ornament.

The entrance alone is an omen. It is flanked by two French soldiers — life size, thank you very much — each sporting a moustache, a jacket pinched back with a half-belt over his lower back, a melon atop his head, a rifle, and a toothy expression. Over the past eight days I have seen more French soldiers at pagoda doors than are stationed at the Phnom Penh garrison. Of course, one should not harbor prejudices. Such statues can be amusing, and the idea of flanking temple entrances with two threatening guardian statues goes back a thousand years. The sanctuaries of Angkor were guarded by *dvarapalas*.[31] Well, today the *dvarapalas* have become French soldiers. So what? But these — these are jumping jacks,[32] stupid, sadly grotesque, devoid of verve, utterly lacking even in rancor!

The rest of the entrance follows along the same lines, with little round mirrors set into the concrete, like lights on a marquee. Ten meters beyond lies the house of the monastery chief. The house has a pediment, and the pediment — will the reader believe me? — has a plaster clock, complete with pendulum. This exquisite motif, having escaped our hearths some thirty years ago and become, as one can see, specifically Cambodian, is to be found on the plaster decor of the house's roof. It reads six o'clock.

The pagoda's interior, never completed, still bears traces of formwork. One can almost make out the whistle of a train rolling into the station. Empty barrels of cement are stored behind the altar and beneath the upright, interlacing iron bars that await the gravel-flecked skin of the next Buddha. The veranda's balusters, reproduced to infinity in a mold whose halves no longer joined, are laid out in courses like bottles. They have already been whitewashed, and thus look like bottles filled with toothpaste. They are drying, and the toothpaste decomposing, to grind between teeth.

---

31 Powerful human or demonic figures that flank temple and palace doorways to protect the holy places inside. They are often fierce looking and armed. As Groslier points out, however, some modern pagodas substituted concrete statues of French soldiers.
32 Jointed toy puppets animated to raise their arms and legs with strings or sliding sticks. In the late 19th and early 20th century mechanical paper dolls with articulated limbs (called Pantin) were also popular in France. [see www.EKDuncan.com]

For three years the monastery's fifty bonzes have been working away on this horror, having already raised some eighteen thousand piastres from the diocese faithful. A further ten thousand are needed to complete the work, which was suspended six months back. No need for pessimism; the ten thousand will be found.

From the peristyle of this factory I look at the old, abandoned pagoda, standing a hundred meters off. She is rotting in the sun, under her aged gold, in venerable wood that men in their idleness have not seen fit to succor, with wounds that no merciful hand has salved. The old and loyal wife, bedecked in her jewels, is disdained and replaced.

Here as in all other parts of the country the old sanctuaries are making room for reinforced concrete. With this material the new builders hope to imitate the old structures, but they only compound their work's incoherence. One can accept a new pagoda in reinforced concrete, as long as it does not copy its ancient predecessor! Notre Dame du Raincy? Bravo! But the Sainte-Chapelle redone in iron and cement?[33]

The development is beyond puerile. It is destructive. For one thing, when a monastery lacks the money to put up a new building it goes to work on the old one. Wooden pediments are replaced with cement ones. The framework might sag underneath, but at least part of the building will be up to date and fresh from the mold. The same goes for sculpted listels and antefixes.[34] It is so easy, it so swells the chest, that the satisfactions of replacement begin to pale. The game moves on to additions: a little lion, a little console, a little French soldier, an alarm clock. Beaming bonzes watch all day long as the old tree, a little late in life, begins producing artichokes, apples, lanterns, and fish, its tremulous leaves filling with cement.

This is not the sole metamorphosis we witness. All around is the pure and simple destruction of old sanctuaries deemed unworthy of a transplant. Their sculpted beams are used as footbridges in the scaffolds erected around the monsters now rising from the ground. So as not to lose the precious gravel,

---

33 A church near Paris built near Paris ca. 1921, and thus less than a decade old when Groslier wrote this book. To underscore his point, he posits a hypothetical version of the Sainte-Chapelle (a thirteenth-century Gothic chapel in Paris) in modern materials.

34 Listels (from the Italian *listello*) are thin decorative bands. Antefixes are ornaments placed on the eaves of classical buildings to conceal the ends of joint roof tiles.

Sainte-Chapelle. Postcard engravings by Charles PINET.

the whole is ringed with a wooden wall. Let us have a closer look at this wall. We see sculpted animals leaping in trees, mythological heroes, all upside down... What is this? Seek no further. It is hundred-year-old bas-reliefs. They come from the abandoned pagoda. Green Rama, whose arrow never misses its target, has become the construction yard's watchman. Objects that can serve no purpose, whatever they might be, are left to the termites.

But let us take a little rest inside a pagoda, dilapidated or new. Here at last we find the traditional ex-votos, kept safe by religious ritual itself: old abbot chairs, lecterns, little votive trees,[35] glass displays made in the pagoda's image, lamp stands. Are these too made of cement? No. Or, at any rate, it is impossible to tell anymore. It all lies disassembled and rotting in a calamitous heap. More handless alarm clocks, carafes of cloudy glass. Jars used in France

---

35 For a definition of *ex-voto* see fn. 20. Here we have *petits mâts votifs* (small votive masts). Here, Groslier is referring to *bcisei*: multi-tiered, vertical displays of rolled leaves, flowers, eggs, incense and/or gold foil, etc., used in rituals and given as offerings in Southeast Asia.

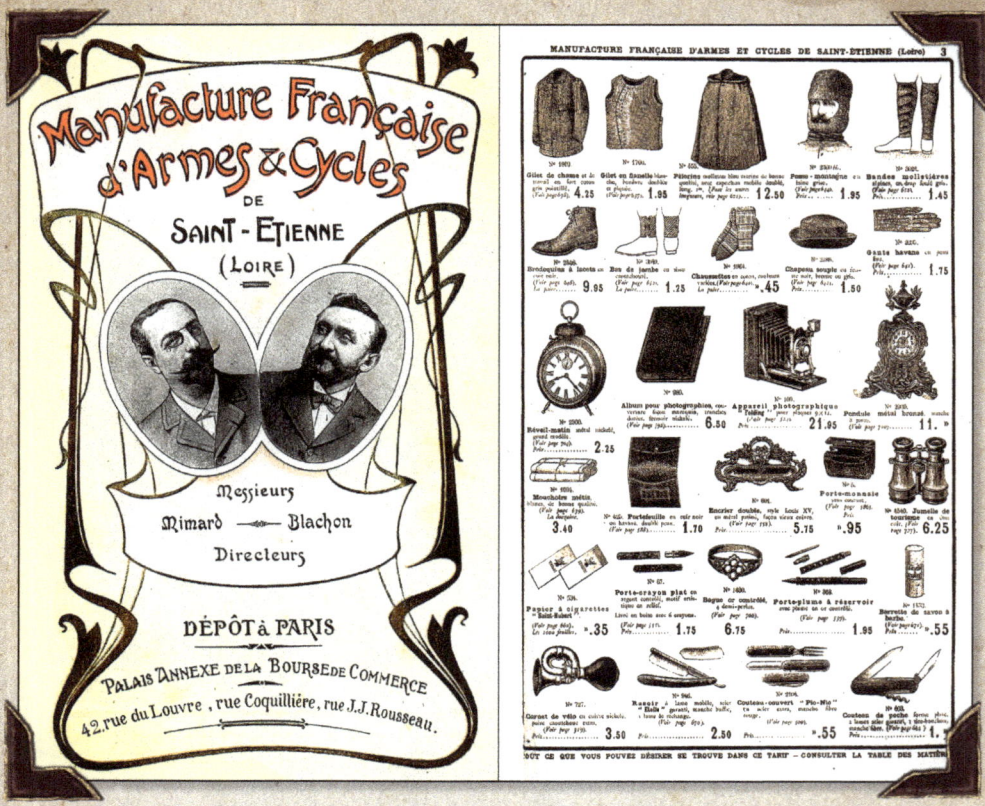

"This is what we Europeans sell to these artists."

to store pickles are here used to replace the elegant, locally crafted funeral urns. They are filled with small bone fragments and artlessly aligned. And the lamps — a museum of lamps: Louis-Philippe hanging lamps with globes, with lamp shades, with neither globes nor shades, standing lamps with bases reading Manufacture Française D'armes et Cycles de Saint-Étienne,[36] lamps with broken springs, storm lanterns, tea lights, railroad lanterns, oil lamps, kerosene lamps, pressure lamps, petrol lamps, acetylene lamps. A Siamese Buddha statuette of engraved metal. At the Buddha's feet, the drum containing the petrol. Next to the Buddha, a beer bottle containing the kerosene. There ought to be a box containing the carbide, too, but the monastery chief keeps it hidden in his room, because young miscreants filch his "lamp stone" to make will-o'-the-wisps

---

36 Also known as Manufrance, this company pioneered mail-order retail in 1888. It specialized in shotguns and bicycles but also rebranded products from third-party manufacturers, such as the aforementioned lamps.

with saliva and a match. Also to be seen in the lamp museum are flowers of paper or fabric, under globes, of tattered fabrics; spider-web garlands intact and hanging; Chinese banners; umbrellas; colored images under glass, printed in Germany, copied from Hindu models, imported from Siam by Chinamen who sell to Cambodians; pots full of sand to stick incense sticks in; and on and on...

This is what we Europeans sell to these artists.

"The old sanctuaries are making room for reinforced concrete."
[Groslier]

30 September

Kampong Cham

"Eh!"

"Bat!"

The acuity of the man's ears is incredible. He was at the back of the launch. I said "Eh!" in a sigh, and: "Bat!" In ten days he has failed to respond only once: yesterday, when he was drunk!

We were stopping at Kampong Cham, one of Cambodia's most important centers, and I had given the crew the afternoon off. I saw Eh! leave. Instead of his sailor's shirt, he was wearing one of those little jackets... Disdaining the prestige of his uniform, he had dressed in his civvies! The crew returned drunk as skunks, the pilot at their head, piloting.

I called Eh!, who did not reply but simply came over, plastered like a pagoda, mouth agape in a godlike smile, eyes looking past their focal point and glazed over in a kind of beatitude. The crew were gathered on the launch's roof, cackling, calling out to the people on the banks. The pilot was no doubt steering with his feet, but that did not worry me, for a Cambodian can do just about anything with his feet. My real concern was that he would mistake a shoal for an abyss or take it into his head to steam across the countryside.

Anyway, Eh! arrived. I no longer recall why I had called him. I saw his black teeth, thinking at first that I was looking at more of his lips, but in fact he was laughing. I had never seen him laugh, and here he was laughing while looking at me. This clued me in that he was drunk. I told him to get the hell

The Mekong and one of its islands upstream of Kampong Cham. [Groslier]

out. He gave me a soldier's salute, and the raised arm bared his side, where I spotted a tattoo: a dancing monkey, bisected by a livid scar.

All the way to the next stage, O Rimbaud, our *bateau ivre*[37] staggered along!

In two days we ran the Tonlé Touch upstream and down, and then, at Kampong Cham, returned to the great river. A night storm to celebrate our return. At eleven o'clock great flashes like the light of day struck at the bank from a terrible sky. We were nestled in at the edge of the river, the wind from the open sea hitting us on the beam and pressing us aground, our port side molding the soaked earth. To starboard we were open to the river's full breadth and were hit with low waves, a stemmed current, and torrential rains. We had lowered the canvas over our louvers, but the water got in anyway, and I was cold. The crew were huddled aft, slumbering like one man, sleeping off their rice wine. Had the river rounded its back, had the monster that killed Hippolytus lifted us up and set us down on the bank, I alone would have noticed.[38]

---

37 *Le Bateau ivre* (*The Drunken Boat*) is a hundred-line verse poem written by Arthur Rimbaud in 1871, when he was sixteen years old. Groslier's own first work, published in 1904, when he was seventeen, was a book of poems: *La Chanson d'un jeune* (*The Young Man's Song*).
38 In a tragedy by ancient Greek playwright Euripides (ca. 428 BC), an innocent boy named

Tonlé Touch – Chinese Influence

The land around the Tonlé Touch, like the banks of the provinces of Kampong Cham and Kratié (tomorrow's destination), is as Chinese as it is Cambodian. Here the Chinese do everything, the Cambodians nothing — rather, the Cambodians cultivate rice and corn, which they sell to the Chinese, and they still serve the Chinese as coolies and pirogue oarsmen. When not engaged in such activity they are idle. In fact, they too are becoming Chinese, by placing their loveliest daughters in immigrant beds. It is an old story, going back at least eight centuries, and probably twenty.

The Chinaman[39] arrives. He is handsome, muscular, light skinned, hardworking, up for anything, a nice fellow, a merchant of all things saleable, a businessman, an errand boy, a travelling cook. He is a buyer of hides, birds, rice, and all things up for sale. He is a jobber, a produce farmer, a carpenter, a mason, a specialist in reinforced concrete, a fishery farmer, a holder of backstairs games of chance, a peddler, a distiller, a usurer. He can do it all. He thought it all out on his way over from China, travelling as a coolie in the hold of an ocean junk, and he was ready when he disembarked.

In a few months he has learned the language, or else attained fluency with gestures and his smile. He displays his cheap wares, carried about in a bundle, then, with his fingers, shows the price. It is not long before he owns a cart or a sampan with which to transport that bundle. A few months later he settles on some patch of ground. If a village already exists there, so much the better. If there is no village, one will emerge. A house quickly goes up. Bamboo trellises around twelve square meters of beaten earth. Four empty kerosene drums. In each our proprietor has replaced one side with a sheet of glass, to make a showcase. He has scarcely put down his roots before a new, somewhat bigger sampan — capable of transporting fifty sacks of rice, or five hundred kilos of something transportable — comes to replace the old. The oarsmen on both boats are

---

Hippolytus is cursed by his stepfather, through a misunderstanding, and dies when a sea monster sent by Poseidon frightens the horses drawing his chariot.

39 The editor recognizes that modern dictionaries identify this as a derogatory term. Here, the translator uses the archaic demonym *Chinaman* to maintain the informal character of Groslier's narration and usage consistent with the era (1931). Like current use of the terms *Englishman* and *Frenchman*, Groslier's use is not derogatory, as is clear from his respectful description of the subject.

A prosperous Chinese family in Cambodia, circa 1920. [Montague]

Cambodians, all working off debts: that is, the Chinaman has loaned to each the sum of fifty piastres, which they may not pay back in money. They pay off their debt in work, at an estimated rate of $0.10 per day. If they were free workers, the same Chinaman would have to pay them $0.50 per day. Of course, we must also reckon the interest on the loans. In any case, everybody is happy.

The Chinaman is not slow to notice among his clientele a girl of seventeen years, with black skin, thick hair, two ripe oranges, two silver anklets, and a cotton sarong. The father gives him the girl, even if he has no debt with the Chinaman. The Chinaman removes the girl's anklets, to show that she is no longer to be courted, and exchanges them for two gold bracelets, to show that she is his wife. He quickly proves it by siring her child. Do you expect her to marry some rustic Cambodian, some fellow even darker than she is and best suited to become a bonze, a pirogue oarsman, or a debtor to the Chinaman? And with the Chinaman himself knocking at her door? No, sir. She marries well.

Every year from now on she will give birth to a lovely child, with lighter skin and a more elegant body than hers. Sons will help Father at the store. Daughters will sport the chignons of paternal grandmothers they will never meet. They will also mix their dress, wearing Chinese pantaloons under a long Khmer jacket. This generation will be split between paternal and maternal stock, lightening the complexion or darkening it up again as the case may be. Thereafter the mixture of bloodlines will stabilize.

Such is the old Sino-Cambodian race making up nearly the entire population of all prosperous, convenient, accessible regions of Cambodia. The reflective Cambodian, the dreamer, the musician, the chatterbox, the good and disinterested Cambodian trusts his merchants. To him belong the highlands, the harsh lands, the rice paddies he cultivates, the rest of the country, remote and sparsely populated. He goes from hut to pagoda and back, never straying beyond. The time he spends not serving the bonze he spends, finally, tending to the Chinaman.

For the Chinaman does arrive one day. He might be up to his belly in water or lolling his tongue with thirst, but he passes through. In passing, he buys the harvest before it is reaped, paying in advance, getting a good price, dazzling the Cambodian. The following day the Chinaman returns and invites his vendor to play a round of "*bacoun*" or "thirty-six beasts."[40] Everyone is happy. Life is beautiful. Guitars and flutes madly resound in the huts. The Chinaman leaves town with the money for the harvest, having won it back from the Cambodian. He shall return two months later to collect the harvest, but by then nobody will want to play.

From Kampong Cham to Kratié the river is Chinese. But doesn't the river too come from China? And what about all the launches? Chinese owners and crews. Stung Trang, Krauchmar, Chlong, Kratié, all those great riverside markets? Chinese and Sino-Chinese population, stores, and commerce. Those enormous junks that in all auspicious times gobble up the fruits of the earth by the ton? Chinese. In short, Cambodia is but inert flesh draped over a robust and supple Chinese and Sino-Chinese skeleton.

However much they hate the Annamites, though, Cambodians love the Chinese. When trouble arises, and a band of drunken peasants sets out for some pillaging, a Chinese shop here and there will go up in flames along with the owner, if he has not managed to escape. It does not happen more than twice in a decade, and on such occasions the Cambodians seem to recognize

---

40 See "The Game of Thirty-Six Beasts," on page 229 in the appendices.

"...the thoughtful best friend who causes antlers to sprout from one's head."

the Chinaman as the thoughtful best friend who causes antlers to sprout from one's head.[41] But on the morrow everybody gets along again.

For the Chinaman stakes his claim peacefully. He imposes nothing, calls on no one. He abides by custom in handling his affairs. Of course, it is he who has been steering custom, nudging it along on the sly for the past ten centuries, but nobody pays any heed. He endows pagodas and gives back to the country a part of the money he earns there. He takes on the work that the Cambodian rejects. He is, in a word, present. He is present whenever needed. He is patient, his hands are diligent, and his belly is extensible.

Fifteen years ago — I shall never forget it — I trekked for eight days from Stung Treng to the northwest, through a deserted region at the foot of the

---

[41] Male victims of marital infidelity, or cuckolds, are figuratively said to wear horns in English. In French they are figuratively said to wear antlers. This makes sense, as the horn-wearing was originally a reference to the sexual behavior of stags, which when defeated by another stag abandon their mate (the doe). Illustration above shows antlers sprouting on members of the French aristocracy, circa 1815.

The author on his northwest trek at Preah Vihear in 1913. [Groslier]

Dangrek chain, which separates Cambodia from Siam.[42] I was at last coming to the final village in the north and hadn't seen a living soul for two days. There were about twenty huts. Alighting from my horse, I was about to shout that I had reached the end of the earth! Clouds a thousand meters up crowned the solitary peaks, but below them was a Chinaman enthroned in his store. My sweat ran cold. A voice was singing: "Ah! I'm giggling! I'm so pretty in the mirror!"

The Chinaman's phonograph.[43]

---

[42] Groslier recounts this journey in *A l'ombre d'Angkor* (1916), now available in English as *In the Shadow of Angkor–Unknown Temples of Ancient Cambodia* (2014, DatAsia Press).

[43] Justifiably surprised, Groslier is hearing in the wilds of Cambodia the "Jewel Song" from Charles Gounod's grand opera *Faust*, first performed in Paris in 1859. The aria is sung by the opera's romantic protagonist, Marguerite, in the third act.

Canéphore by William-Adolphe Bouguereau (1852).

1 October

Canephorae – Men of the Cloth

These bonzes, they live surrounded by women, all day every day! It is, of course, Holy Week, but, well... Bah! I know all too well that it's always more or less the same thing. These women arrive at all hours, on foot, by pirogue, by cart, bearing offerings of every color, the loveliest fruit, flawless betel leaves, platters heaped with brimming bowls of refined soups and cigarettes and bottles of lemonade — anything that one might chew on, suck on, breathe in, feast the eyes and stomach on.

The young Canephorae[44] don their best finery, sashes dyed by the *Badische Anilin Fabrik*[45] of Ludwigshafen and bracelets like those found on the bas-reliefs of Angkor. They file in behind the old women. From three leagues around the women come. They gather in the *sala* for half the day. Then, after washing their feet, they move to the house of the monastery chief. A few of them clean up the monastery and show great devotion to the anchorites. I smell sandalwood and things less orthodox — the redolence of humanity and kitchens snaking its way into an atmosphere of incense. A flock of Chinese half-blood women leaves. Entering to replace them is a band of Cambodian women, grey, dirty, trembling with piety and old age: among them, like flowers on a dusty shrub, some girls.

---

44 Literally "basket bearer" in Greek. Honorific office bestowed on certain unmarried young women (i.e., virgins) in ancient Greece and granting them the privilege of leading sacred processions at festivals. The Canephora's duty was to carry the first offerings of grain or fruits and ritual instruments through the city and to the altar. The duty strongly resembles that of sacred dancers in royal Cambodian rituals.

45 Founded in 1865, now known as BASF, and currently the world's largest chemical company.

'A people and their bonzes living along a river, in happiness and solidarity, for the past twenty centuries.' [Montague]

The monastery chief, consular in bearing, pollen-swathed in his toga, sits at the foot of the altar in a sacerdotal chair with a flared back. He is surrounded by four novices and reads his *kampi*[46] in a bell-like voice. A boy fans him, performing the great, isolated thrusts as if throwing stones. The chief reads on, pauses to spit, rests, takes a quid of betel — to suck on, that is, for he is toothless. A novice prepares the quid, crushing it in a copper tube, plunging in a piston by the seashell handle.

Thus proceeds the easy-going sermon, with its intermissions. The crowd is gathered below, the cooing pigeons above. Dogs fight off to the side, emitting hideous cries. From atop the *sala* one of the faithful pitches one of the three hearthstones at them. His aim is true, and it lands with a thud amid the raging pack. The prayers begin again. The pigeons have not stopped cooing. These hours are for families, for the people — hours of simplicity and easy mysticism.

I watch as before the preacher they lay out a mat and white linen, packets of candles and incense, tobacco for quids, French sous[47] and piastre coins in a cup (for the future concrete pagoda), slices of sugarcane, slices of sugar-palm, flowers made of sugar, sweetmeats, and all manner of sugary treats for the dear old lips to suck on once the prayers have been said.

Women to one side, men to the other, children to both. The men are starched up, their foreheads tense, their faces all business. Carefully, from right to left or left to right, they pass around a cone of betel. They want to keep the cone moving, so that, wherever it happens to be, it will enhance the spread, rendering the still-life still more voluptuous — for they expect the bonzes to return half the spread to them. There are, finally, Cambodians at work, struggling through life's worries and troubles. They suck on big cigarettes as if on baby bottles

---

46 The *Kampi prah Thomma Chhean*, a Buddhist work in Cambodia's native language of Khmer.
47 The sou was one-twentieth of a franc, or five centimes. After the First World War France minted coins, in nickel or cupro-nickel, in denominations of five, ten, and twenty-five centimes (one- and two-centime coins were discontinued in 1920). The coins had a distinctive hole in the center. The silver piaster (see fn. 31) also circulated in bronze (one-cent coins) and silver (ten-, twenty-, and fifty-cent coins).

and readjust their *krama*[48] with every gesture. Whenever some authoritarian old woman voices an opinion or barks an order across the *sala* they make a little show of shrugging it off and then waddle along to do her bidding.

A permanent gathering of an entire people and its clergy around a feast, amid polished columns, under a scintillating roof, in an atmosphere of incense and fermentation, in the friendly warmth of shadows, for a period limited only by the monastic tam-tam. A daily meeting of the idle of all ages.

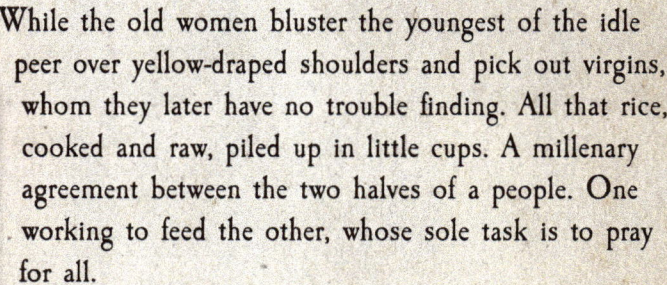

While the old women bluster the youngest of the idle peer over yellow-draped shoulders and pick out virgins, whom they later have no trouble finding. All that rice, cooked and raw, piled up in little cups. A millenary agreement between the two halves of a people. One working to feed the other, whose sole task is to pray for all.

And those ten thousand men of the cloth. Sworn to poverty, they drape themselves in silk. Sworn to solitude, they live their lives with a country's population passing continually at their feet. Sworn to a life of begging, they are served like princes. Sworn to abstinence, they enjoy food and sweets in abundance. Sworn to a life of renunciation (for every desire leads to pain), they hang like fruit from a filtering tree that feeds them nothing but its most succulent sap. Sworn to humility, they are addressed only by people who kneel, hands joined.

"I have a flask of Curaçao that I had forgotten all about."

---

48 A multi-purpose Cambodian garment made from a rectangular bolt of fabric, traditionally red or blue, used as a sash, bandanna, or covering for the head or face. It is also used to carry children or goods. An equivalent garment, the *pha khao ma*, is prevalent in northeastern Thailand.

A people and their bonzes living along a river, in happiness and solidarity, for the past twenty centuries. Perhaps I am mistaken, but it seems out of the ordinary, and worthy of some reflection.

Tonight, having written my page, I feel like a little treat. Nine o'clock. My coffee was good. The launch is dozing, tied up to a tree. I have a flask of Curaçao[49] that I had forgotten all about.

"Eh!"

"Bat!"

He isn't asleep, the rogue. I ask him for a liqueur glass. I haven't brought any along, but I figure that the boat's government supplies must include a set. Nope. No liqueur glass. Eh! returns with the porcelain egg cup, and it's just the thing. But doesn't Eh! always set the table with it, using it as a salt shaker? Where has he put the salt? He points it out to me, on a corner of the table. Did I think he would throw it out? I sip my Curaçao.

"Eh!"

"Bat!"

"Done."

He takes back the egg cup. He washes it, leaning out over the river, and dries it off with the hem of his sailor's shirt. Then, with a twisted index finger whose nail is a chip of bark, he sweeps the pile of salt back into the egg cup — salt shaker to liqueur glass and back to salt shaker.

I wonder: would Eh! use the egg cup if by chance I had hankering for a soft-boiled egg?

---

49 A popular, thirty- to-eighty-proof liqueur flavored with the peel of the fruit of the laraha (*Citrus aurantium currassuviencis*) tree. Related to the orange, laraha fruit is so bitter as to be practically inedible. The tree is in fact a mutation of the orange trees originally planted on the Caribbean island of Curaçao in the early sixteenth century. The liqueur is clear until distillers add orange and blue food coloring.

2 October

Kompong Réap — Viléa

I have just witnessed the death of a tree, in broad daylight, right in the water. A proper death for a tree in this neighborhood, the epilogue to a fight of perhaps thirty years between it and the river. Two times a year the river would rise and roll around at the foot of this tree, pay its respects like an old, hypocritical snake, and then gradually recede, having gnawed away a little ground.

What botanical name should we give the tree? Three meters about the waist and a shady cupola, an underbelly of foliage as dense as rock, through which the sun long ago stopped penetrating. The big, top-heavy clod was already leaning off the bank. Two-thirds of its roots were naked, exposed to the air, washed. They were whitish, emaciated bones, a crypt of a hundred prancing columns, the lapping waters sounding at every flood like oars.

The tree's weight had meanwhile grown ever more terrible, and the tree had cast out distress cables — rectilinear, bulging like veins — to the opposite side, toward solid ground. Futile tactic. It would better have sent them out from the trunk and branches, at an angle, like the stays and shrouds of a mainmast. But the poor giant lacked the craft! Was it counting on the birds to keep it erect? Of course, it could not retreat either, or beg the river to spare its patch of ground. With its vegetal credulousness, with its heedlessness of God's faults, did it ever notice, I wonder, that a handful of future was carried off with each passing flood?

By the time the tree felt the first wobble it was too late. We were leaving. The sailor who had cast off our cable was climbing back aboard. I heard the groan of ten, successive cracks, an abominable arpeggio a hundred meters behind us. I looked. The great body traced an arc. The canopy whistled like escaping vapor. The river absorbed the tree with retreating waves, which caught up to us and lifted the launch. Roots atrociously stretched in futile resistance were still cracking. Thick, red dust rose from the ground, and a spray of water rained down where the hole of the impact had already been filled in, onto waters foreign to the tragedy and already mistaking the corpse for an islet of verdure.

☙❀☙

How to explain the variety of welcomes I get in villages and monasteries? In the former it's as if any wife were mine for the asking. In the latter I would probably be shot down on sight if there were any rifles handy. Fortunately, these hypothetical welcomes lie at the two extremes and are thus rare. In the range between them I never know which way the welcome is going to tend, and I have never been able to establish any correlation between the welcome and population density, wealth, geographic remoteness, or current fashion.

The *mê-srok* (village chief) of Kompong Réap sees the launch coming, leaps into his sampan, and skedaddles, faster than a cormorant. Night falls, leaving the village dark. We call out, but it is as if the place had been dead for a hundred years! We settle down for the night on our own. An hour later this same village infers that we are passing it by. The animal has remained in its shell and means no harm. In every hut a torch is lit, and the village becomes a constellation.

On the morrow we pull in at Viléa, asking for nothing. I have not yet finished shaving when a brouhaha on the bank draws my attention. Viléa is the seat of the provincial governor. He has come with his entourage to welcome me. His silk jacket is fresh from the wardrobe. In a mere five minutes he has summoned the *mê-srok*, the *chantop*,[50] a secretary, and guards. Add to them twenty curious bystanders, gathered of their own volition. Congratulations all around. I take the occasion to ask whether I might purchase — purchase, I stipulate — three chickens: the *mês-srok* runs off. A dozen eggs: sudden departure of the *chantop*. Fish: too late in the day for fish, but I am promised some for tomorrow, before my departure.

---

50 An assistant appointed by the French.

Byrrh aperitif ad, circa 1910, by Belgian artist Edmond van Offel (1871–1959).

The Governor invites me to his house for a rest. In florid terms I decline his invitation. He asks my permission to withdraw. I grant it.

Then begins a torture opposite to yesterday's. A guard arrives carrying a basket: a gift from the governor. In this basket are a bottle of cognac, a bottle of anis, a bottle of Byrrh,[51] two bottles of Médoc,[52] two bottles of beer, two bottles of lemon soda, a tin of Japanese fruits, and six tins of California sardines. On the lids of these last items is the image of a whale-like fish. That poor devil of a governor has just purchased it all at the Chinaman's as a gift for me. I accept only one bottle of lemon soda, explaining that this selection brings me more pleasure than the whole. Confounded, the porter dares not leave. He insists. I point to my little launch and say it would sink under such a cargo. Everybody laughs, and the porter departs with his parcel. Ten minutes later he returns with a dish of lemons. I accept the lemons. He departs. Ten minutes later, a cage with five lovely chickens. How many? Look here, man. Take them. They're a gift: the Governor's chickens. And I must accept with a courtesy equal to that of my kind benefactors. For a moment I fancy myself a bonze!

Yet this very afternoon, at another village, I was begging to be sold a chicken and was told by everybody that there were no chickens. An old crone washing I don't know what in river water injuriously exclaimed, as if I were stealing her water: "This season I have eaten chicken only once." But I could hear hens cackling in the village, running between the betel poles.[53] Cocks — as if it had rained cocks — were frolicking right up to the edge of the water, piercing the air with their crowing. I don't mind being told there's no fish in the river, since I can't go look for myself, but to have been told that this henhouse village had no chickens!

---

51 Marketed as a "health drink," this French apéritif was invented in 1866 by the Violet brothers who blended red wine, mistelle (grape juice with added alcohol) and cinchona (a quinine-rich flower).
52 Red wine from the Médoc region of France, on the Gironde estuary, north of Bordeaux.
53 Betel leaves, used as a mild stimulant, grow on vines of the Piperaceae family, which includes pepper and kava. Betel poles organize the vines' growth and increase leaf output.

A solitary monk's cell. [Groslier]

Kâs Chrèng – Bey Pey Island

The only person I saw in the Kâs Chrèng pagoda was a twelve-year-old boy who had not had time to flee. He went to fetch the sanctuary keys at the chief's house. The chief did not trouble himself and kept me waiting twenty minutes. The bonzes watched me from their cells whenever I was not looking at the cells. If I turned toward them they would withdraw from the windows. We dusted off the altar for a photograph and set up our stand in front of the western pediment. No one came. It was the Sleeping Beauty of pagodas.

Then, ten kilometers farther on, we found the monastery chief of the island of Bey-Pey[54] already awaiting us with the launch still a hundred meters off the bank. A majestic old man. I observed him from below — a Roman statue on high. The brotherhood surrounded him. He was already talking as we tied up, greeting me, beginning his account of the history of his wretched hermitage. Like Sim, the old bonze whom I had awakened in the sculpted cell, he took my hand for the grand tour. Sweetly sincere and trusting, he was also voluble, as if he'd been waiting for my arrival on the island since his youth. I had to enter his cell, and then I had sit on the monastery's only chair. I somehow managed it without having the leg go through the slats of the parquet floor. A novice scaled twelve meters of palm tree and knocked out some coconuts for us. They were filled with moonlight. I was given a basket of guavas. Farewell, courteous, fearless, unimpeachable monks! I shrank into the distance. Lined up on their hospitable bank, they honored me with their immobile presence until they were no bigger than daffodils.

---

54 Now called Kaoh Krabei, the island lies between Kampong Cham and Stung Treng.

3 October

A Morning Massage

We were chewing the fat, the old Cambodian woman and I. It was daybreak, and the crew was loading up on wood. Passing by, she had seen the launch, peered in through the cabin window, and spied a Frenchman. She had stopped.

"Eh! old woman," I say to her. "How is your family?" She replies with unction, rests an elbow on the gunwale, and observes my toiletries case. I tell her where I come from. Without further ado, she comes in. A jacket, formerly white. A plaid sash worn as a baldric. Pierced earlobes, light streaming through them as if through a pair of portholes.

She is headed for the pagoda but is in no hurry, for at this hour the bonzes have not yet risen. Me too, I say. I am headed for the pagoda. I have done nothing but go to pagodas for the past ten days. I have already visited ninety-four of them, my dear, and I think I'm turning into a bonze! We laugh. Her wrinkles swell with malice. I add that I am tired, that I haven't had enough sleep. We spend half the night developing photographs, I explain. She invites me to lie down and offers a massage.

To receive a massage is a great honor in Cambodia, and old women excel as masseuses.

Is she perhaps going to give the monastery chief a massage at the pagoda? She delivers a blow to my arm, offense in her features.[55]

How old are you, old woman? Sixty-eight.

I stretch out. She pulls up the legs of my pajamas and opens my jacket. A few children watch the tableau from the bank. Eh!, come to clean my cabin, turns around and departs with his deck swab.

It was excruciating!

The old woman grabbed me by the belly and wrung me out like her dirty laundry. She sank two rattan-like fingers between my abdominals, grabbing at deep fibers unknown to me, seeking to yank and release them as if plucking a lyre.

---

[55] In Cambodia women are forbidden to touch monks and vice versa.

"The old woman grabbed me by the belly and wrung me out like her dirty laundry." [François Pochon, 1970]

I will tell the whole story. The purpose of the operation, it seems, was to release the wind accumulated overnight in the abdomen. The old anatomist gave me the name of the muscle she was trying to grab: "the muscle of the morning zephyr." I translate literally, except for one word that seems a little too short in French.

Then two scrawny spiders took hold of me by the hips. I must have screamed when they separated the biceps from the humerus, or when they pulled on each toe until it cracked. How could so old a body produce such prodigious force?

I gave her twenty *sous*. She wrapped them into a corner of her *krama*. With them, she said, she would buy a few things for the bonzes. And thus the bonzes of that bank will have their ounce of fat from me as well.

The rapids of Prah Patang between Kratié and Stung Treng, at high water.

[Groslier]

Stung Treng to Kratié

Upstream from Kampong Cham the Mekong exaggerates everything. It gets even broader, but higher land hems it in better, stamping on the mind the idea of a limit, and thus of proportion. My reproaches of days past fall away. We steam on upstream, and at Stung Treng the river achieves full, definitive majesty, without a hint of devastation or disquiet. Here the banks rise abruptly to a height of some fifty meters, dominating an immense bend in the river, countering its forces with rocky structures of a tragic pink. A line of vegetation crowns them like a concave diadem. Then, from Stung Treng to Kratié, nothing but a fringe of giant bamboo, spurting like geysers, splayed like posies whose stems are clenched in a fist.

Here, unable to spread out, the current is ruder, and certainly more capricious, than it is downstream. Our bottom grinds some sand. We take on water at the

"We encounter timber rafts, some of which exceed half a hectare."
[Groslier]

stern, and the wind combs a reddish mane onto the wave crests. A bend in the river, and now not a breath of wind. The waters turn to mercury against the sky, to green oil against the bank. Lapping the land, they turn yellow. If not for the dead trunks, rough, round, and gleaming like the backs of crocodiles as they float past, one would think the water still. A cormorant is caught unawares. Lacking the time and the courage to fly off, it dives in, speeds along underwater, and comes up for a breath here and there. Only the reptilian neck and soft beak, swiveling in every direction, break the surface. Then the launch suddenly begins to pitch, halting my pen. Lurking beneath the slick surface waters are powerful undulations, flattened out by reverberation.

We encounter timber rafts, some of which exceed half a hectare[56] in area. Logs of rough timber are floated one by one down the two thousand kilometers from Laos and collected in northern Cambodia after the Khône rapids.

---

56 5,000 square meters, or about an acre and a quarter.

78 Water and Light

What a strange livelihood these tree-fishing pirogue-men have. Watching from the riverside for the enormous, precious amphibians to float down on the water's momentum. Paddling out to give chase, capturing them, chaining them up with rattan cables (which also float), dragging them in to the bank, and then, once their monstrous flock is gathered, yoking the trunks together one by one with bamboo, to keep them parallel. Thus the mass departs, reaching the sea a month later. Somewhere upon that jolting parquet, whose bottom is the river's, stands a thatch hut, sheltering inhabitants: the helmsmen of the drifting floor and the accountants of a fortune entrusted to watery currents.

4 October

Lacquered Nudes

Another day comes to an end on a bank where everything is a swaying in stillness. Not a single hut visible, but a village present, behind the crowing of cocks, a smattering of human voices, and bindweeds draped from tree to tree. The gangway and a cable — nothing else tethering us to the land or to the tenderly silver hour into which the twilight has just vanished.

Women are bathing with their children under my foreign gaze, which for them does not exist. Has this not been their hour since childhood? Is this instant not essential to the rhythm of their life? Almost all of them, under that pointy shell of a chignon, are of mixed blood. A few have light skin, and theirs is the sole pale matter in the landscape, capturing all the light. They make their way here by retracing their own footsteps, laid down in the morning. They set down their clay jugs, and upon the fruits there they lay the jackets and dry loincloths that they will don after their bath. Then they enter the water, gradually rolling their sarongs up over their breasts. And thus, all along the immense river, thousands of women bathe and change their clothes without ever baring more skin than is on their shoulders and legs.

But the water is a varnish, tightening the silk, making it silkier still, and every sarong clings like a second skin. For all the women's modesty, what rises from the river are nudes, lacquered nudes, ebony nudes with shoulders of ivory and jet black heads, nudes aquatic in their gleaming rivulets and terrestrial in their flesh. They smell of milk and charcoal. Breasts young or withered, crushed beneath the knot of a loincloth. Never a wasted gesture. Children stir up the water, whitening the bank with froth, and from it the women emerge softened, with an Athenian, animal, barbarous tranquility.

![Pagoda image]

One of the pagodas in Kratié with finely carved doors. [Groslier]

To the left, a man sits on a sampan. The waves generated by the bathing bodies catch up to it and rock it. Athletic shoulders over the waist of an ephebe,[57] feet dangling in the water. He must be one of the husbands. He watches the females of the village, seeing none of them. I observe his vegetal stillness, his sated expression. This life, so foreign to me, has been rooted within him for centuries. At first I believe him insensible to the visions that move me, but I look again and see that in his attentive hand rests a fishing line, which he watches carefully, ready for the slightest tug.

---

57 Greek term for adolescent male.

10–20 October

Pursat River

The launch runs aground at her center on a bed of sand, pivots, and comes to a halt at a perpendicular to the current, which tips her sideways. Eight in the morning. We are at the entrance to a village, about even with the pagoda that the pilot was supposed to steer us in toward.

For the bonzes it is a first-rate show, and unexpected to boot. Seated in a line, they observe the French launch in its ridiculous posture. Backward propeller, switch, forward propeller: for half an hour — in vain! I hail the bonzes, ask them to fetch the village chief, but they are deaf. There are a lot of deaf bonzes in Cambodia. A sampan, with two rowers, appears. They see us, make a beeline for the bank, disembark, and disappear. Eh! and another sailor then leap into the water and swim off in search of the village chief.

The chief arrives by pirogue, and I already know what he is going to say. Ever since we ran aground all the able-bodied men of the village have felt a need to tend to their rice paddies, even those who have no rice paddies, even those who were on their way back and learned that a French launch had run into trouble on the river.

And here is the *mê-srok*. I show him my papers and the official seal and offer him a cigarette, which he places behind his ear. Then I suggest that perhaps about fifteen men... He rises, promising to fetch them. No, no, you crafty old man. Stay here with me, call out with that well-known, authoritative voice of yours, and get somebody to carry forth your orders. Of course, it will take two hours to gather the men this way, but I see clearly that if I let you go...

Pursat *"Kampong Luang des Lacs."* Floating village, circa 1910. [Montague]

So the *mê-srok* hails the bonzes. The bonzes are no longer deaf, and a novice goes to the village. Pirogues appear and do not turn around. Fifteen men? Twenty hurry over, each with an opinion. Nothing but goodwill! We cast out a cable, too short for all the haulers now racing over to help. If we wait a little longer women, children, elders — even bonzes — will hop to it! In five minutes the launch is free. I hand out three piastres for our saviors to buy cigarettes with. They are rejected. In this country effort is no big deal, but getting it...

☙❀☜

Stung Srèng – Bak Préa

We leave the Great Lake and head for Stung Srèng, across a plain that lies under three meters of water.[58] We navigate an area where six months from now carts will be kicking up dust on paths. The pilot sniffs out a course amid bush summits and trees with submerged trunks. Their reflections are a little less sunlit in the still water and lie atop viscous shadows. With great difficulty we turn about in place, by rudder or by long poles, which the crew plant in the foliage and lean on.

Like a buffalo harassed by flies, the launch rubs its flanks against trees. Boughs sweep the bridge, depositing ants and caterpillars. From time to time a sailor dives in, machete in hand, to free the propeller from a tangle of underwater plants. It is so quiet during his work, between his breaths at the surface, that the launch, engine cut, seems defeated, crestfallen at the prospect of wandering this suspended, temporary world, a world where the water itself is foreign and simply lies there, mute, thick as a gel, and ignorant of its own course.

At last we encounter a junk nestled against some tree like a beast outside an inn. The owners are eating. Nearby sleeps a familiar, red-legged wading bird, head tucked under a wing. A cylindrical fish farm of woven bulrush floats at the end of a rope, and creels are drying on the junk's roof. Smoke rises, a copse masking the tableau — incomprehensible, in a desert that has hitherto seemed endless — of floating, familial life: the life of men who never feel the dusty earth beneath their feet.

We encounter the same tableau yet again, so close to the first that our immediate impression is of coming up against the same junk as before. But,

---

58 The Stung Srèng is a tributary of the Stung Sangke, a river that feeds the Tonlé Sap Lake from the northwest.

no, we are entering the suburbs of Bak Préa, a village of one thousand souls, a center for fishermen and for wood merchants, those astonishing lumberjacks who work from the perch of their sampan, decapitating trees, gradually working their way down as the waters recede.

A hundred houses built on rafts of great bamboo logs, linked by sagging planks or sampans: that is the village, ever mobile in its immobility, anchored to a ground that never appears.

The water here is both foul and magnificent, black as coffee, mottled with oil slicks that the sunlight trims with metallic pinks and violets. It is covered with detritus, the scales and entrails of fish, ash, floating plants. It swarms with alevins,[59] with little hopping shrimp, with insects and larvae. Fish come up to the surface vertically from the bottom. The air and light send them reeling back, like a wall making elastic balls rebound, and they dive down and disappear as suddenly as sparks. It seems to me that they bump into the surface, that their impact results in bubbles and an inaudible rending. Other fish come in schools, at an angle, parallel with one another, and yawn, their round mouths poking holes in the water.

Crowds and crowds of children everywhere. They mass onto hut platforms and gangways throughout this village of relentless instability, where everything slides, slips away, slopes down and up, and bumps into everything else. They sit in little pirogues, where the single passengers who manage to squeeze in must constantly use their foot to bail out the water taken on. They look out from the poop of great merchant junks, with no guardrails to prevent a fall.

Those who cannot yet walk crawl. Who watches over them? The others. With so dense a population, it seems to me that ten divers would fish out any child who fell in long before he could drown. In any case, children here learn to swim as early as they learn to walk. Never in her life will that five-year-old girl paddle along better than she does now, beneath my gaze. Generations of amphibians.

Two hands plunge between zigzagging planks to wash a pot. Here man lives in a crouch, his feet always wet. He drinks that water, boils his rice in it, relieves himself into it. Launches empty their burned oil and ash into it. Animals die

---

59 Young fish, from the Old French word *alever*.

and rot in it. Earth and verdure decompose there in a gruel that a paddle can penetrate as far as one cares to push it. At the stem of a pirogue a young girl washes herself with the water, pouring it on voluptuously as the crows pass overhead — a lukewarm bath in plasma and rot.

Emerging from the water: men of fine physique, bound-up old women who spend their lives here, children by the swarm, live-eyed little acrobats, born of the women's dependable fertility. How many die of it? Many, no doubt. But do they die? Consider the solitary, deserted little house floating opposite the village on bamboo pontoons. It is painted sky blue with rosettes of a bombastic red. It is surrounded by Chinese pots, in which grow carefully pruned bushes decorated with paper flowers. It is festooned with fabric banderoles. Paddlers passing by bow before it. It is a sanctuary. It floats like a bouquet in front of the vile, noxious village — and its gods take nourishment from the same water.

The Red Ant

An ant, transparent like a drop of honey, advances along the handrail. Thorax angled up, goatish head aloft, she carries a cooked grain of rice in her mandibles and hurries along, as proud as can be. She is a red ant: the most ferocious beast in the land. Sensing the slightest danger, she will bite immediately, wherever she is, and cede no ground. She digs in her two sharp mandibles, rights her belly, braces herself with her legs, and pulls and pulls. If the elephant and panther were as courageous and aggressive, man would no longer walk the earth.

She is the scourge of travelers, and she is everywhere, the dirty little thing! At this season and in this flooded region the trees are covered with her like. Not long ago, when I was in northern Cambodia surveying the ruins of Banteay Chhmar, there were so many of these ants that I nearly gave up my research. They would slip into my clothes and feast on my skin. Oh yes, I would have given up had it not occurred to me to strip until I was nearly naked. With mine enemy thus exposed, I had a coolie dust me off with a broom of leaves.[60]

But let us return to the ant on the handrail, this Amazon turned housemaid, who transports her grain of rice and aims to return to the tree whence she fell, though she is in fact now herself transported on this launch. I bar the way with a finger. She tries to go around. I advance. She flees to the left. The obstacle

---

[60] Groslier's work at this remote temple was unparalleled until modern efforts began in 2007. For details see *In the Shadow of Angkor: Unknown Temples of Ancient Cambodia*, DatAsia Press, 1914, which includes Darryl Collins' article "Banteay Chhmar: First Automobile Visit by Groslier in 1924." Devata.org features an online translation of Groslier's 1937 article, "Une Merveilleuse Cite Khmere–Banteay Chhmar." For a comprehensive look at the temple see Peter Sharrock's 2015 book, *Banteay Chhmar: garrison-temple of the Khmer empire*

"Surveying the ruins of Banteay Chhmar, there were so many of these ants that I nearly gave up my research."
[Groslier.]

again. She rears up, vibrates — things are taking a nasty turn! In her anger, she comes to believe that she is gripping my finger rather than the grain of rice. She squeezes her mandibles, and the grain, cut in two, falls to the sides.

If on this beast the Creator has bestowed a bit of vanity to go along with the courage, the fierceness, and the bullheadedness, imagine the vexation that must be welling up in that tiny brain! With two flicks I pitch the grain halves into the water. The ant turns about, seeks its goods, and departs. I leave her to her double humiliation.

❧❀☙

Last hour of daylight. We can no longer see well enough to advance any farther in this liquid labyrinth. In the grey light — ah! — the melancholy of white egrets, taking flight in flocks, like a sash unfurled to brush the water's surface. We see it, but it tears and vanishes in an instant. Was it an illusion?

We tie up to a bush, having first beat it vigorously with poles, so as to flush out any reptiles that the waters might have chased into it. I hurry to dine without the lamp, before the mosquitoes come, for yesterday I witnessed their strange assault. I had closed my mosquito net with safety pins, and the invisible cloud gathered round with its muddled riot of whines by the thousand. It felt like being at the literal center of a gaseous sphere several meters thick, isolated from the world. In this flooded region there are only anopheles, the fever-carrying species.

Kampong Chèn — Stung Chèn

Meeting at the ends of their respective courses, the muddy waters of river and lake mingle, deposit their impurities and become astoundingly transparent, but the vegetation decomposing there still lends them a mahogany tint, and in the shadows of the foliage they seem made of the same stuff as scales.

After this first metamorphosis the flooded forest thins out, and the last trees vanish. Bushes and reeds stud a sad, sun-beaten landscape. A pole pokes about from the launch to help steer a course.

Then, gradually, the world is reassembled. Weeds reveal a rise in the earth, which now lies no more than sixty, then forty, centimeters down. Once again the horizon changes. Great trees appear, trees never touched by flood. The hitherto flaccid river begins to take definite shape. Another hour, and the ground finally emerges, black and sticky. It snags detritus, for a light current has begun to flow. Thus this monstrous river is born, emerging from chaos right where it vanishes.

This illusion of creation becomes more and more striking. The banks organize. The water, now contained, picks up speed and silt. The bend straightens. The launch turns freely and steams ahead full. The villages multiply. This morning, at the estuary, there were a mere six meters between the two invisible banks. At noon the Stung Chèn,[61] sixty to a hundred meters wide, gallops between flanks of naked earth crowned with mango trees and human life! We round

---

61 Most likely the Stung Sen at the south end of the lake flowing NE.

harmonious bends, the sun bouncing from bank to bank as if on a pendulum. Forces mobile and immobile join in common victory, and the sandy beaches born of their struggle shine like dazzling rounded backs.

Yet this morning, as we sought the mouth of the river in a lake with invisible shores, I felt uneasy, oppressed by the river's persistent desert aspect. On we went through a trunkless forest where all things were incomplete, as if stuck in some motionless catastrophe. My eyes could find nothing familiar to settle on. Now, between lovely, steep banks, imprisoned by great masses of trees, I find myself ineffably free. Everything is in such perfect balance, and the balance has emerged so naturally before my eyes, that if I continued to follow the course upstream, if I continued to follow this river born under my gaze, I would eventually see it vanish into the earth and die at its source.

Part Two
Low Water

15–26 February 1930

Water and Light

"We set out yesterday evening at moonrise, with the moon full for its second night."

Danseuse dorée (Rôle religieux) — Golden Dancer (Religious Role) [Groslier, 1912].

15 February
Phnom Penh to the Sea

After a four-month hiatus I have once again taken up my visit of the pagodas of the Mekong. My travels along the great river are finished, and I shall now be travelling in its two western branches, one descending from Phnom Penh to the sea, the other from the Great Lake to Phnom Penh. The waters are at their lowest level, peaceful, and partly relieved of their silt, but they are nevertheless not very transparent and in sunlight turn greenish against sandy bottoms.

We set out yesterday evening at moonrise, with the moon full for its second night.[62] Phnom Penh, a city as Chinese and Annamite as it is Cambodian, was celebrating the Feast of the Dragon.[63] A cortege advanced, dragon unfurled, along the quays, trailing the crackle of firecrackers and the flaky light of lanterns. Stragglers from the crowd gathered around altars of bloody crimson, gleaming with gold and alight with flames. Amid the firecrackers and the crash of gongs, Chinese girls, braced with invisible supports, stood tall in the light of acetylene torches before symbolic landscapes, tableaus erected on moving carts — trucks covered with rocks and Elysian pavilions made of fabric. Penetrating the night with their glimmer, the girls looked artificial and inanimate, their expressions set in porcelain. The only sign of life was the occasional fan, extending out from an opulent sleeve and beating the air. Children carried luminous fruit and mythological animals, with candles flickering like beating hearts within ribcages of rattan.

---

[62] Groslier's second Mekong trip auspicious begins during a full moon, the indispensable witness of all important Cambodian festivals.
[63] The Sino-Vietnamese New Year, which is of utmost important in Vietnamese culture and better known as Têt. Celebration last for days and always include a parade with a large Mua Lan, a dragon-lion animal symbolizing strength.

I made my way through the crush of people, a crowd congealed with sweat, dust, and light; through shadows and the smoke of burning oil and saltpeter; through the legends; through odors of gasoline, human warmth, cries, and pyrotechnics bursting between naked legs, bursting behind the dragon as it undulated upon its porters and frenetically shook its head. I went down a dark riverbank, where the launch awaited me. A few minutes later, as the crackling fête moved on beneath its nebulous halo of dust, I entered suddenly into the liquid silence of the river.

Stripped of the opaque red, the moon turned a glacial, translucent saffron-white. It pierced and saturated the clouds with its light, and they in turn enveloped it in their pulp, coating it like a hard seed. Moonbeams pranced on the water, then sank into it in sinuous lines. The cool forced me to close up my cabin and wrap myself in a blanket just as a fog was settling over the river. And I have just awoken.

We are at pains to avoid the sand bars between dried-up banks. Not a drop of rain has fallen in four months. The trees that the floodwaters had undermined at the base, and to whose trunks we tied up at high water, now tower over us with their flood-washed roots, extending some five disheveled meters overhead. They remain upright by miracle and are arrayed as if depicted on a botanical plate. Those that have fallen are now stripped of their foliage and punctuate the river with their heaped remains. Decimeter by decimeter, in great patches, the land that the water has uncovered, stratified, and fertilized is now crumbling and sinking. Raw inlets and lustrous, monstrous cavities have opened up. Some have been filled in to form slopes, upon which human feet maintain gleaming paths. Elsewhere on the new flanks young tobacco plantations have already sprung up.

Every year, at an unimaginable rate, the fluvial landscape is recreated between two upheavals. First, the rise of the waters, which we saw thread their way between the piles of huts that now stand eight meters above the river. Back then the river covered the area as far as the eye could see. Livestock were perched on platforms. Everything was moving water and mud. As the days elapsed and the tree trunks floated past with the speed of galloping horses, there came a time when the native fixed his eyes on the watermarks of floods past and prepared to gather his meager belongings for a flight in his pirogue.

"The trees now tower over us with their flood-washed roots, extending some five disheveled meters overhead." [Groslier]

Today the bank has reemerged, and he does not recognize it. Either the current has hacked at it with mighty hatchet blows, or a beach has softened the old contours. The tobacco field is already spreading its broad leaves in the very spot where, as the adolescent recalls, launches would until very recently draw up. Exhausted and lacking a true current, the river now crawls along a new course, feeling its way. From dried-up tributaries only riverbed vegetation now flows in. Where a cruise ship could once pass, a junk now runs aground. But the tranquility will just have settled into its rhythm when a new shudder runs through the water. It will take up a course and mount an assault that is already taking shape five thousand kilometers upstream, on the slopes of Tibet.

16 February
Bassac River — Chinese Junk

We draw up alongside a great Chinese junk. She passed us in the night, hugging the bank, mute, shut down, betrayed only by the water lapping at her belly, pulled along by the current and steered by invisible men bearing poles. These people travel by night and work by day. The junk is a grocery crammed with merchandise, which she sells and replaces as she purchases new stock. Her owner salutes me politely with a characteristically Chinese smile, triggered by a string, wrinkling the bottom of the face as it reveals the teeth. And so the smile remains, serious and stuck on, until the string gets a second, releasing tug.

I cannot help but visit the junk, for I must cross it to reach land. The stem is kept clear for customers. A scale occupies the center. The entrance under the roof, open from one side to the other, is framed with gold-speckled red papers. Upon them, like strange insects on pins, are characters supposed to bring luck. Painted on the lintel are two crossed eyes, one on either side of the registration number and a date: 1920.

Only the entrance lights the inside. There is curry in Perrier bottles, sacks of garlic and onions. On shelves: bottles of lemon soda, beer, and Chinese wine. Lined up along the planks: jars of fermented sauce, spherical, black, gleaming like cannonballs. Baskets of vermicelli. The air smells of brine and wood oil. Just about everywhere the labels on Japanese preserves, firecracker packets, and bundles of incense sticks enliven the floating boutique with multicolored splashes. Coiled iron cables and tools by the bunch hang from the ceiling. Hardware takes up one side, stationery in a showcase the rear. I take two steps and, without entering, peer into the owner's cabin. Mats cover the floor. It is dirty and shiny, open to the poop and beyond, onto a small garden and a clay oven. Two human feet, from an invisible body, are sticking out, toes splayed. Dry linen on the monumental tiller. Held in place by two hapchots,[64] this beam, under its protective cover, traces against the sky the long curve of a mare's back. The red-brown sail is furled in rattan rings. The roof is covered with crates, barrels of carbide, and skins. Finally, at the base of the mast, an astonishing, fantastical porcelain fish, streaming with jade-green and shrimp-pink enamel, gorged with air and more humid than if it had just come out of the river. Held in its mouth is a bundle of incense sticks. I leave the junk, and the Chinaman collapses his smile like a fan.

She is returning to Châu Đốc,[65] steering hard against the bank, following every bend. Wind lets up? The crew rows. Water level drops? Poles replace paddles. By night the two protruding eyes on her prow descry the smallest fire; by day, even the gesture of a child. It is from this drifting booth that these men peddle their wares. They tie her up for an hour, spend a day at the foot of a village. They buy fish oil and skins, sell petrol and playing cards. They trade iron for kapok. They also have chrysocale[66] bracelets, which they proffer to women who coarsely submit in return, at locations agreed upon three months in advance.

༺❀༻

In this country, so hostile for Westerners, one hour of the morning and one of the evening make up for the scorching, implacable day. Everything is so fresh, so gay, so delicate at sunrise — portent of the coming day's despondency — that the landscape turns feminine. The sky covers it with a crystal cupola, suffusing it with a charming, reflective light.

How will I muster the courage to leave this landscape, formed from nocturnal contemplation like diamond from a mass of coal? It surrounds me at such harmonious distances that my gaze surveys it whole in one smooth pivot. A whistle blast from the launch, with musical intervals of elegant ratio,

---

64 Hatchets used in France to chop certain pine woods.
65 A city bordering Cambodia in the Mekong Delta region of Vietnam.
66 The modern if rare English word *chrysocolla* refers to an attractive, blue-green mineral. Groslier's French word *chrysocale*, however, undoubtedly refers to a brass alloy that resembles gold.

16 February ❖ *Bassac River – Chinese Junk*

"...an island whose land has the luster of steel and whose prow is fit to serve as a battering ram." [Groslier]

returns three times to us at this miraculous center and glides jubilantly over sky-filled waters.

The bank lies behind me, backlit, cracked with ravines and faults, revealing strata like a transverse geological cut. To my eyes it resembles, on a tiny but nevertheless imposing scale, the cataclysm of a cordillera.[67] A patch of undermined land has slid down vertically, preserving its grassy crown. For the first time in millennia, the nascent light reaches the muddy matter freshly exposed by the landslide. The water's surface is flush with the layer of clay. Above this rises a surface that perspires with juices, where rootlets trace out a nervous system. Farther up, the trees loom in silhouette. This prehistoric screen, gnawed away at the edges by a halo, repels me toward the river.

Two cable lengths[68] to the north an armor-plated old-timer lies moored stem and stern: that is, an island whose land has the luster of steel and whose prow is fit to serve as a battering ram. No masts, but a crew of gorses[69] leans over a massive hull of white plumes. Near the water on the spur-like prow lies a little votive altar dedicated to the spirits of the current and extending out to them a banana trunk into which lotus buds have been stuck.

A quarter-horizon rests atop the river, upstream, so far off, on so fine a line, that it would be invisible if not for a black point: a junk revealing the water's surface; its sail, the atmosphere. The opposite bank, two hundred meters away, scintillates in shadows, cut off from an estuary gone dry and spanned by a bridge. Pieces of new tile can be seen on an old roof. The oxen of this steep bank drink with heads low, bodies supported on their front legs. A milkweed plantation, with its horizontal branches, overlooks the hillock of a beach divided up into tobacco and tomato fields. The beach ends in a point of pale sand, sprinkled with a colony of egrets. Behind this spindle of land the bank retreats, then heads off with the river toward a distant cul-de-sac, where the ochre land turns blond and the foliage turns silver.

Then — I have completed my tour of the horizon — this supremely delicate, almost immaterial downstream region is interrupted by the savage silhouette

---

67 I.e., of an extensive mountain chain. The term is often used for the Andes of South America. In French Indochina the Annamite Range is also known as the Annamese Cordillera.
68 French nautical unit (*encablure*) equal to 120 fathoms or 200 meters.
69 A dense, spiny evergreen shrub with fragrant yellow flowers, common in Western Europe. Groslier must have seen a similar plant, for plants of the gorse family seem not to exist in Cambodia.

French seaplane in lower Laos, circa 1920s. [Montague]

of the bank where I have settled to write: a ridge as sharp as a plowshare, and still dark. Herons startled by our siren blast fly over it.

Seaplane Survey

About ten days ago I myself had a chance to fly over the region, at an altitude of twelve hundred meters, in a seaplane surveying for the land registry.[70] There had been four months of drought, and I thought I would be looking out over dusty, parched land: the sort of land one sees when traveling on its paths and through its reddish dust. Imagine my surprise on discovering that there was far more water than land, as if I had left Cambodia and was flying over some new, totally unknown country!

I saw nothing but lagoons, ponds, marshes, holes shimmering like mirrors, all the way to the horizon; a map of puddles between dried-up streams; a mosaic of backwaters and lagoons, of dazzling green, mother-of-pearl grey, or black,

---

[70] Groslier was an aviation pioneer, taking his first balloon flight in 1908 and serving in the French balloon corps during WWI. See "Le Khmérophile: The Art and Life of George Groslier" by Kent Davis, in George Groslier's *Cambodian Dancers: Ancient & Modern*, DatAsia Press, 2011.

left behind four months earlier by the flood. The islands of the Bassac — going around them today I see only the emerging land — had their underwater foundations exposed. The sandy deposits at their endpoints were like undulating fins and fletching. The river water, visible only in its deepest parts, traced out in blurry hues a second, astonishingly sinuous bed within a vaster one. Viewed from an angle, a patch of forest looked like a piece of astrakhan over which the plane's shadow ran.

All farming ceased no more than one kilometer from each side of the river, and thereafter the land was deserted, uncultivated, rough, squalid, clean shaven by great rocky slabs, still mottled with ponds. River aside, nothing was stranger than that band of cultivated, intensely green land, twisting in a narrow arabesque across the immense, wild basin below us, its edges lost in the metallic grey of the distance. The villages remained invisible, with only the areca plantations signaling their presence. Seen from above, the white trunks topped with dark plumes, those trees seemed like bunches of darts stuck in the ground, as if we ourselves had cast them down. Only by the flash of a paddle could we tell that the slim shuttles below, the pirogues, were moving. Birds flew, their shadows following along beneath them. On a road, dust trailing behind a scale: the roof of a cart. The straight line of our flight cut across three meandering bends in the river, which seemed to flow in every direction, as if twisting before my very eyes. Here and there the rectangles of rice paddies advanced right up to the water, coming to so clean a break that one might have expected some pompous disembarking to follow, a munificent municipality rolling out fine carpets.

17 February

Bak Nam

Embarking the other night at Phnom Penh, I saw a sailor squatting on the wharf and preparing the boat's acetylene lamp. He was swearing at it, going on about the vermin in somebody's mother's belly. With the poor syntax of the spoken Khmer, I could not tell whether he was referring to his own mother or the lamp's. And it was Eh! — an unrecognizable version of him.

I had not expected to find him again, first because I had been assigned a launch of lesser draft than last time around, and then because each government launch had its own crew. Learning that I would be setting off again, however, my man had requested permission to go along. It was the right time, for his boat was being repainted. We establish little sympathies like this in life, and they reveal themselves when we least expect it. I had reencountered the black brute, the little rascal — had found him abusing the lamp that would illuminate my cabin. He could have chosen to sit idle as his boat dried, but he had arranged to accompany me, and I was not a little moved.

In a few months Eh! had been transformed. He wore white pantaloons, a new shirt, and — here's where things get interesting — a white sailor's beret with blue piping. The piping, having faded strangely, had become a sort of caterpillar wrapped around the beret. Eh! informed me that his wife had died (of a disease for whose name I have searched the lexicons in vain), leaving him with a four-year-old girl: a girl who was, in fact, another man's daughter. And we cast off.

I watched another sailor untie the cables, push off the launch by executing a split, and leap back on at the very instant I was sure we were going to sunder him, leaving half his body on the wharf and carrying off the other. These, of course, were the duties I was used to watching Eh! carry out. But Eh! was squatting up front and giving the orders. From this I gleaned that he had been promoted to first mate and was training a second. And so do peoples evolve, outside one's notice. In regarding merely myself, I would never have suspected just how much change a few months can bring into a man's life.

Ever since our departure, then, Eh! has kept to the roof of the launch — I was going to write poop deck. I call him, and he responds with the usual speed, but it is the second mate who shows up. Eh! nevertheless continues to disembark with me and carry the photographic equipment. He is now aware of the noble and vulgar sides of the role of up-and-coming sailor. Refilling the acetylene lamp, deploying my mosquito net, carrying an 18×24 view camera in varnished wood: this formerly fed his pride. The rest, not so much: fit for a second mate! To each his rank!

Besides, the tour of pagodas that he made with the aforementioned crew is today but a stroll in the park. We draw up to the bank properly. No more mud, no more pirogue gymnastics. If it once humiliated him to have mud on his thighs and water in his hair, he has more than made up for it over the past two days. Ah! The beret! Sometimes it covers the man's forehead, sometimes it falls over his nape. At one landing it is flat; at another, bulbous. At the entrance to monasteries Eh! halts, sets down his gear, and, preserving his respect for his god and his monks despite the promotion, removes the beret, folds it into a ball, shoves it into his pocket, and takes up the gear again.

☯❀☸

Bak Nam, the last Cambodian village, situated at the estuary of a stream and of the Bassac. Cochin China begins properly a hundred meters farther down, but it is already here in the form of Annamite huts. The Chinese predominate, incidentally, and this far out there are only a few Cambodians to be seen. A kilometer from here they have a tattered pagoda, covered with thatch, but in the village stands a rich, lovely Annamite pagoda, low and solidly built.

A tributary of the Mekong from its estuary. [Groslier]

The banks are everywhere studded with ovens in series. A strange mixture bakes inside them, under hemispherical, leaf-covered vats, and a nauseating odor wafts forth. Annamite coolies in disgusting clothes plunge long ladles into pots. At the foot of each kitchen, screens form an enclosure and fence off a rectangle of running water, into which the cooks ladle a dirty, yellow, lumpy, viscous scum. Every enclosure is covered with the stuff. Overhead: an unsparing sun, crows, fish-loving birds of prey. Ducks by the squadron, tails quivering ridiculously, circulate in the open water between noxious pieces of moiré fabric stretched and interlaced between the racks. Nets tied to enormous stakes block off the current every hundred meters. An accursed spot!

Bak Nam is nothing but a fish-oil works. The coolies cook the stuff in those pots by the hundred-kilo batch. The oil that spews forth is what they pour into the reservoirs, where it floats and coagulates. They recover it, cook it again, and collect it in drums. Chinese junks arrive empty and depart full of these drums. Lamp oil.

The season is in full swing. The suitable fish have been mature for the past month. Within a month they will have melted in boiling shops, and for the rest of the year they will burn in smoky flames in the huts of the land. Everything is so neatly arranged that a month after the fish vanish the waters rise, submerge the ovens, and break them up, for the ovens are dug right into the bank. Then the river recedes again. The cooks rebuild their ovens, patch up their oil plants, and deploy their nets. And then little fish by the quivering ton leap into the pots.

Each party has kept this annual appointment for probably the last century. Suppose one year the mother fish all agreed to lay their eggs fifteen days late and advised their children to do the same. In six years the scaly tribe would be appearing with a three-month delay. And what would stop them from carrying out the plan? There is no winter here. With this plan, no more boiling shops on flooded banks, no more oil works to be carried off by the current! I laid it all out for a little fish stuck in a pirogue that had taken on water. But he'll pay no heed. Just watch.

18 February

Anlong Chèn – Chrui Kéo – Native Forms

The vegetation of the Bassac lacks all the allure of the Mekong's. Not that it's ugly, but its melody plays an octave down and lacks variety. Milkweed, often closely planted, predominates. The early trees, having lost their leaves, carry only seed pods, which dangle like bats. Their horizontal branches form a rather monotonous grid with their trunks, giving the banks a graph-paper backdrop. There are tufts of bamboo and a few great trees, their bald roots exposed to the air. There are no great junks, as for two months the shallows bar their passage beyond the island of Anlong Chèn, twenty kilometers from Phnom Penh. The population is dense but idle in this season. The rice harvest is over, the tobacco is sprouting, and this is not a fish-farming region. We will find fish farms in the other branch, past Kompong Luong.

Yet a few more fish-oil works. They figure among the charms of low water. We will see many others. In the Tonlé Sap, where they use a bigger species of fish than in the south, only the heads, guts, and swim bladders are boiled up. Cambodians from the interior supply more such waste tissue, by cart caravan, and trade it for flesh that is just beginning to spoil. All month long the paths and roads are poisoned by a powerful, warm odor of rot trailing behind the carts. Certain villages become unapproachable. The already worm-eaten flesh is heavily salted, macerates a few days more, dribbles its juice, and ferments. The resulting greenish cheese is preserved in jars. It will serve as the basis for soup broth until next season.

I prefer fresh fish! It is abundant, and I eat it for breakfast and supper, making up for last time, when I had to go without. At dawn the fishermen gather, six or seven pirogues at a time. Women paddle at the rear. From the prow the

Buffalo cart caravan in Phnom Penh, circa 1910. [Montague]

men cast their nets all together, at a signal, and an equal number of crackling circles slice into the water. What lovely gestures, balanced for an instant at the center of broad aureoles that flit from open arms and fall in cupolas! Then the pirogues turn, and the men, squatting, collect their rope-work, silver leaves ensnared. The great catch is rare, and nets often return empty. Still, ten or fifteen casts usually suffice for the daily nourishment of a village.

My launch stops near one of the groups, and I always find supplies available, as do the crew. The round basket held out to me drips with water. Inside I see a flat, copper-yellow fish with three black, oblique stripes; a shrimp of faded green as big as a lobster, with vestigial claws on long stalks; and other, transparent, astonishingly buffed grey bodies, with backs that end in abrupt humps right over their necks, making them look like yoked oxen. Their flesh is white and as tender as snow. The vertebrae beneath have the same mother-of-pearl luster as the scales. If I were a naturalist and had to give this plain but ravishing fish a name I would call it "water light."

We have visited only about fifteen pagodas, all fairly uninteresting except Chrui Kéo, built well within the tradition some twenty years ago, by H. M. Sisowath. The interior is covered with the most beautiful murals known to me in Cambodia. No caricatures of French soldiers at the gates. Instead, good-old guardians: stiff, well proportioned, with diabolical masks and princely dress, hands resting on solid clubs.

At high water these pagodas would take on the look of pagodas previously described. One would reach them by pirogue, and their courtyards would ring them with fetid waters. Today they crown the high edge of the banks and watch the river's approach in the distance. They have traded their reflections in the water for a pedestal. Thus elevated, they unfurl in their train a staircase carved directly into the emergent ground.

The dogs have put on weight and can find themselves a patch of warm, dusty ground to sleep on. There is a thick layer of dry leaves spread under the trees. In front of the monasteries the hibiscus are bursting with flowers of a vibrant red. The shadows, no longer reflected in water, have lost their violet tinge. They now have some substance to them and lie thick like a spread fabric. As we pass they seem to tear beneath us and release the freshness of the earth.

With no monsoon sweeping across the atmosphere, the nearest features of the land are blurred by the overly dense air and seem more distant than they really are, as their mass and discernable details prove. And thus beyond the first layers of foreground, with their overly stark contrast, the landscape disintegrates into a light that seems intense but is in fact merely shattered. All that is land vaporizes, and the rarefaction acts as a prism. The air has a gelatinous aspect. I compare three planes of trees: the first is of an acid green; the second, barely a hundred meters off, assumes an olive hue; the third, still taking shape, and where white trunks gleam, is suffused with a sunlight that is already too weak to travel back to me.

Around this faux sparkle, the sky is cylindrical, flat on top, full of a water vapor too thin to form the slightest cloud, sufficiently dilute to remain invisible, but so permanent as to exhaust all color. This sky flows downstream with the waters, reflecting them. When the waters halt under the exposed tree roots, the sky finds a perch on the treetops. Between these two disks, while they exchange their heat in massive silence, human life yields to the life of material things. Noon.

Landing platform at Chrui Kéo. [Groslier]

≥☙❀☙≤

Women on the bank. We have just passed two paddling with exquisite ease and youth, tunics of faded indigo molding their breasts. Every such encounter stamps this notion of human perfection on my mind, and for the hundredth time I wonder what it suggests to me.

≥☙❀☙≤

These women are unaware of their beauty, do nothing with it, do not seek to bring it out individually. They have kept it collectively and unconsciously in clothes that have remained uniform for centuries. Necessary chores have made them supple and distributed the flesh on their bodies better than any principle of balance could have. The principle at play is well-being. This sort of grace defies all definition. Do I believe that these rustic females feel in their souls the same satisfaction that they give me? Do I believe that they mold themselves within just as the light by which I capture them molds them without? Of course not. And this state of self-ignorance in which they face the world (accompanied by nothing human that I could understand) no doubt helps make them both animal and inaccessible.

They are crude and perfect. And the only exchange between us occurs between their bodies and my mind. No desire for them ever infuses my flesh, and thus I follow them all the better in their plastic perfection. How could I have invented them? How could I have endowed them with such perfection? Without their example I would never have conceived of it. They are foreign to me by their race, their customs, their sentiments, their love — but all it takes is a minute, and everything they offer me matches up with the means at my disposal. Perhaps they benefit from a prestige that I bestow on them. But how could I pertinently imagine any such prestige if they did not supply me with the means to bestow it, or if they were not fit to receive it?

Little by little, things boil down to this: in terms of plasticity, Western individualism and fashion make each woman into a different watered-down, incomplete, and often unrecognizable type of woman. Whereas here each woman represents a pure and complete type, the entire sex condensed and expressed in one shot. She is not a self-limiting or arbitrarily composed form, subject to provisional conventions and the tastes of average intelligence. She is the permanent sum of man's feminine needs.

The native man is no less beautiful. But, in rising to meet or oppose the same set of ideas, he seems incomplete. Though he is just as perfect in design, though he is an agile climber and swimmer, supple, and clever in his truck with earth and water, I am physically and intellectually stronger than he. A yielding servility and insufficiency contribute to his wife's beauty but undermine his own, which could hold up only if I considered him my equal. With these things at variance, this feminine man disappoints me in his masculine forms. They lie! I find it repugnant to dominate him, precisely because it so pleases me that the lovely paddler is a slave. With his handsome muscles and solid limbs, I would like him to be tougher, more savage. I would like him to stand up to me, spy on me to plot his betrayal, show some hostility. Instead, he is always smiling, languid in his mediocrity. Rather than carry a bow, the imbecile wears a sash!

19 February

A Stowaway

The sun declines, and I climb onto the roof of the launch, painted white and still scalding. The black chimney is red hot on the sunset side. In its shade Eh! is scrubbing his toes. The pilot, still dazzled by the afternoon sun and sitting cross-legged, holds the helm in a limp hand.

In the shadow that his little tent casts onto the bridge I see a pile of rags. From underneath protrude two miniscule feet. They belong to a four- or five-year-old girl, asleep, her head resting on a sailor's shirt, a cotton cord knotted around each ankle. Who is this stowaway? She is Eh!'s daughter! And she has been aboard since our departure from Phnom Penh.

How can I have failed to discover her until now, after a few days' steaming on a boat where we are tripping all over one another? True, this evening is the first time I have climbed onto the roof, eight meters long, two wide, cluttered up with the life raft, the water tank, and the hen cage. For several days the girl has lived up here, without my hearing her. Her mother, Eh! has told me, is dead, and so man sails with girl. If it kills her, too bad. Couldn't she tumble into the water from that roof, especially since there's no handrail? Eh!, carefully reassuring, says no, as if my hypothetical situation were crazy.

"And you think the girl's having fun on this white-hot stove top?"

Eh! makes no reply.

"What does she do all day?"

"She watches the river."

She watches the river, the trees, the people. True, I don't do much else myself. She will do nothing else for the rest of her life, and at times I would like my destiny to mingle a bit with hers. Already tested by the rude climate, the little creature is at present asleep. She bakes in the sun, her fragility withstanding an onslaught that plows me under. Her existence is nevertheless so slight that for several days she has lived just a few meters from me, overhead, never giving herself away with a laugh or a cry or a frolic. Even on discovering her I see only a shape quashed against her father's shirt, which twists her mouth. One hand is flipped over and holds the other. My impression is not of childhood or of a blossom. It is a brutal and disillusioning sight: thirty pounds of human flesh.

༄༅༄

Imagine this: a staircase carved into the bank climbing amid tall grass. At the top a single tree looms. At the foot of the tree, a little bamboo chapel, on piles, made in the image of an exquisitely proportioned hut, standing out against the sky between the verdant cupola and the crest of the bank. It is an accursed place, for sixty years ago a fornicating bonze was killed there by the husband of his mistress, and the assassin hanged himself from one of the tree's branches.

The water laps. A black and white bird with the squat look of a kingfisher freezes, watches its prey, drops vertically into the water, and departs. The sun sets plainly, colorlessly, in a sky that instantly turns grey. And I watch as a marvelous boat drifts gradually down the river.

She is bedecked with banners, and a long, serrated flag flies aft. She has the profile of a junk and a caravel. Her poop is covered with gilded paper. Is it the carrack of Jaufré Rudel?[71]

No. She is scarcely two meters long. She passes at my feet, and I discern the ingenious bamboo frame at her heart. At the center a little pile of rice, bananas, and half-wilted flowers rest on a platter of woven leaves. The flanks

---

[71] Twelfth-century seafaring troubadour who explored the topic of "love from afar" in ballads. The little evidence available suggests that he died in 1147 AD and was thus a contemporary of the Khmer king Suryavarman II (ca. 1098–1150 AD), builder of Angkor Wat.

are made of oil paper and distempered in vermillion. She spins as she waddles along, under a torn sail of vibrant pink. She is an ex-voto launched by a village to appease the water spirits of the cholera.

As if a pilot familiar with the bank were at the helm, she gets tangled in the grass and bumps against the stairs, water-borne woe caught up in the woe of a place.

20 February
Samphan — Angkor Borei

The pagoda of Samphan is the one hundred third that I visit and the first where I find an ancient statue, preserved in a corner, covered with dust, transported there from no one knows where. Yet the region is poor in ruined monuments from great eras. The archaeological map pinpoints about ten: brick towers, earthen levees, vestiges, most dating back even further than the prosperous days of Angkor. Yesterday afternoon we were near an old capital, Vyadhapura, now Angkor Borei, a few kilometers from the Bassac, on one of the tributaries.

It was a few years ago in the neighborhood of this ancient city that we had the good fortune to find two extraordinary Buddhas, broad hipped, in the Greco-Gupta style (more Greek than Gupta), exemplars of an art imported into Cambodia in the fifth or sixth century at the latest and not yet assimilated by the Khmer mind. They seem to have been the prototypes of a secondary art that we call *pre-Khmer*, others call *primitive*, and still others call *pre-Angkorian*. Cambodian archaeology is not yet well established! The successor art, already degenerate, was the art of Angkor, which brings us into the fourteenth century. From the fifteen century on, the Siamese influence permeates the dotty old style — itself descended from other dotty old styles — and keeps it breathing.

The statuette found this morning is an example of passable pre-Khmer art: a thick-necked god. One arm is missing. The remaining hand once held some sort of attribute. The face, under a cylindrical chignon, is vaguely Semitic, the unsure execution mixing its blood. The body lacks all jewelry and is nude except for a short sarong knotted in front. While having the statuette washed for a photograph, I spotted the current Buddha, of gilded cement, at the back of the sanctuary, his eyes cast down on his miniscule sandstone ancestor of fourteen centuries, as if to furnish his references.

The country seems primitive and men's lives elementary. Except along the banks of the river, these regions are more or less deserted. Wooden carts, clay ovens, pirogues dug out of tree trunks, the same draped clothes of a thousand years, people in misery, a few songs, almost no literature, unfurnished huts of thatch and bamboo. It is as if we were meeting adolescent populations that were feeling their way along, their development at its earliest stage, at but a slight remove from their original poverty.

Then, when one makes the smallest effort to get a better look, one sees that the child in fact bears the burden of an old man, that he has built fortified cities and immense temples, withstood several successive civilizations. Like ash, his language bears the brands of Sanskrit, Pali, Malay, Chinese, and Thai. The bonzes we see proceed from the Brahmans who once covered the land and have vanished. Generations of philosophers have held forth in the monasteries. And one soon comes to recognize that nothing is born, that nothing can be born, of this exhausted human turf, which now lacks even a memory.

Eh!'s daughter — that obscure little bud scarcely emerged from the plasma, that barbarous little girl — is a prodigious half-blood matron, the daughter of half-bloods. She has been a princess and a slave, a merchant, a royal dancer, a sacred dancer. She has roamed other countries and returned as a female bonze. In the twelfth century she was secretary to a king and an astronomer, a prince's singer, then a Chinaman's wife, regent of the empire, concubine of a mandarin, embroiderer, rice pounder, sampan paddler, mother of ascetics and great generals. She has seen battle and laid pious foundations. She has had every human virtue and every human vice. She has been clad in gold, brocade, and vermin. Eh!, her brute of a father, since abandoning the caves, since stripping off the seashell necklaces one finds underground in Samrong Tong,[71] a hundred kilometers from here — well, the room would start spinning if I tried to establish Eh!'s genealogy up to his promotion to first mate aboard this launch.

---

[71] In Kampong Speu province, west southwest of Phnom Penh.

We now exit the whimsical detour in my meditations and return to Eh! and his daughter, for this very morning, when I awoke, they perfectly matched the ideas I have just expressed. I heard water splashing, raised my shutter, and saw Eh! bathing his daughter. She was floating in front of him, and he held her by the arm. With an open hand she wiped away the water slicking her face and blinding her. She did not laugh, did not cry, said nothing. He would sink her entirely into the water and lift her back out. For a while I thought he was going to wring her out like a towel. Her head is shaved except on top, and the hair that has been permitted to grow there, wild, is knotted up in a tight, snail-like chignon.

At last Eh! headed for the bank, gradually emerging from the water, his daughter straddling his hip. She was pale and minuscule next to her bulky father. They seemed linked to each other by the light of the dawn and the water streaming from their bodies. The little body protruded from the man's, from his hip — as if made from his rib. In a flash I had a vision: an act of creation occurring before the earth of a bank where no vegetation had ever sprouted, a bank that had emerged from the same water as the couple.

I called to the original woman. She dropped from the man like a fruit, and I glimpsed the narrow dent of her belly. She donned a torn, greyish sarong. Her precise little steps brought her onto the gangway-plank, which did not bend. And here she is standing before me.

"*Sampeah, louk!*"[72] her father cries out to her.

She kneels and holds out her joined hands. Droplets roll off the snail, onto her forehead, then onto her cheeks: tears. A broad nose, a tiny crescent of a mouth, features already sharpening out of their childish blur. Age will accentuate them no further but only make them bigger — all except the eyes, which have already achieved their definitive breadth. A skinny little neck on a rounded but overly tight thorax. I set the little animal on my lap.

As a father who for twelve years has been holding children close and caressing them, I expect limpness, that hardy abandon typical of tykes. Reaching for

---

[72] *Sampeah* is the traditional Cambodian greeting of respect, in which both hands are held together prayerfully in front of the chest. Based on the Indian *anjali*, the gesture features prominently in ancient temple carvings and in the Cambodian dance tradition. *Louk* is the Khmer (and Thai) word for *child*.

pulp, I take hold, instead, of a hard, stiffening little body, cooled by the water evaporating from it. She is scared but looks me square in the eye. She neither tries to leave nor abandons herself. A dreadful passivity.

"What's your name?"

She replies with a rolled R:

"Trâp."

Which means eggplant.

"Don't be scared! Laugh! Laugh!"

Her mouth breaks into a laugh, and I see that she has lost her upper baby teeth.

I ask another question:

"You like riding on the river, eh?"

She says nothing and will go on saying nothing. I set her back down on the plank. She turns her back, looks around for her father, but does not leave, dares not leave, until I tell her she may.

When she does she is holding at shoulder height, in an upturned fist, the twenty-cent piece that I have given her. She approaches Eh! and shows him the coin in a half-open hand before inserting it carefully into her chignon.

21 February
Tonlé Sap River — Chruï Changvar

Back in Phnom Penh to embark on the fourth branch of the Mekong, the Tonlé Sap. We entered the astonishing fluvial crossroads at five o'clock. I arranged things so as to observe it at this loveliest of moments, a daily ceremony officiated by water and light.

Behind us the Bassac has nearly touched the sun, which is already riding low, as if sucked down by the river, in a blaze of light that defies every gaze.

To our right, the southeast branch is obliquely lit and smothered with lusterless reflections, and the bank beyond is rendered so thin and taut by the distance that it vibrates like a saw blade.

Ahead, imperially spread, the high river flows from the northeast under moiré lilacs in pastel, hoisting sails that it seems not to carry. The sails are lit up by the sun and seem yellow flames stabbing the sky. The sky serves as the waters' backdrop. Sunset hits the peninsula of Chruï Changvar with a broadside, leaving not a spot of shadow.

At last the northwest branch, flowing in front of the peninsula, equally lit up, and rife with river craft, turns gold — buttered and saffroned — at the foot of Phnom Penh, which spreads there backlit, raising its sacred spires above the vegetation.

Thus four rivers — the first of mercury, the second of tin, the third of a celestial mother-of-pearl, the last of honey — open around us, heading off in the cardinal directions. They mingle between banks so far apart that one is barely in view of the other, though they are peninsulas arranged tip to tip. Four skies yawn over the four paths, for they are too vast for a single, necessarily precarious dome.

21 February ❖ Tonlé Sap River – Chrui Changvar

As we navigate through this watery split that stretches off to the four horizons I try to open my spirit, which wavers like a magnetic needle over the winds' rosette. I sense the ruddy, white-headed ospreys as they pass overhead. They soar over lands that seem to float, lands tenuously linked and stretched out in distant fringes; a city of one hundred fifty thousand souls, ten kilometers long, lacking the thickness of my finger, and shading off to blue. I feel as if I were discovering a liquid architecture, a cathedral laid on its side. If I cried out my cry would quadruple. The vastness above is a knot untying.

Low water. The majesty is but a dying down. The currents of the great river and of the Tonlé Sap, nearly exhausted, join over a sandy bed and depart once more with but the slightest divergence. But in a few months the crossroads will rise eight meters. Waters come from Tibet, China, and Laos will rush in and swirl in massive volume. They will seek some egress, momentarily breaking their speed. Some, brushing past the sands to the east, will make off immediately. Some, having crossed the sands and gathered new silt, will be diverted into the Bassac. The rest, coming abruptly to a halt, frothing at the bit, mane cresting, will veer around and break off for the northwest, nearly heading back whence they came, to fill the Great Lake, and eventually to overflow....

Then there will come a moment of solemn equilibrium, during which this reserve of spent water will become still, held captive by the three other rivers, themselves settled in to the rest of the country. But one day the original river will incline its back and recede, and the great lake will thereupon release its waters to the south and empty out. Having nearly swollen to bursting for the previous six months with venous blood thickened with fish spawn, the heart, for another six months, will expel an arterial blood dazzling with scales. And thus twice annually Phnom Penh watches a river change direction, passing to and fro at its feet; it watches another river spill into the first; and it watches yet two more depart from the first as if born of it.

The shift; the pulsing of the lake; the back and forth of the Tonlé Sap; the grandiose oscillation between two moments of immobility, first with the watery forces equally matched in confrontation, then with other waters arriving flat and insouciant, just as we see them today — once all this has become familiar, the look of this already unique place takes on even greater significance.

"With a great cortege in tow, the king rides out to the cord on his floating house and cuts it." [Montague]

This evening, over the low waters, I watch the rivers at their moment of greatest effort. Within a minute the currents are reversed, exhausted, and reborn. A vertical rhythm — high water, low water — is at work in the horizontal effusion, and as time goes by the august landscape breathes, losing none of its vastness or geological expression, transforming everything to match its own scale.

Remembering the November Festival

Every year at November's full moon, when the current reverses itself, a cord is stretched across the Tonlé Sap, and there is a festival.[73] With a great cortege in tow, the king rides out to the cord on his floating house and cuts it. With this symbolic gesture he releases the waters, eliminating the barrier that had

---

[73] The Cambodian Water Festival (*Bon Om Touk*) remains one of the biggest celebrations of the year and also marks the end of the rainy season.

"...for the three days framed by those sacred nights there are pirogue races. [Montague]

held them captive, and thus allows them to rush off to sea. For three nights the court singers, all female, salute the moon with the songs of Sakrava,[74] and for the three days framed by those sacred nights there are pirogue races. Thus one of the kingdom's most beautiful feasts: the water festival.

The slim pirogues that we saw up on blocks in the pagoda enclosures, under the trees, take to the river for the occasion. The accumulated leaves are bailed out, the gilding is shined up, and they are shoved out into the water. They set off instantly, like long, reanimated saurians.

Each of the racing pirogues is dug from a single tree trunk, and some reach a length of forty meters, with a mere meter's width at their widest. They scarcely touch the water and almost taper off into the air. Crews for the largest consist either of more than forty rowers seated in pairs, three pilots, a buffoon yapping at the center, and a leader clutching the prow, or of twenty standing male

---

[74] Festival songs honoring the king, generally sung by his concubines. See "Sakrava – The Moon Songs" on page 195 in the appendices.

"Every pirogue rides slowly upstream, passing very close to the king's floating platform."
[Groslier]

paddlers. A silken panel, two cubits long[75] and framed with tassels, hangs from the tip of the prow. A pendant of flowers floats aft.

At race time the sun drops below the bank on whose slopes the crowd has gathered. The season's great clouds loom opposite, reflecting an already red light. Amaranths and violets roll in the water. Every pirogue rides slowly upstream, passing very close to the king's floating platform. Forty little paddles dip simultaneously, and spattered water streams down the paddlers. At the center, establishing the rhythm, the buffoon contorts his body and calls out light, satirical phrases, to which the paddlers respond with a regular, joyous cry. It has two parts: "Ha" for the lifting of the paddles, "Ya" for the dipping. "Ha!... Ya!..." The joyous, masculine sound rolls along, supporting the pirogue. The pirogue, lifted whole, stem to stern, advances in regular leaps. As it passes by it shows its paddlers in pairs, then its helmsmen. "Ha!... Ya!..." And off

---

75 I.e., two forearm lengths, from the tip of the middle finger to the elbow bottom.

she goes. And now that she's moving away and we can see her from behind. Between the regular lifting of paddles and their superposition in perspective the pirogue looks like a woodlouse with gleaming legs. About thirty more just like her will be setting off, from about two kilometers upstream.

They suddenly reappear, expanding by the second, approaching at an incredible speed, vying for position three at a time, the water alongside chopped up, white, vaporized. Arms paddle like mad, and the pirogues' flanks seem to expand and contract in a pant. A paddler clings with his legs to the prow like the bridle of a runaway horse. He brandishes a gilded oar, so as to cleave imaginary obstacles. The scene blurs, and that is the point. A clamor of shouts hits the bank and washes over it with the great waves raised in the assault. Paddles up and running on headway, the pirogues trace a vast circle.

The stampede quickly settles down, and the pirogues take on a melancholic air, as if suddenly recalling the great trees that they once had been, on the banks of this very river, at this crepuscular hour, their foliage quivering under an airy caress.

(194) CAMBODGE : Pnom-Penh - Arbre du voyageur et escalier du Pnom.

The stairway to the Phnom, hand-tinted circa 1920. [Montague]

22 February
A History of Phnom Penh

Phnom Penh is a girl entering puberty, and the growing pains are bringing about its disgrace. Block by block, on a plan that could be grandiose, they are erecting a suburb. Lining boulevards twenty meters wide are villas proper to a French town like Viroflay, ringed with stingy little gardens abloom with household laundry set out to dry. A small park had been planned around the Phnom: a breast-like hillock, crowned with a three-hundred-year-old stupa and a pagoda. But the pagoda was old, so they made it over in concrete. They laid stairs into the hillock's sides and covered them with moldings. It was an exquisite park, so they put in an electric plant. To make the boulevards they used land dredged up from the edges, and thus for thirty years the boulevards have regularly become dykes, with the city sinking steadily on either side. Now they're stopping up all the holes. The houses were built at the projected street level and thus wait on piles for their embankments to be laid. Daylight is visible under the partition walls.

An old canal, broadened to supply land for the two boulevards alongside, splits the city in two. At low water it is dry. Its bridges span vegetation, and the sewers empty into it uncovered. At high water those same bridges are inundated and imprison all watercraft for two months. So they're going to fill in the canal. Paris wasn't built in a day.

No site for the port has yet been found anywhere along the river. The port is therefore everywhere. A ten-kilometer stretch of banks before one of the most beautiful panoramas in the world serves as avenue, quay, dock, shipyard, warehouse, wharf, street, and esplanade, where a hundred Chinese launches

Phnom Penh, circa 1885. [Montague]

drop off and take on passengers day and night amid a thousand potbellied junks. Hides, cement barrels, wood, coal, stones, casks, iron — all things fit to be swallowed or spewed — are loaded and unloaded smack in the center of town, in view of the chief stores, the circle, the pagodas, the school, and the hospital, or along the grand avenue running from the headquarters of the French Protectorate to the Royal Palace. Ceremonies of official pomp thus take place amid coolies, who like to watch them and will set aside their sacks of rice and their baskets of charcoal for a while, wiping the sweat from their nude torsos. And in fact the scene simply becomes all the more picturesque.

Chinese city to one side, European city to the other — with the Cambodians to the south, on the outside, populating the outskirts. Despite the division, however, a Chinese pagoda stands in the European city, with groceries between the two riverbanks, while the large garages and some of the French government's offices sit smack in the middle of the Chinese quarter.

In 1863 Phnom Penh was nothing but a village of three hundred thatch huts much like the ones we have just seen all along the river. It had not yet become the capital again, as it had many times over the past few centuries. Since then the town magistrates have been trying as best they can to keep up with the city's development, sewing new bits onto a garment that perennially comes up short. And this rather young city seems to have foundered with every endeavor, from its port, which silts up at low water, to its turn-of-the-twentieth-century European style, which has never taken hold. Aside from the occasional pagoda, with an allure scarcely greater than that of the pagodas we visit from one end of the country to the other, the city boasts no building of authentic native design. Rich Cambodians and opulent Chinese retirees, meanwhile, embrace the comprador style with childish delight.

In 1903 there were 350 Europeans. Last year there were 1,450, troops excluded. Over the course of thirty years the ranks of French merchants have swelled from 20 to 160. They sold only 1,800 bicycles in 1921 but unloaded 5,450 in 1929. In 1910 the first automobile made its appearance, on the eve of the war there were 35 in circulation, and in 1929 the city's five garages held 2,930. Roads had to be built for them. There were 50 kilometers' worth in 1900. Today Phnom Penh sits at the center of a partly gravel, partly tarmac asterisk boasting some 2,400 kilometers of roadway. And circulating within the young city are 25,000 Chinese, 22,000 Annamites, and 350 Malays and Hindus. The Cambodians, meanwhile, are seldom seen outside their neighborhoods and number 36,000.[76]

These figures and dates suffice to define the city. They explain its destiny and, in part, its misfortune and merits. How could it achieve unity? Its past is gone without a trace, its future indeterminate. It is a government and commercial city, above all a city of Chinese and shops. One would expect to hear a monastic hum and see venerable gilding in the royal quarter and around the palace, but instead these places have been entirely rebuilt in reinforced concrete and gleam brand new in the sun. The same is true even of the stables for the white elephant, that sacred princess, herself a youngster.

☙ ❦ ❧

Let us now leave behind this city emerging from the river and the marshes. Let us travel back in time, erasing the city with a cinematic dissolve, and on the

---

[76] A few pages earlier Groslier cited the population as "a city of one hundred fifty thousand souls." The cause of this discrepancy is unresolved.

foggy background produced by our little artifice let us superimpose the first historical Phnom Penh, just as the impeccable George Cœdès[77] has evoked it from chronicles.

Incidentally, our trip along the river has done more, far more, than the work of our official architects to help us to recognize the old village of Phnom Penh in the modern-day city. This evening we pull in, like the two mandarins whom King Ponhea Yat sent in the fifteenth century for their knowledge of favorable spots. The capital of wood and thatch that our projector will now gradually project, as the historian opens the aperture, took the name "Capital of the Four Branches, fortunate mistress of Cambodia, new Indraprastha, noble, rich, and royal frontier." A simple name like that.

The king ordered a mass conscription of men subject to the corvée,[78] had the riverbanks shored up, so as to keep the river from flooding the city, and thereby prepared the port-boulevard of 1930. He had the earth transported in from the west. This left behind a vast marsh that has just been filled in, thanks to a machine devised in Amsterdam to aspirate river sand.

The palace of Ponhea Yat stood on the site of the current market, the Bank of Indochina, and the Residence/City Hall. To supply the palace with water, the fifteenth-century builders dug a canal, which they covered with stone slabs and earth. This is the same canal that the city magistrates of 1880 expanded and that those of 1931 are going to fill in.

To fortify the city, a moat, which came to be called the "stream of the Chinese forgers," was dug to the north, because that is where His Majesty had located the armament manufacturers. The canal still bears that name and is spanned by a stunning bridge built forty years ago. A roadway dangled on chains from the four square towers and was to be lifted to let junks pass underneath. It was never put to use, however.[79] The chains were removed, and the towers of the immobile drawbridge now serve as the city's northern gate.

---

77 George Cœdès (1886–1969), French scholar of Southeast Asian history and archeology recognized for his epigraphical analysis of ancient Khmer inscriptions.

78 The conscription, throughout medieval and ancient times, of citizens for labor on public projects in lieu of or in addition to taxes paid with currency.

79 The De Verneville Bridge was such an expensive fiasco that it was finally called the Bridge of Dollars. Initiated in the mid-1890s by the eponymous chief French official, it was finally demolished in the early 1930s, shortly after Groslier published this book.

'A roadway dangled on chains from the four square towers... It was never put to use, however.' [Montague]

To the south the "Capital, happy mistress of Cambodia," was defended by another still-extant stream still bearing its old name: the stream of Old Man Kev.[80] The present-day city thus still fits within its former limits, within which civil servants and civilians built their dwellings as they liked. Also, two of the king's sons built palaces there: the first, to the south, is that inhabited by King Sisowath Monivong; the second stood on the site of the city's current dump. Things change.

Sixty years earlier the hillock that would give the city its name, the hill of Lady Penh, had already been raised. This woman had land brought in to build up a little hill in front of her house, so as to deposit there five Buddha statues, four of bronze and one of stone, that had miraculously been found in a tree trunk floating on the river. The trunk was used to build the frame for the idols' shrine. When Ponhea Yat arrived the shrine was a near-ruin. He ordered the shrine restored, the summit of the Phnom covered with gravel, and a great stupa, perhaps the current one, raised.

---

80 No modern name is found, but near the modern Chroy Changva bridge in Russey Kev district.

The Cantino planisphere—named after Alberto Cantino who smuggled it to Italy from Portugal in 1502—is the earliest surviving map showing early Portuguese navigation. Peninsular Southeast Asia at lower right.

This 1619 map of "India Orientalis" by Gerardus Mercator and Jodocus Hondius shows the expansion of European familiarity with Southeast Asia, a little more than a century later.

22 February ❖ A History of Phnom Penh

The first Europeans arrived fewer than a hundred years after Phnom Penh's founding and called the city Churdumuco, after its Pali name, Catummukha: the four faces. They were Portuguese clergymen and adventurers from Malacca. So as to follow their adventures closely, let us switch historians and leaf through a little volume in quarto, with full-calfskin binding and raised bands, decorated with golden fleurs-de-lis, published in Valladolid in 1604, found and enthusiastically translated by Mr. Cabaton.

I myself cannot imagine that they would have worn helmets or colonial dress at the time. I see our Castilians disembarking at the Four Branches with flat berets on their heads, armholes ornamented with spaulders, codpieces shaped like seashells, strapped-on knee breeches, and perhaps gaiters in soft leather.[81] Short hair and pointy beards, because of the ruff,[82] which they probably did not bother with in that heat... And, finally, of course, a long sword in the belt, a dagger on the right hanging from a cord, a well-secured pistol, and a powder horn worn on a scapular. Yes, well armed, as we will see, and with curled moustaches.

And lovely names, to boot: Diego Belloso, of Amarante; Pantaléon Cornero, of Lisbon; Francisco Machado and Blas Ruiz, Chul de Diaz and Col de Monteiro. And the conquerors never missed a chance to knock up a lovely Khmer woman. Great-grandchildren in present-day Phnom Penh carry their names as if carrying a red flower in their mouth. Sonorous patronymics recalling the history.

The curtain that had come down before the monuments of the Angkorian stage was still swinging from its recent descent. It rose again on new men, men who carried a rondache on their fist and an arquebus under their arm.[83] The Castilian novel arrived to run its pen through the smoke of sacred fires and the murmur of Sanskrit chants in the monasteries. Chinese junk encountered

---

81 Spaulders are plates worn on the upper arms and shoulders. Codpieces are metal, leather, or fabric pouches that cover and usually accentuate the male genitals. Gaiters are protective coverings for the lower legs.

82 Ruffs are voluminous ruffled collars that were popular from the mid-sixteenth to the mid-seventeenth centuries.

83 The rondache is a circular shield carried by foot soldiers; the arquebus, a portable, muzzle-loading, long-barreled gun popular in fifteenth-century Europe.

Variations of military garb, circa 1608 by Dutch painter and engraver Jacob de Gheyn II.

Portuguese fluyt. The Kshatrya,[84] descending from his battle elephant smeared with human bile,[85] watched *condottieri*[86] disembark. The last inscription had hardly been inscribed before the king it celebrated was receiving the friendship and counsel of two swashbucklers: Blas Ruiz and Diego Belloso.

How had they come to find themselves at the hillock of Grandma Penh in about 1590? Nobody knows. Belloso was married to a princess, a relation to the monarch. Blas Ruiz had already been a slave in Champa and was scarcely more than twenty years old. The king sent him to Manila to seek help from the Spanish government. Halfway there he and two companions were captured by the Siamese, placed on a junk, and tied up, but our singular prisoners managed to escape, killing the Siamese and taking the junk.

What was there aboard that monster-headed boat, long, riding low in the water, and looking as if it had popped out of a bas-relief? Perfume burners, little bells, mosquito nets of Chinese silk for the divinities? Was it a grocery boat, like the one we boarded four days ago on the Bassac? No. What Blas Ruiz found aboard were five hundred arquebuses, a hundred culverins,[87] fifty falcons, a hundred jars of gunpowder, iron masks (?), lances and morions,[88] ten thousand caltrops.[89] Satisfied with his inventory, Ruiz simply continued on his way to Manila, arriving at the same time as Belloso, who, believing his comrade dead, had mounted his own expedition to carry out the mission.

They obtained the help sought by the Khmer king and set off for Cambodia

---

84 Members of the warrior caste, one of four Indian social orders.

85 Bile, or gall, factors into Cambodian history and culture in interesting ways. According to thirteenth-century Chinese author Zhou Daguan (*The Customs of Cambodia*), the king of Champa, during an annual "gall harvest," would receive as tribute an urn filled with human gall bladders. (What the king did with the gall Daguan does not say.) Michael Freeman (*Cambodia*, 2004, pp. 129–31) expands on the legend, noting that bitter gall is an important ingredient in certain Khmer cuisines and that eating the liver of an enemy was "connected with the idea of acquiring the energy, the spirit, of the slain. In particular it was a custom of wartime."

86 Mercenaries. *Condottieri* were originally soldiers contracted by the Papacy and Italian city-states from the late Middle Ages to the Renaissance. The term later came to denote hired soldiers in general.

87 Firearms, ranging from the musket-size hand culverin (like the arquebuses the ship carried) to the field culverin, a cannon weighing up to 4,800 pounds.

88 Military helmets, famously worn by Spanish conquistadors.

89 Ancient equivalents of the landmine, meant to wound or impede horses and foot soldiers. Often tetrahedral (like four-pointed pyramids), caltrops resembled children's jacks, the spikes arranged so that one would always point up no matter how the caltrop lay.

with one hundred twenty Spaniards and an admiral — along with some clergymen — aboard two junks and a frigate. I leave it to the reader to imagine the mugs on these volunteers! They arrived at the Four Branches only to learn that the king had recently fled to Laos with his family and that a usurper now sat on the throne. Had they gone to all that trouble for nothing?

Their first act was to lead sixty men into battle against three thousand Chinese. They killed three hundred. Then, having thus limbered up, they captured their goods and the junks, along with the goods and junks of the Chinese who had fled. Back then the *chinchoes* (killings) began less peacefully than they do now!

Having developed a taste for conquest, Blas Ruiz and Belloso then besieged the Royal Palace, blew up the powder magazine, and killed the usurper by arquebus — no more, no less.

Now thousands of Cambodians attacked and pursued them. It rained torrents. They swam across rivers and, as our good Dominican father naively adds, "covered the arquebus bassinets with the rondaches to keep the powder dry."

The Khmer chief took too great a risk and — whoosh! — found himself cleft in two by halberd blow, his amulets notwithstanding. The Castilians returned to their ships and left, "regretting that they could not do better or accomplish more."

Ruiz and Belloso were with them, but only to tour Indochina on the admiral's frigate. They disembarked on the coast of Annam and set out west on foot, crossing the Annamite Range and the vast savannahs of the plateau,[90] braving all manner of perils, and quite simply heading for Laos in search of the deposed Khmer king. They were not easily put off.

Knee breeches doubtless worn out, puffy sleeves doubtless gone flat, they arrived as naked as Moses[91] — except for the belt to pass their swords through. They found their king, rekindled his courage, stirred his ambition and spiced up his memories, bucked him up, took a few years off him, grabbed him by the shoulders, took him back to Cambodia, and set him back on the throne. There was a grab for power, and each found himself governor of a province and showered with favors.

---

90 Groslier calls the plateau "Interland."
91 In the Old Testament, Moses is found in an ark among the Nile's bullrushes by the daughter of Pharaoh when he is three months old, and presumably naked beneath his swaddling clothes.

What repose! I can see it now. Debauch after debauch, dear reader! Orchestras playing madly every night. Fine silk sampots to wrap around their thighs. Brocade imported from Bombay to make skirts for the dancers and coronation garments for kings. Showers with cool, cool river water, with macerating jasmine flowers. Massages with coconut oil and administered by hands other than those of my old witch of Viléa. Cigars as big as trees. Well-appraised jewelry. Near at hand, swords with openwork guards!

But our two governors soon learned that two Spanish frigates had been attacked and captured by some Japanese and Cambodians under a Malay chief, and they abandoned it all: the cigars, the dancers, the soft silks, the cool water — all but their flame-bladed swords. They flew to the rescue of their countrymen, fell into an ambush, and were massacred. Their heads were carried off in cages, like a pair of turtledoves....

From Phnom Penh to Kompong Luong, which we will pass tomorrow, sagas begun in the sixteenth century continued on into the seventeenth. Missionaries evangelized after the killing of Father de La Bastide.[92] The Dutch came to the rescue and opened a trading post in 1643. Regesmortes, who ran the place, was killed at the instigation of the Portuguese. The court switched riverbanks, moved up- and downstream in keeping with the intrigues, usurpations, and assassinations. Then, one fine day, a new Portuguese adventurer, Melchior Díaz,[93] arrived from Brazil. He acquired a princely title, by means unknown, and married a Cambodian. His children received from the king a province conceded in appanage.[94]

Meanwhile, perhaps as part of the guerilla war, the Siamese and the Annamites mounted incursions. Sometimes the king would fortify Phnom Penh, or whatever the capital happened to be. Sometimes he would pack up and flee, either to the north, if the Annamites were coming, or to the south, if the Siamese were pouring down from the north. As soon as things seemed to have

---

92 In 1588, Spanish Dominicans Father Maldouat and Father de la Bastide tried to settle in Cambodia but the king forced them to leave. In an attack as they returned to their ship Father de la Bastide was killed, becoming the first martyr of his faith in Cambodia.

93 A century earlier, a Spanish explorer with the same name worked in the New World before dying there in 1541. The editor found no record of an Asian explorer by that name (or with the Portuguese spelling "Dias").

94 The bequeathing of an estate, title, office, or anything else of value to the younger brother of a sovereign's first-born son.

settled down the king would have a palace built wherever he was and sign an order bestowing upon a class of mandarins the right to carry a seal decorated with a circle of leaves and a double parasol. Afterwards a usurper would kill him and there would be war within the court until the legitimate branch or an able minister retook power in a regency.

One of these kings converted to Islam, currying favor with the Malays. Another married an Annamite princess, whose countrymen thus gained entry to the court. Then the Siamese returned to restore order, burning the villages and leaving with an army of prisoners. A respite would have followed that bloodletting if not for a provincial governor who, under pressure from an enlightened bonze, rebelled and marched on the capital. He was stopped by floods so violent as to devastate all the lowlands. Big cats took to the highlands, vying for refuge against the inhabitants.

In 1816 we find a certain Monteiro, a Portuguese of mixed race, and a prevaricating minister, "who also fornicated with the women and concubines of other men, whom he would lure to his house and appropriate." He was taken prisoner, escaped, and was taken again and decapitated. His son, who had helped him escape, was also arrested, but the king pardoned him, "because he had acted in filial loyalty, as he ought to have done."

Then, under Annamite domination, the crown went to a woman. She was soon accused of being the mistress of the enemy ambassador, and the accusation drove her mad. Phnom Penh took an Annamite name: Nam Vian. Three envoys from the emperor Ming Mang administered Cambodia with such discretion that they imposed the Annamite dress and chignon on Cambodian civil servants. So the people revolted, called on Siam for help, and got it. After four years of war they succeeded in driving out the Annamites. A new Khmer king on the throne in Phnom Penh (1845). The fortresses were demolished and their bricks used to build pagodas, but Cambodia was once again a Siamese vassal.

In 1855 Mr. de Montigny, a Frenchman — the first, I believe, to appear in any chronicle — arrived with orders from Napoleon III to establish a treaty of alliance with the Cambodian king. He arrived at Kampot, on the Gulf of Siam, and found the weather too hot and Phnom Penh too distant. Declaring himself fatigued, he returned without having seen the monarch, who was impatiently awaiting him.[95] If only that most singular diplomat had been Blas Ruiz...

1859 saw the arrival of Mouhot, a French naturalist on a mission for England.[96] He crossed Cambodia and discovered Angkor, which had been discovered previously by the Reverend Père Bouillevaux and yet three hundred years earlier by a pair of Dominicans: Fathers Dorta and Luis de Fonseca. Our naturalist searched for little grasses and butterflies but engaged in no politics. Briefly suspending his search, he was received by the Khmer king at the palace in Oudong, thirty kilometers north of Phnom Penh. After this audience Mouhot pressed on and died of exhaustion in Luang Prabang.

Soon thereafter the king of Oudong died, leaving behind three sons. One was crowned, one of the two others objected, and the land was once more awash in fire and blood. Meanwhile the new king fled to Battambang (once again in Siam) with the royal attributes. A legless cripple was seen leading troops into battle against the royals. He was killed, hung upside down, and eviscerated. If not for the sun and the scavengers he would still be swinging from his tree.

At the same time a French naval lieutenant arrived on a small gunboat. This was in April 1862, during the present season, at low water. His name was Doudart de Lagrée, and he was our first representative in Cambodia. His mere presence pacified a country that had been boiling over for centuries. Who in

---

95 According to Georges Maspero (1872–1942; sinologist, governor of Indochina, résident supérieur of Cambodia, and co-founder of the École Française d'Extrême-Orient):

"M. de Montigny, to whom Napoléon III had previously entrusted several diplomatic missions in Bangkok, Annam, and China, received orders to meet with the king of Cambodia to discuss terms for a treaty.

"Knowing little of the relations between the two countries, the diplomat made the fatal mistake of disclosing his mission at court in Bangkok.

"The Siamese king, fearing Cambodia might slip from his grasp, quickly drafted a letter to King Ang Duong and dispatched it with a mandarin, who followed M. de Montigny to Kampot, whence the embassy was to make its way by land to Phnom Penh.

"As soon as he set foot on Cambodian soil, the Siamese envoy hastened to the capital, presented himself haughtily before the king, and threatened him with the hatred of Siam if he acceded to the French envoy's demands.

"Thoroughly frightened, Ang Duong made apologies, found a pretext, and stole away, with the result that Monsieur de Montigny, reluctant to undertake a long land journey from which he expected little profit, left Kampot for Hué, never meeting with the king. He had failed in his mission (1855)."

96 Henri Mouhot (1826–1861) is the French naturalist and explorer generally credited with the rediscovery of Angkor. While other Europeans knew of the lost jungle city, it was the posthumous publication of Mouhot's travel diaries that brought the Khmer civilization to the Western public's attention.

French explorers of the Mekong Exploration Commission at Angkor Wat, 1866. From left: François Garnier; Louis Delaporte; Eugene Joubert; Clovis Thorel; Louis de Carné and Captain Ernest Doudard de Lagrée. Not pictured is renowned photographer Émile Gsell. [*Voyage d'exploration en Indo-Chine vol. 1.*]

France knows his name? He had all the boldness of an adventurer, but kept his sword in its sheath. He had an iron hand, but never clenched it. It sufficed for him to raise that hand. Just passing through, he picked the country like a fruit, enthroned the kings who have reigned ever since, and dissipated the factions, all without unlacing the covers on his cannon. Then, having raised our colors over a still smoking Phnom Penh, he once again took up his scholarly mission, reaching China, where he died.

Not long thereafter another Frenchman, Auguste Pavie,[97] a former postman of small stature, came on the scene. He had marked out the route for the Phnom Penh–Bangkok telegraph line and because of his excellent ability was entrusted with various missions. Passing through, he recruited Cambodians and set off under a broad-brimmed velvet hat, treading on his long beard. It hardly mattered, for the conquering explorer was marching barefoot. After

---

[97] Auguste Jean-Marie Pavie (1847–1925) was a soldier and diplomat who worked extensively throughout French Indochina and became known as "the barefoot explorer" (*l'explorateur aux pied nus*). For detailed information and photos visit www.pavie.culture.fr.

Auguste Pavie (right center standing) and Pierre Lefèvre Pontalis (left center) with Cambodian interpreters at the Colonial School in 1893.

traveling around Cambodia he went up into Laos, like Blas Ruiz and Diego Belloso before him, crossed it south to north, without a single weapon in his bags, mapping it along the way, telling stories every night at camp, and every now and then planting a tricolor flag. After a few years of such wandering this secular bishop had all the earth of Laos clinging to his bare soles. Laos had become French.

In ten years two Frenchmen, unknown then and nearly as unknown now, had conquered these volcanic lands, where adventurers of every stripe had been foiling plans amid incredible political disorder. They had delivered the region from its nightmares, the one sweeping it with his gaze, the other with his beard. They had worked gradually, with meager means but grand ideas, injuring no one's conscience, and leaving only one death, a single, small native death, in their wake — only thousands upon thousands of villages on the riverbanks and in the heart of the land, all of them gazing out into the distance every night, to see whether the travelers might yet return…

24 February

Kompong Luong

Setting off from Phnom Penh on the Tonlé Sap one navigates between banks nearly free of Cambodians for some thirty kilometers. In their stead is a population of Catholic Annamites and Mohammedan Malays. One leaves behind the capital's Cambodian and Chinese pagodas only to find the cathedral, a seminary chapel, and a Carmelite convent here in the suburbs. Crosses crown the doors and tile rooftops of the huts. There is a mosque.

Then, whereas the left bank flattens out and becomes abandoned and fallow, on the right bank a narrow curtain of trees and Malay houses rises. This continues all the way to Kompong Luong, the "Royal Riverbank," the court's last capital before the French Protectorate raised its flag over the kingdom. To the west, upon gently sloping hills some hundred meters tall, the fine silhouettes of royal tombs rise into a pale, dense sky.

The lovely pagoda of Kompong Luong dates to this historical period, so recent and yet already opaque to us. The pagoda is of markedly mixed race, but venerable and run down. Its gate and surroundings are Chinese. Its windows are framed with stucco-work vaguely inspired by the Louis XIV and Louis XV mirrors and armchairs that the East India Company used to import from Siam. The rest is lovely mid-nineteenth-century Cambodian art. A few gutter tiles survive, their butts decorated with a praying woman. Inside there remains an exquisite secondary altar, finely sculpted in the form of a slender tower and serving as a display. There is also a strongbox with a slit for the insertion of offerings.

"The lovely pagoda of Kompong Luong dates to this historical period, so recent and yet already opaque to us." [Groslier]

The old palace once stood about five hundred meters to the southwest. The sole traces are imperceptible undulations in the ground, covered with tufts of bamboo, amid rice paddies stretching out as far as the eye can see. An old architect sketched the layout of the caravanserai for me from memory and hearsay, and I have provided the sketch elsewhere.[98]

It bears no relation to the idea we have in France of an Asian royal palace. It was a sort of thatch village with a little lake surrounded by palisades. The monarch had wooden quarters and an adobe throne room. The archives, carpets, and treasure were locked up in a pavilion built on piles in the middle of a pond, to protect it from fire and termites. The naturalist Mouhot gave a good description of the palace when he passed by it in 1859. Life on the river has changed little since then. The same blazing light covers the banks, along with, perhaps, the last of the intrigues that brewed in the palace and spread like dew in the course of mysterious nights.

---

98 Groslier cites his drawing from page 334 of *Recherches sur les Cambodgiens*, 1921, Challamel, Paris. For readers who don't have a copy handy, his sketch and description appear on the next page.

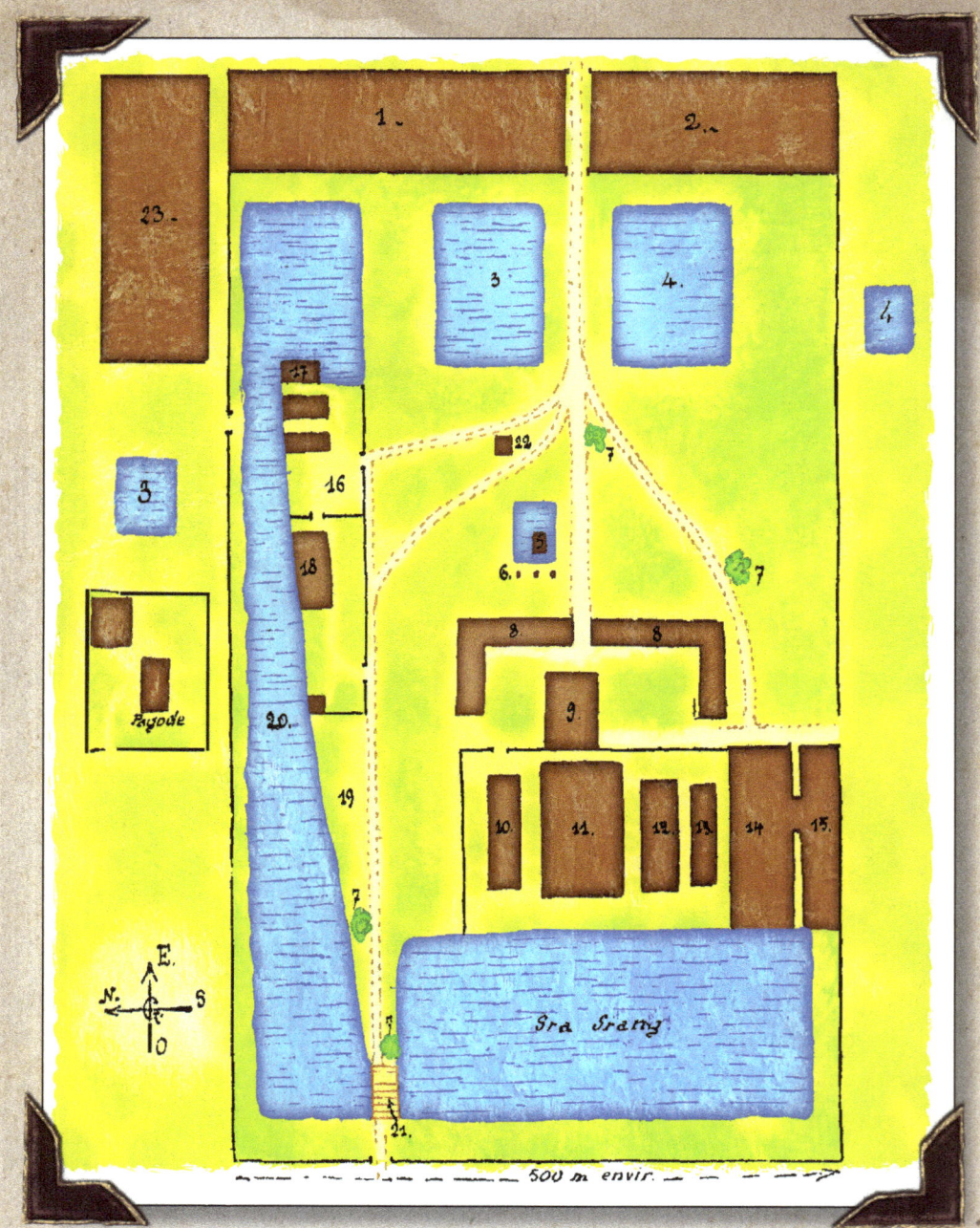

Plan of the Royal Palace of Oudong (recreation). [Groslier]

1, 2, soldier's quarters. 3, 4, ponds. 5, storeroom for silver objects, textiles. 6, offering gates. 7, large trees. 8, gallery. 9, theater hall. 10, King Norodom's sister's home. 11, king's mother's home. 12, 13, home of the palace ladies. — 14, king's nephew's home. 15, servant's quarters. 16, royal apartments. 17, floating house. 18, women's quarters. 19, storerooms. 20, great lake (pirogue racecourses). 21, wooden bridge. 22, library.

From *Monsieur de la Garde, Roi* by George Groslier. Illustration by Charles Fouqueray.

This is the setting for the three days related in my novel *Monsieur de la Garde, Roi*, based on events and characters — king, princesses, and brethren of the coast — sifted from three centuries of history to fit my plan. I copied the chronicles and took from them whatever I found striking, just as I copy what I see in this travelogue. It is unfortunate that I included so much heroism to stoke the adventure, that instead of a weak, mediocre hero I chose a passionate man whose gestures are shown off like a peacock's tail, an adventurer drawn like Belloso to great events, and who pounces on his destiny tooth and nail. It is, as I said, unfortunate, because that sort of heroism has gone out of style, and editor after editor politely returns my manuscript.[99]

Eh!, first mate, friend, with one of the Ramayana's apes tattooed on your side, black Cambodian in whom I see the amulet-covered chief whom Blas Ruiz cleft in two with a blow from his halberd: pray, let us leave behind these banks of ill inspiration.

---

[99] Groslier's persistence paid off when the French magazine, *L'Illustration*, published his novel as a two-part series in 1934. Working with the Groslier family, DatAsia Press is preparing modern editions in French and English.

25 February

Fisheries

Past Kompong Luong the fisheries begin. They have just been set up and will multiply up to the Great Lake. I stopped counting them yesterday. What is a fishery in Cambodia, at this season, on the Tonlé Sap? I have had the launch weave its way through and examine them, and can hardly believe what I have just seen. My eyes still burn from the sun-drenched waters. I have been dazzled by strange visions, by I know not what chaos of mercury, mother-of-pearl, and steel, and human bodies dipping into it with muddled gestures.

First, a known favorable spot — an estuary, a bit of land jutting out from an island, a bend in the river: a place discovered generations back by aquatic men who knew every rivulet of water down to its taste. Next, at the observance of certain seasonal signs, of secret omens, the isolation of a hectare of river with a rattan screen, a mobile, vertical wall planted in the mud, opened with a device upstream and hermetic everywhere else. Within this camp, dead branches and trunks are submerged to serve as shelters. Two weeks' or a month's wait. The current descends once more from the Great Lake and plays the role of beater on a hunt. Finally, on a day deemed propitious, the fishery chief goes to the bank and lays out offerings for the spirits. The great trap is closed, and about twenty men leap into the water.

The men use prudent, measured maneuvers, and the walls gradually close in. Screens left out as the trap area shrinks past them are rolled up and carried off in sampans. The original perimeter is finally reduced to a channel some three meters wide and fifty meters long. Never throughout the long, painstaking reduction is a space of more than an arm's breadth left open.

Thus "compressed," the water is already wrinkling with a strange quiver. Fins, some sharp and stiff, others long and undulating like bat wings, constantly rip through the surface everywhere.

Then at one end a transversal screen begins its piston-like advance, pushed along by men standing shoulder to shoulder. With every meter they must tie it to the corridor walls and rest. Following behind is a second screen, in case some fish escape the first, and dragged along behind that is a net, on the off chance. Gradually the corridor is reduced by half, then by two-thirds...

We come upon a fishery at that extraordinary moment. It is half-past noon. Two large sampans are tied to the downstream end of the corridor, a pocket seventy meters square and one and a fifth meters deep. Into this terrible impasse the fish have been squeezed together since dawn yesterday. The most desperate, swiftest flights of these fish, which for the past month had been accumulating and teeming in a hectare of water, have irresistibly driven them there.

The water boils, flashes, and bursts under their senseless leaps. A hundred beasts vault into the air at once, reaching heights of up to two meters. They twist and fall, collide obliquely, slap against the screens that squeeze them together. Enormous bodies fall with a din, having blended their gleaming, speed-blurred forms with the sunbeams. Fine rockets as sharp as squeaks trace out the parabolas of projectiles. Three men still caught in the cauldron stagger and cling to stakes amid the scaly bodies. They suffer the impacts of soft muzzles, the scrapes of fins, and the whipping of nervous tails as they bathe in this inconceivable multitude of crossed sabers.

I leap onto the first sampan slated to receive the flesh, a sort of screen-covered skiff, whose capacity I estimate at about five cubic meters. Others are brought along in reserve. Around the skiff, with hatches open, they have half-submerged some rattan boxes, so as to keep the choice fish alive. Everything is ready. Women and children, the reinforcements, arrive on pirogues. This entire Annamite world is born with fish, lives off it, until death.

They toss a sturdy cylindrical basket to the men still in the fishery. These take it by the handles, plunge it in, and with monstrous effort pull it back out. It vibrates and blazes while other men take hold, and in one swoop thirty kilos of fish roll into the skiff. In half an hour the skiff is full, sunk to the gunwales under an agonizing, animate mass. Another skiff pulls up... And while this impoverishment of the river proceeds I think of the hundred other fisheries just like this one operating at this very hour, stretching all the way to the lakes a hundred kilometers away... I think of those that have been operating for the past month, and will operate for another three... I think of the banks of the Seine, of a fisherman casting in his line from the Pont Mirabeau... And I consider these five cubic meters of fish, in the crush at my feet, there, under the sun, two tons, perhaps three, this magma...

Some have reptilian bodies. Others are flat, like soles. A woman pulls one out by the tail. It is a meter long. Once again I encounter my "water light," but they weigh twenty pounds and sport six black half-moons on either side of the belly. Many drool with the blood of broken, bleeding barbels. Others are tiled with scales erect in anger, like the bristling hairs of dogs. Bodies of roof-like, triangular cross-section, with flat bellies and heads. There are cylindrical fish, serpentine fish, club-like fish, fruit-like fish, fish resembling torn, meaty leaves. Living fish swim through dying fish. The dead are revived by the contact and whip the air with an electric crackle. An atrocious, desperate frenzy. The sun shines on bloodied eyes. The soft, moving, sucking mouths! The white of the bellies is glacial, the green-grey of the backs sticky. Crawling. The vast, opaque river, the empty landscape, the drab sky, and all that unsuspected, secret life laid bare, revealed in a few instants, enormously heavy, enormously spasmodic! Red blood seeps from the white, metallic flesh.

Little girls set aside the cá lócs[100] — kings among fish, flecked and green finned — along with other tasty species. Saltwater fish that have adapted to the river make an appearance: soles, small mackerel, and a monstrous ray that will not fit in the basket. The coolie lifts it, ten fingers sunk into the flesh, while a tail as fine as a strap whips the air.

And suddenly... I lean in, cock my ear. What is it? The wet rubbing of bodies? No. The clash of fins? No. The discharge of scaly mouths, the tearing

---

[100] The Vietnamese name *cá lóc* describes the snakehead, a freshwater fish of the Channidae family. The species with green fins is the most popular in Cambodia where it is known as *trey chhdor*. It may be grilled, then opened in a fan shape to be salted and dried, or half fermented to make fish sauce (called *nước mắm* in Vietnam or *teuk trei* in Cambodia).

In the original text, the word appeared as "caïlocs" because Parisian typesetters often altered Vietnamese spelling by applying French accents and transliteration while combining multiple words into single words.

of gills gone too dry? No. It is a murmur of deep little cries, shrill and near-imperceptible, a jingling in hideous sadness. I reckon the odds that I am misconstruing this, but I need convincing that in fact I am. I hear a murmur of surprising and pathetic agony. Whatever the dictums, these fish are sobbing. No doubt the learned are already aware of the phenomenon, but I am just discovering it. Each sob is brief. Its timbre is that of a taut cord snapping. In isolation it would be imperceptible, but a thousand fish are dying at once just fifty centimeters from my ear.

This fishery, of moderate size, permanently employs about fifteen coolies. A hundred women slit the fish open, gut them, and set them out to dry in the sun. Over the course of three months every year eighty tons of fish are taken from the river, and their heads and swim bladders generate ten thousand liters of oil. The value of the equipment — the rattan and bamboo, the creels, and the river craft — is estimated at ten thousand piastres. The chief earns a net profit of five thousand. So he says while serving me tea on his junk.

The junk is luxurious and varnished. The altar for his ancestors gleams at the rear, between two miniature, century-old trees, planted in porcelain pots. Two panels in precious wood, incrusted with mother-of-pearl, bear the name and profession of the master of the house. A band of red silk, embroidered in gold thread with characters of good omen, crowns the chapel. A flat, round guitar made of pale wood hangs from a partition, amid family photographs. The deck, still damp from a swabbing, reflects the sky, whose light streams in through a window. A parrot-beaked sunfish, gutted and dried in its circular form, hangs like a lantern over a cot that gleams as if liquid.

The junk's salon opens onto a terrace. There, at the master's call, a coolie brings me about ten fish arrayed in a star on a flat basket that looks like a cross between velvet and tinned iron. These, I am told, are the best fish one could eat.

"And the cá lóc?"

The Annamite responds to my question with a look of disgust, and I realize that next to these lozenges the cá lóc is a poor man's fish. So I ask why the cá lóc is absent from the market of Phnom Penh, since it is in season. My host's expression of disgust turns into a superior pout. The species is very rare. The rich Chinese will pay any price to get it and have first pick of the fisheries' deliveries. Also, the Europeans (bigwigs included) have never seen it on their tables, because they understand nothing about fish markets and their cooks get up too late in the morning. Besides, if by chance the cooks found one of those fish at market they would keep it for themselves...

How difficult it is to get to know a country! For fifteen years I have made a profession of studying it, and I travel through it at all seasons, yet only today have I discovered that the fish here sing like swans, that the fish that grace our most reputed tables and to me seem excellent are in fact the fish that the Chinese have rejected! Imagine, if you will, how effusively I thanked my rich fisherman, and the recommendations that I made to Eh! when I saw him take charge of our provisions under these most propitious circumstances.

But I should have left him to his own devices, for with his zeal duly stoked he wrapped the fish in the black drape of our camera!

26 February

Kampong Chhnang — The Great Lake

From Kampong Chhnang, "the cooking-pot riverbank," to the Great Lake, the river is nothing but a vast fishery. It splits into little branches in which the water returns from the lake, and which on a map evoke the circulation of blood.

Almost no vegetation on the low banks that regularly flood. We pass village after shadeless village of fishermen and fishmongers. There are few pagodas, for the population, mostly Annamite, appears only at fishing season. We see bamboo scaffolds four or five meters high and about a hundred long, where seines set out to dry emanate a brown brume that puts a glaze over the sun.

Three bamboo shafts laid flat on the water. The launch steers clear. Lashed together with rattan, they do not move. They are the floats of dormant nets that partition off the river. The mesh is calculated to snare certain fish species up to the ears and keep them pinned to the invisible walls. We find these bamboo everywhere we go. No pirogue without its fishermen armed with framed nets or shrimp nets. Deposited everywhere on the banks and suspended from huts are complicated creels, marvels of rattan workmanship, divided with a disconcerting shrewdness into compartments. These were withdrawn from the water this morning and will be plunged back in this evening. One of them, attached to the rear of a junk, serves as a cage for a pair of mandarin blackbirds.

The current carries down a vile and foul-smelling foam, the detritus of rotting fish, upon oil-slicked water. It leaks from a village entirely bedecked in little

"We see bamboo scaffolds four or five meters high and about a hundred long..." [Groslier]

kites — the color of straw and amber, hanging on taut cords from bamboo T's — and as many gutted fish set out to dry. Groups of women, their arms bloodied and flecked with scales, tirelessly prepare the fish, with hacking knives. They must work fast, to prepare within the hour the manna that spills from every sampan, lest it spoil — and the water that once carried the living beast now carries away the scraps. The ichthyophagous[101] birds do not wait around. They have given up searching and turned to theft, and now pick wearily at the piles. In three months all the fish that two million people will eat over the next year, that hundreds of junks will carry to Singapore and the Malay coasts, is fished out, gutted, and dried in this region. Here the entrails rot, the oil boils, and the scales scintillate.[102]

This, then, is a lethal place, probably unique in the world. Nowhere else do so many creatures gather every morning to die without a struggle, their

---

101 I.e., fish-eating.
102 Groslier's note: "Last year [1928 or 1929]: 120,000 tons, of which 24,000 were exported (official statistics)."

only defense a futile flight. In short, nowhere do so many die without man's killing them!

Even this late in the game, because there still remain a few acres of open bank and too much water for a net to filter and too many living fish, we encounter companies of fishermen coming upstream to set up. Tugged behind a panting launch like a bunch of grapes are about thirty junks and sampans. They follow along flank to flank and prow to prow, sails furled, rudders unmanned, carrying new nets, rolled-up screen, traps, stakes, ropes — and personnel lying amid stacks of supplies, under tents of straw.

Editor's Note: Groslier's two river tours end here.

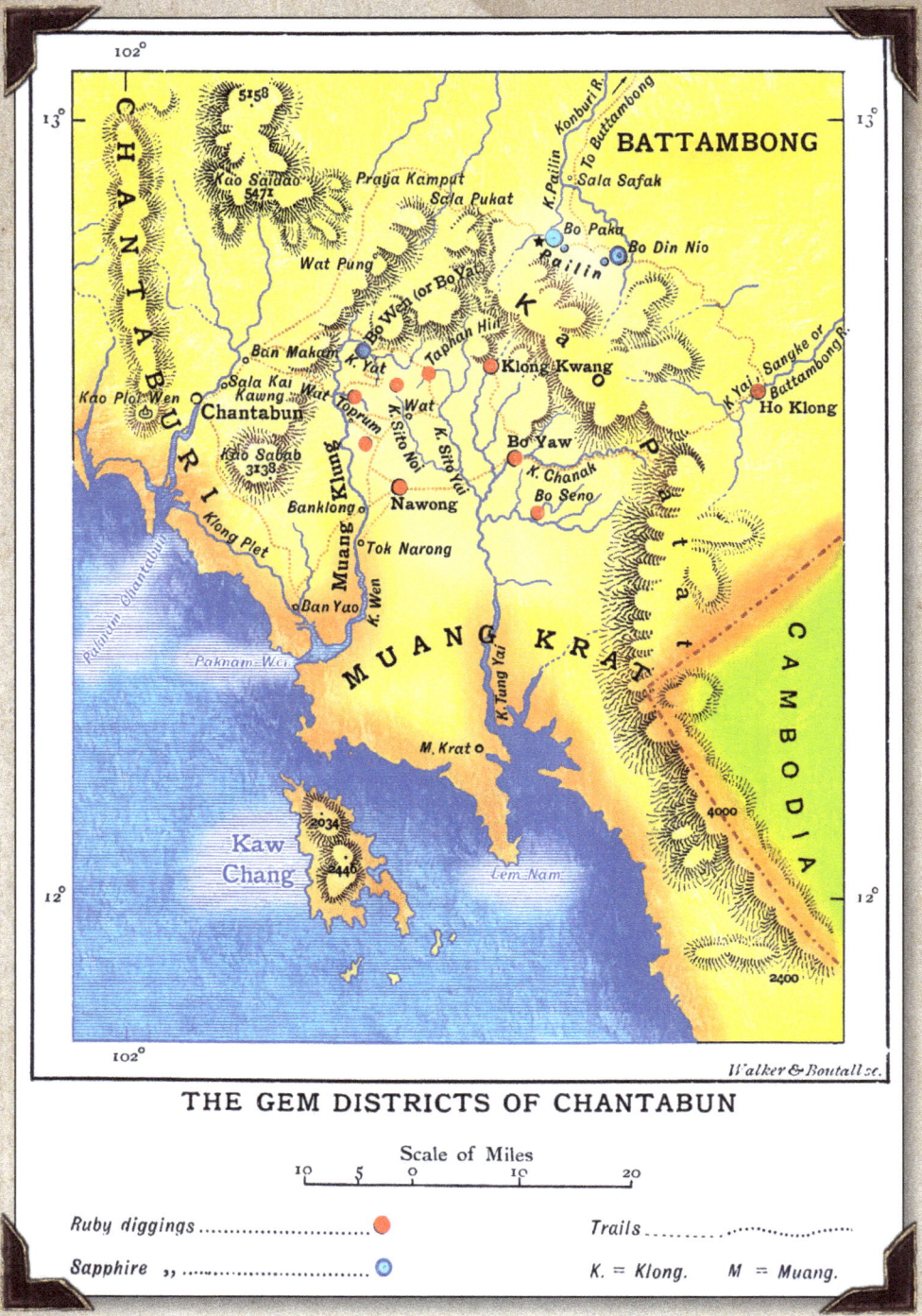

THE GEM DISTRICTS OF CHANTABUN

"The Burmese colony settled into the hollow of Cambodian land, which took the name of Pailin." [*Five Years in Siam*, H. Warrington Smyth, 1898.]

14–15 March, 1930

Pailin

Half a century ago a Burmese hunter arrived in northwestern Cambodia, a few kilometers from the border of Siam, in a cirque of hills and mountains, one of which was nearly a thousand meters tall. How did the hunter reach that spot, crossing Siam from west to east? Nobody knows.

On the ground he found bluish-black stones, like clots of lacquer. The region's Cambodians made casual use of them, to produce sparks for their lighters. The traveler placed a few in his belt and returned to his country, where he learned that the lighter flints were sapphires. He immediately returned with a hundred of his compatriots, panners and gem cutters, a few lapidary wheels. The Burmese colony settled into the hollow of Cambodian land, which took the name of Pailin (pronounced pie-lean).

It did not become Khmer for two reasons. First, the export of sapphires to Bangkok, and then to Europe, had soon abundantly compensated the expatriates, who had then brought over their parents, wives, and friends. Second, the first colonists had died off quickly: only a few remain today. Fifty years later, however, a second village had been built a few kilometers from the first. Five or six pagodas, in the Burmese style, had been founded. And now this miniature Burma has a population of three thousand souls. They live the life of the old country, and dwelling in every house, or nearly so, is a miner, cutter, or merchant of sapphires.

A thousand Cambodians serve them as coolies and cultivators. The groceries are, of course, Chinese. We are in the French Protectorate of Cambodia, but

Gula horseman
Pailin

By 1892, more than 400 Gula (Burmese) prospectors were mining for precious gems near Pailin. [*Five Years in Siam*, H. Warrington Smyth, 1898.]

these Burmese write their business papers, invoices, and receipts in English, and part of the merchandise sold by the Chinese is Siamese, as well as English. It is an astonishing mixture, to which any frequent traveler in the Far East, getting his taste of it here and there as necessity dictates, quickly grows accustomed. The result is a homogeneous whole, with a markedly Burmese flavor.

We are in mid-holiday. Yesterday was the full moon of March, the one the Burmese most sumptuously celebrate in the year. Mong Phothy, a Burmese, representative of the lapidaries of Pailin and shopkeeper in Phnom Penh, where he sells fabrics, alarm clocks, faux stones, just about everything but sapphires, walked into my office. He had a big belly and the gluttonous face of a Vitellius.[103] He bowed and invited me to attend the festivities. Pailin is 400 kilometers from Phnom Penh.

We left the following day before dawn. My Burmese man left me just enough time to grab my toothbrush, assuring me that I would find everything I needed at his sister's house, where I was to accompany him. We sped past Kampong Chhnang, where I had briefly stopped with the launch eight days earlier, and at Pursat ate a breakfast of piping-hot Chinese soup. Between there and Battambang we passed a cart transporting an eight-foot beam and, as luck would have it, were rammed in the rear mud flaps by the same, since the cart was turning as we passed. And at noon we entered Pailin, which was like another world.

༄༅༅

It is, as I have said, a village ringed with mountains and hills. The village begins at the foot of one of them and stretches to the center of the cirque in the company of a river. A sanctuary crowns the hill, and the landscape opens around it like a corolla. Instead of stamens, a forest of coconut palms. Large insects have made their niches there to gorge themselves on pollen: the pagodas. What a contrast with the river and its flat banks! The red-ochre land is unspeakably rich, and I ceaselessly wonder whether by nourishing the thick, fast-growing vegetation one mightn't make the land sweat sapphire.

The gemstone is everywhere. Even in the village itself, you can just scratch the

---

103 A Roman emperor who reigned for less than a year in 69 AD. His bust in the Louvre suggests that he was a rather stout fellow, and the description by Suetonius bears this out: "He divided his feasts into three, sometimes into four a day breakfast, luncheon, dinner, and a drinking bout; and he was readily able to do justice to all of them through his habit of taking emetics [to induce vomiting]. Moreover, he had himself invited to each of these meals by different men on the same day, and the materials for any one of them never cost less than four hundred thousand sesterces.... Being besides a man of an appetite that was not only boundless, but also regardless of time or decency, he could never refrain, even when he was sacrificing or making a journey, from snatching bits of meat and cakes amid the altars, almost from the very fire, and devouring them on the spot" ("Life of Vitellus," *Lives of the Twelve Caesars*, Loeb, 1914).

"Nonchalant and gay, they dress in all their jewels and wrap themselves in large-patterned sarongs, with little flowers stuck in their chignons."

[Burmese women, late 18th c., Felice Beato.]

ground, wash it in little vermicular watercourses, and find the gems in your basket. They are not of very great quality, often flawed and clouded, but they trade on the European market. Such lapidary considerations hardly matter: the blood of this land clots blue. One can also, though more rarely, find topazes. These are rough and emerge from the ground swollen and humid, like tears.

Feast day — but is not every day a feast day in this rich village, isolated by its race, its soul, its foreign traditions, by a cirque so remote from the rest of Cambodia?

A long, sloping road snakes through the large plank houses, expertly built, covered with thatch, some with upper floors and balconies or openwork friezes with sculpted decor. Each opens entirely onto the street, like a shop. Inside one sees small, flower-bedecked altars honoring a framed image of the Buddha or Buddha statuettes in showcases. One sees rocking cradles and tranquil men, thighs sheathed in tattoos, seated with their backs to the street before horizontal wheels that they work with one foot. The stone rustles softly like tearing paper, and its whisper continues from house to house.

The young women, who do not hide away like their Cambodian counterparts, tend to their little household chores. That is, they do nothing. Nonchalant and gay, they dress in all their jewels and wrap themselves in large-patterned sarongs, with little flowers stuck in their chignons. The parquets maintain their gleam under the ceaseless passage of bare feet.

Small gardens two cubits wide bloom like household altars before these houses, between them and the street, one thing blending into the next. Their bushes — rosebushes, gardenias, jasmines, frangipanis, hibiscus with lantern-like suspended flowers — are enclosed in bamboo, to keep the goats from ravaging them. Magnificent coconut palms — taller here, it seems to me, than anywhere else in Cambodia — rise above the rooftops.

༄༅༆

My courteous Burmese had time to wire his family the evening before, so the house is ready for me when I do arrive. A single room ten meters long, eight wide. The same dimensions from parquet to topmost beam. A high room juts out like a balcony. It has a sculpted frame and is accessible from the inside by a ladder. This is the room reserved for me. From it, like a caged bird, I overlook the vast room and, beyond that, the street.

I am not the sole occupant. There is a Buddha, seated on a lotus in his altar just as I am seated in my room, and the altar overlooks the room just as my room overlooks the house. The god is surrounded by paper bouquets, themselves behind three votive flames. This morning the daily offering — a plate of rice, a glass of water, a banana, and flowers fallen from an invisible frangipani tree and arranged around the food — has been laid out before the altar on a pedestal table. A cot, a very white mosquito net, and everywhere new mats for me to set my feet on. How better to describe the urbanity of these Burmese people?

Mong Phothy's sister, widow, solid matron some forty years of age, merchant of precious stones, lives here amid family and servants. All that I have seen of her so far, so dazzling was the garment, was an astonishing sarong decorated with guitars, geometric bands, and extravagant flowers, all of it colored and randomly arranged against a background of burnt topaz. An English fabric specially made for the colonies, patterned after local models to appeal to native tastes (we in France do not know how to do this). Near the matron is her last daughter: the last of I know not how many. She is eight years old and has dazzled me even more than her mother's sarong. They tell me her name in Burmese. Her uncle translates into Cambodian. In French it would be "Emerald."

Emerald and Eggplant, the aristocrat and the commoner, the daughter of rich bourgeois and the daughter of a first mate, the lapidary and the cook. Between them: two races, two civilizations, two castes, and names that happen to stake out the difference. In Emerald I find an exquisite synthesis of all the cute little girls I have seen pass by since this morning, each already looking every bit the lady, except in hairstyle.

Hair so black as to seem heavy and mineral, and glazed with coconut oil. First, a well-smoothed, neatly trimmed fringe three fingers wide goes round the head. The chignon is knotted above the fringe and the blue line that separates it from the rest of the hair. It is not the miserable little snail atop Eggplant but a conical chignon, run through with a large rose if not a golden flower. At its base, a crown of pale-yellow orchids, analogous to the buttercups in our fields. A flaring, very short blouse,[104] buttoned under the arm and white, or of a very tender and unfaded color: a color just coming into being. And skinny hips wrapped in a perfectly smooth sarong. Dressed in this way the little Burmese girls go about, striking from afar the profiles of women.

Their elder sisters wear turban-like chignons. The fringe is gone, but not the crown of flowers. Their skirts have great leafy patterns. Their clogs knock out two notes — click, clack, click, clack — on the floor. The men, meanwhile, with their proud bearing and grave faces, knot a handkerchief around their ears, like Corsican bandits.

ಌ✽ಌ

---

104 Called a *caraco* in the French text referring to a tight-fitting jacket or camisole.

"Their elder sisters wear turban-like chignons."

Burmese girl holding a local cigar. [Watts and Skeen albumen print, circa 1890]

I am drinking a warm soda imported from Siam. It is mint green and tastes like lipstick. Emerald prepared and lit the lamp, which she placed on the floor. It was then, with the light suddenly bursting from her hands, that I observed her, the chignon, the little flowers. We could have ended up together. And she held the lamp out to me like as if it were an offering.

The table is covered with an openwork cloth. Resting at its center are two glasses, one containing a bouquet of yellow roses, the other a bouquet of cigars. These are twenty-five centimeters long. The tobacco is in a tube of thick paper. They resemble mirlitons.[105] There are cigarettes in a silver cup, its granular surface deeply embossed with mitered characters.

Emerald pours me some tea. She watches me and refills my cup as soon as I have set it down. I am not thirsty and don't much like the tea, but I drink. I drink so as not to trouble the little girl. Every time I tap out some ash she takes the ashtray outside, empties it, wipes it, and brings it back. She

---

105 Kazoo-like musical instruments.

understands neither French nor Khmer. But she would be equally silent if I understood Burmese, for I am infinitely big and powerful and she is infinitely humble and small. It would only frighten her if I paid my respects. I am not to notice her presence. She was dispatched by her mother to keep an eye on me, empty my ashtray, and fill my teacup, always stepping noiselessly on the parquet. She wears a pale sapphire in each ear, tiny gold circles on her wrists, and a five-pound coin, stamped with the profile of Queen Victoria, empress of the Indies, around her neck.[106]

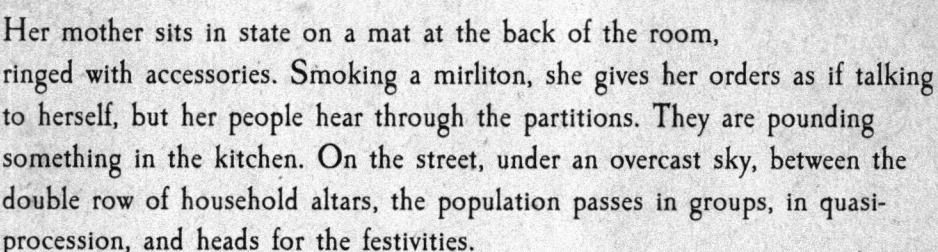

Her mother sits in state on a mat at the back of the room, ringed with accessories. Smoking a mirliton, she gives her orders as if talking to herself, but her people hear through the partitions. They are pounding something in the kitchen. On the street, under an overcast sky, between the double row of household altars, the population passes in groups, in quasi-procession, and heads for the festivities.

The men keep to their side. The young men, lanky, are half dressed in European clothes, which make them look like thugs, and half dressed in draped fabrics, which suffice to make them seem princes. One passes by on a bicycle and brakes by pressing a big toe onto the tire. An imbecile puts on airs, sporting a balaclava.[107] Where could he have got it? The mature men are less Westernized, old brigands with pierced cheeks and dark-red or jade-green headscarves on heads that still sport the chignon. These are the men who, they say, would in times of trouble transport their precious stones by inserting them under their skin, letting the slit heal before setting off, and opening the wounds once they had reached the distant destination of Rangoon. These groups alternate with female groups, never mixing.

---

106 This necklace—such as the 1897 example above struck on 39.67 grams of gold—had substantial value in 1930. According to MeasuringWorth.com, £5 has a buying power of £234 in 2009. More telling is that a wage of £5 in 1930 has a value of £960 in 2009. That, of course, was in UK. In Cambodia labor was far cheaper, and thus the value far higher.

107 A knit, pull-on hat, not unlike a ski mask, that is traditionally made of wool and covers the head, ears, chin, and neck but not the facial features. While Groslier characterized the wearer as "putting on airs," ski masks are now common throughout Cambodia and Thailand. Natives often wear full head coverings when working in the fields or on construction sites.

The women are the same in their lines, their style, their stride — but different in their colors. The path slopes downward, so they land awkwardly on a bent leg with each step, their torso angled back a bit. They carry flat parasols ribbed with bamboo, showing spokes in their transparency. They ceaselessly twirl them in their fingertips, the spinning halos of painted paper hardly shading them at all. Nowhere among them do I find the closed expression or haughty step of Cambodian women. I find instead an insouciant sweetness, some secret gaiety that pours forth unintentionally and is rendered precious and untouchable by the flowers in their chignons and the evident care that has gone into arranging their hair. The mothers, the old women, and the servants follow behind the ravishing youths, like a nice breeze impelling leaves.

⁂

They were more beautiful yesterday evening, in the light of the full moon, when the glimmer of the silks split into unknown colors. Conversations would cease in my presence, and the sound of the passing cortege was reduced to the click-clack of clogs. The yellow flowers were white. So were the little jackets that appeared pale pink or bud-green to my eye during the day. There was a lantern near me, and beyond its light, a few steps off, the original colors would reappear. A silvery grey turned almond green, then, back in the moonlight, silvery grey. I would catch the gleam of invisible jewels only to lose it instantly. The women passing were not those I had seen approach, yet I would recognize them again as they went off into the distance. The chatter would revive when the colors split apart again. For more than an hour I watched these sapphire girls parade by, alternately lunar and fleshly.

I came to an analogy in no way fortuitous. It obsessed me as soon as I seized on it, and it became more and more striking as the minutes passed. There was, I found, a Baudelairian[108] rhythm to the cortege, to the channeled, mysterious flow. The only thing equal to the abandon of these passers-by was their artifice. Jewels revealed and melting away! Enameled chignons! The gliding

---

108 In the style of French poet, critic, translator, and hedonistic freethinker Charles Pierre Baudelaire (1821–1867), who wrote some of modernity's most influential poetry. Though not disavowing classical models, his poetry at times verges on prose, deals with opiate-induced hallucination, and links love with death.

"For more than an hour I watched these sapphire girls parade by, alternately lunar and fleshly." [Burmese lady, circa 1920s.]

gaits and swinging arms! The twin artificial lights of moon and lantern! Yes! This was indeed the hour when each flower, vibrating on its stem, when each of these women would evaporate like the smoke of a censer! It was the hour of charcoal, of silver. Sapphire underfoot and palm leaves overhead....

What the poet's genius had been able to create with full-blooded artifice and passionate research — ah, how could such a thing be possible?! — was being recreated with the same cadence before me, in this far corner of the earth. The prudent mouths, the groups alternating like stanzas, the silken profiles, the girls beneath their flowery hair, the old women who had given birth to these shimmering beings — together they murmured:

"Listen, my darling. Listen to the sweet, strolling night."

❀

An hour later I went to the festivities, on the great square that dominates Pailin, where the village begins, at the foot of the hill. I could no longer see the hill itself, but only the pagoda at its summit, lit up and standing out against a clear sky. I always felt the same surprise whenever I looked away from the crowd, the shops, the open-air theater, all lit up by well-designed kerosene pressure lamps, and caught sight of that great nearby star up there in the night, shining in symmetry with the moon. And only when I had thus located the summit could I locate the hill, which had become as imponderable as a fog.

I mixed with the people, entered a jubilation distilled by the night. Men gathered around lamps and gaming tables, where the game of "thirty-six beasts[109]" was especially popular. Little cafés lined the square beyond a narrow canal of flowing water. These miniature, flag-covered shops of thatch and bamboo served only tea, coffee, and lemon soda. Opposite them, the crowd lined up against a row of lit-up stalls, with smiling, dainty female vendors squatting behind skewered slices of sugar cane, green mangoes, cakes of amber-colored sugar-palm fruit, cubes of pineapple, and pompons of flowers. A silent perambulation. Orientals feel joy in their eyes and hearts. They do not leap or cry out, and not a petal drops from a chignon.

---

109 See "The Game of Thirty-six Beasts" on page 229 in the appendices.

A carnival troupe of Cambodian dancers was putting on a play. In this foreign milieu the Khmer seemed plump cheeked and vulgar. Their women's short hair stood on end like a brush, looking elementary and rude next to the languorously, painstakingly turned Burmese chignons. Entertainers were performing in a well-lit thatch hut. Still and contemplative, the Burmese women of Pailin had settled onto raked seats to watch. They would suddenly join in laughter over the clowning of the buffoons and just as suddenly fall back into their attentive, silent tranquility.

What a mosaic! The powerful colors that I had seen during the day were now absent from the same fabrics. The colors seemed still gayer, still lighter, and ran together to form a celestial blue, a sharp lilac, and a green that I have seen nowhere else: the green at the heart of a cucumber, between the seeds. It seemed to me that almost all of these evening colors were not only light, and vibrant in their lightness, but also cold. Yes! To the raging sun of a blazing day they were instinctively offering up skirts that resembled forests and gardens, woven with gold, blood, and copper, and at night they were wrapping themselves exclusively in fabrics that on every ornament would hold a cold gleam in the moonlight — what a lesson, what discipline in this collaboration between a people and the activity of the heavens!

꿍❀ೞ

I was permitted to watch Emerald's toilette. She had settled onto on a mat before her mother in a pink sarong stiffened with a few silver threads. Her mother had already prepared some powder on a sheet of newspaper and made a little pile of flowers on a square of still-damp banana leaf. The little girl's jewels lay in an unknotted handkerchief.

She kept still. Mute, the matron molded her, selecting each flower and its place. The fringe of hair was meticulously evened out with a comb resembling an engraver's chisel. With every stroke of the maternal finger, a slightly more ornamented little girl emerged from the shadows, a new facet shone from beneath the centenary buffwheel. The powder, applied with the palm of the hand, mixed with the amber of her kneaded face. Her little necklaces were put on, in order of increasing length, and in such a way that a two-hour walk would not disturb them. The child's obedience stemmed from her own certainty. She knew what she was turning into as surely as if she had been shown a mirror. She checked only the clasps of her bracelets. When her mother had completed the traditional work, with nary a correction, the child rose, as an idol. I took her hand, and we set off for the festivities.

My step, as I strode next to her, made the earth tremble. I felt as stocky as an aurochs,[110] roughhewn and barbarous. In former times, while I was still but a mixture of Huns and Franks[111], other men were already ornamenting this cute little girl, making her look just as she did now.

The Buddha had been smiling for her for ten centuries. Despite the quick pace of certain races, there is something that their progress and intelligence cannot quite reach, some prize that only slow civilizations can take.

I was holding it by the hand.

It was floating at my side.

NOTE: Selected chapters of *Water and Light* were also published in French in the review *Terre et mer—la géographie* from September to November 1931.

---

110 Ancestor of the modern cow.

111 Huns were a nomadic pastoral people who migrated into Europe around the fourth century. The Franks were a Germanic people who lived in Europe in the same era. Groslier is describing his sense of awkwardness before the elegant, delicate little girl.

Appendices

George Groslier – A Contemporary Profile
Paul E. BOUDET

The Works of George Groslier

George Groslier Awards
Kent DAVIS

Sakrava — The Moon Songs
Kent DAVIS

Sakrava Songs in *Saramani*
Kent DAVIS

Model Sakrava Lyrics by H.M. King Sisowath
Solang UK

The Lunar Origins of the Khmer People
Paul CRAVATH

The Game of Thirty-six Beasts
Kent DAVIS

George Groslier, circa 1928.

George Groslier:
A Contemporary Profile

Paul E. Boudet

Editor's Note: Boudet's profile of Groslier give us a personal impression of the author and his works. It was published in *Extrême-Asie* in February 1928, a little more than a year before Groslier's Mekong voyage. Boudet's specific comments about *Le Singe qui montre la lanterne magique* have been cut below, but will appear in the new edition of that title.

GEORGE GROSLIER, a smiling, hospitable man who welcomes you with the sort of joyous voice one does not employ on the importunate. The Cambodian house is so very un-colonial, more like a Pompeian villa, with its flagstone peristyle and an impluvium[1] crawling with new leaves. The den of the lord of the manor is in a shady far corner of the gallery, its double doors closing without a sound. Books all along the walls, sometimes jostling for space with a polished, attractive grey block: the head of a Khmer with contemplative eyes. Higher up and all around, the scintillation of Cambodian silks, old sampots of faded lamé, still sumptuous despite the gentle effacement of time. The entirety of Khmer art, the imperishable stones, the extinguished silks, and the lasting jewels, heavy with precious cabochons.

---

1 An apt description of the rear of Groslier's home. In Greece and Rome this was the sunken part of an atrium that carried away rainwater that fell through the *compluvium* of the roof.

The Groslier home as seen in 2012. [Photo Kent Davis]

Groslier's 1928 photo shows the "impluvium" behind his home.

Before he has said a word we have understood George Groslier's whole history: fifteen years in the life of this still-young man are writ here, and each has left its mark around one who, like no one else, can condense and collect the many scattered and disparate traits of a potent personality.

On the walls, canvases, already old, from the writer's brush; in boxes, a trove of ink drawings. All of them attest to the artist's first years, his first vision of the Angkorean forest, of the temples still buried within, romantic like the wellspring of his inspiration, which had initially made him into an artist of the line and color variety, a man devoted to his visual existence as artist-explorer.

He has since been months in the Cambodian forest. When scarcely adolescent he had not yet acquired the means of externalization that would later transform him into both a visionary archeologist and a writer.

Instantly his artistic temperament found his most immediate means of expression: painting. One of the canvases, among his oldest (a temple in a forest), which I chanced on at a friend's house, seems already to harbor the secret of what the man would become.

But it was a long preparation that George Groslier was obliged to undertake—years of solitude in the forest, years of research and tent-bound meditative life, leisure in which a paintbrush strives to express what the man seeks, and then, once more, dogged work to extirpate an active intellectuality from the passive nature depicted by a dazzled artist...

For he is exceedingly young, this artist, and has not yet forged his own temperament before this invasive variety of nature. But he is driven by an obscure force of will that with astonishing speed will unfetter him from lines and matter, lead him to an intellectual and no longer sentimental comprehension of Khmer art; he will pass from things to living beings and on to souls.

In those boxes of ink drawings are the inspiration for his first book: *Cambodian Dancers: Ancient and Modern*. Long before they were described the dancers and poses were captured as they are depicted in that box. The author always proceeds from sensible forms to spirit.

In the Shadow of Angkor is a lovely and already long-published book, which Groslier's early manner cloaks in romantic charm: temples in the wilderness that cluster around ancient Khmer cities—Ta Phrom, Prah Vihear, Beng Méala, Banteay-Chhmar. He spent interminable days traveling by ox cart between them, sleeping nights in the forest, writing when the dense tropical deluge forced him to take shelter.

Recent years have matured him further: the artist no longer paints. *In the Shadow of Angkor*, which seemingly paved the way for him to become a new "Pèlerin d'Angkor,"[2] has no future. Its form, increasingly intellectual, has led to that first-rate work *Recherches sur les Cambodgiens d'après les textes et les monuments depuis les premiers siècles de noire ère* (1921) and to the creation of a collection, *Art et Archéologie Khmers; Revue des recherches sur les arts, les monuments et l'ethnographie du Cambodge, depuis les origines jusqu'à nos jours* (1921-25), in which, for the first time, the author has rendered the entirety of Cambodian artistic life.

It was thus a surprise in 1925, ten years after a purely literary work like *In the Shadow of Angkor*, when the author drew from his boxes to produce a lovely novel titled *The Road of the Strong*.

An unforgettable, palpitating read—the temperament of George Groslier had returned to its primitive, purely intuitive form. In reading *The Road of the Strong* those who had been loath to see him absorbed in the probing of a lost art's traditions, in the painstaking exhumation of a slow, skillful craftsmanship, so as to revive what time had buried, suddenly had the sense that the man had bided his time before revealing certain aspects of his personality, aspects that until then he had purposely kept dormant...

Edmond Jaloux, better placed than any other publisher to judge the flavor of this evocation of the Cambodian forest, enthusiastically retained the book for his collection, and the literary critics were grateful. As Jaloux himself said in *Nouvelles Littéraires* and his much-appreciated chronicles:

> "All of the descriptions are worthy of note. They are not descriptions in the rhetorical and banal sense that we have given the word; they are recreations, a series of living, stirring poems scattered throughout the book, making us feel all the beauty of a little-known land...."

---

2 I.e., a new Pierre Loti, author of *Un Pèlerin d'Angkor* (*A Pilgrimage to Angkor*) in 1912. The book was issued in English in 1913 under the title *Siam*.

And this from the *Gazelle de Lausanne*, which reaches to the very depths of the work:

> "The new perspective M. Groslier has managed to take on the enduring conflict of Orient versus Occident is evident. His book is troubling, sad in its beauty, like Hindu music."

And next we have *Le Singe qui montre la lanterne magique*, which M. Groslier has just entrusted to Extrême-Asie.[3] This latest work is no less surprising than *The Road of the Strong*, or, rather, confirms us in our surprise at seeing the full manifestation of a writerly temperament from which the rigors of pure science had momentarily removed our attention.

The memory returns of charming hours spent with G. Groslier, spent listening to him read other works, some that the author will perhaps jealously keep forever in his boxes. Deep intuitions of a complex psychology where other characters live, but only within!

I see the nervous hand quickly put the pages away, and I wonder what aspect of this artistic temperament will come to dominate in the long run: the novelist of new men, elemental and deep like all that is intimately bound up with action, or other aspects entirely, diverse and nuanced and open to the outside world?

What surprises lie in store for us as this artistic, archeological, writerly temperament that can already externalize itself in so many ways reaches fruition?

>Paul E. BOUDET
>
>Director of the Archives Department and the Libraries of Indochina
>
>February 1928

---

3 Groslier's little-known work appeared as a series in *Extrême-Asie*, with Boudet's biographical profile above published with the first installment. DatAsia Press has a French edition of this title in preparation. Groslier released his next novel, *Le retour à l'argile* (*Return to Clay*), shortly after this article. In 2014, DatAsia Press issued an English translation, including the original French text.

George Groslier at work in his study on December 5, 1922. Above him rests the scupted bust he made of his daughter Nicole. It remained there for the rest of his life.

The Works of George Groslier

Creative, passionate and prolific, George Groslier was a visionary man of many talents. First trained in fine arts by Parisian master painter Albert Maignan, George returned to his Cambodian birthplace in 1911. There, he devoted his life to documenting, preserving, promoting and celebrating Khmer art, culture and history.

Groslier expressed himself visually as a painter, intellectually as an archaeologist, museum curator and essayist, and emotionally as a creative writer. He championed Khmer patrimony in every endeavor, infusing his artistic works with his unique love, respect and sensitivity for Cambodia that ensure the timeless validity of his contributions.

Modern French & English Language Editions

- *La Route du plus fort.* Paris: Kailash, 1994.
- *Le Retour à l'argile.* Paris: Kailash, 1994.
- *Cambodian Dancers – Ancient & Modern.* Holmes Beach, FL: DatAsia Press, 2010; and Phnom Penh, Cambodia: DatAsia Press, 2011.
- *In the Shadow of Angkor – Unknown Temples of Ancient Cambodia.* Holmes Beach, FL: DatAsia Press, 2014.
- *Danseuses cambodgiennes – Anciennes & Modernes.* Holmes Beach, FL: DatAsia Press, 2014.
- *Return to Clay – A Romance of Cambodia.* Holmes Beach, FL: DatAsia Press, 2014.
- *Water and Light – A Travel Journal of the Cambodian Mekong.* Holmes Beach, FL: DatAsia Press, 2016.
- *Road of the Strong – A Romance of Cambodia.* Holmes Beach, FL: DatAsia Press, 2016.

Books
- *La Chanson d'un Jeune.* Self-published. 1904.
- *Danseuses cambodgiennes anciennes et modernes.* Paris : A. Challamel, 1913.
- *A l'ombre d'Angkor; notes et impressions sur les temples inconnus de l'ancien Cambodge.* Paris : A. Challamel, 1913.
- *Angkor...Ouvrage orné de 103 gravures et de 5 cartes et plans.* Paris: H. Laurens, 1924.
- *Arts et Archéologie khmères, 2 vol.* Paris : A. Challamel, 1921-1926.
- *Recherches sur les Cambodgiens d'après les textes et les monuments depuis les premiers siècles de notre ère.* Paris : A. Challamel, 1921.
- *Arts et Archéologie Khmers. Revue des Recherches sur les Art, les Monuments et l'Ethnographie du Cambodge, depuis les Origines jusqu'à nos Jours.* Paris: Société d' Editions Géographiques, Maritimes et Coloniales, 1925.
- *La sculpture Khmère ancienne ; illustrée de 175 reproductions hors texte en similigravure.* Paris : G. Crès, 1925.
- *Les collections khmères du Musée Albert Sarraut à Phnom-Penh.* Paris: G. van Oest, 1931.
- *Eaux et lumières; journal de route sur le Mékong cambodgien.* Paris: Société d'éditions géographiques, maritimes et coloniales, 1931.
- *L'enseignement et la mise en pratique des arts indigènes au Cambodge (1918-1930).* Paris: Sté d'éditions géographiques, maritimes et coloniales, 1931.
- *Angkor, with 103 illustrations, 5 maps and plans. Translated from the French by Paule Fercoq Du Leslay.* Evreux: impr. Hérissey, 1933.
- *Ankooru iseki.* Japanese translation of *Angkor.* Tokyo: Shinkigensha, 1943.

Novels
- *La Route du plus fort.* Paris, Emile-Paul frères, 1926.
- *Le Retour à l'argile.* Paris : Emile-Paul frères, 1928.
- *Monsieur De La Garde, Roi: Roman, Inspiré Des Chroniques Royales Du Cambodge,* 1934, Paris: *L'Illustration.*
- *Les Donneurs de Sang, Phnom Penh et Saigon.* Saigon : Albert Portail, 1941.
- *Le Christ Byzentine,* 1953, Ellery Queen Mystère Magazine, N°69 and N°70.

Graphic Works
- *Les Ruines d'Angkor.* Indochine, 1911.

Archeological Publications
- "Objets anciens trouvés au Cambodge." *Revue archéologique,* 1916, 5e Série, vol. 4, pp. 129-139.
- "La batellerie cambodgienne du VIIIe au XIIIe siècles." *Revue archéologique,* 1917, 5e Série, vol. 5, pp. 198-204.
- "Objets cultuels en bronze dans l'ancien Cambodge." *Arts et Archéologie khmers,* 1921-3, vol. 1, fasc. 3, pp. 221-228.

- "Le temple de Phnom Chisor.' Ibid, vol. 1, fasc. 1, pp. 65-81.
- "Le temple de Ta Prohm (Ba Ti)." Ibid, vol. 1. fasc. 2, pp. 139-148.
- "Le temple de Preah Vihear". Ibid, 1921-1922, vol. 1. fasc. 3, pp. 275-294.
- "Essai sur l'architecture classique khmère." *Arts et Archéologie khmers*, 1923, vol. 1, fasc. 3. pp. 229-273.
- "L'art khmèr." Paris, *Arts et Décoration*, août 1923. vol. 27. N° 260, pp. 34-40.
- "L'art du bronze au Cambodge.' *Arts et Archéologie khmers*, 1923. vol. 1, fasc., pp. 413-423.
- "L'Art khmèr." Paris, *Arts et Décoration*, August 1923, vol. 1, pp. 413-423.
- "Amarendrapura dans Amoghapura." *Bulletin de l'Ecole Française d'Extrême-Orient*, Hanoï, 1924, vol. 24, pp. 359-372.
- *Angkor, Les Villes d'Art célèbres*. Paris, Laurens, 1924.
- *Catalogue du Musée de Phnom Penh*. Hanoï, IDEO, 1924.
- "La céramique dans l'ancien Cambodge." *Arts et Archéologie khmers*, 1924, vol. 2, fasc. 1, pp. 31-64.
- "La vie à Angkor au XIe siècle." Saigon, *Pages Indochinoises*, 15-1-1924, N.S., vol. 1, pp. 9-17.
- "Les empreintes du 'Pied du Buddha' d'Angkor Vat." *Arts et Archéologie khmers*, 1924, vol. 2, fasc. 2. pp. 65-80.
- "La région d'Angkor." *Arts et Archéologie khmers*, 1924, vol. 2, fasc. 2, pp. 113-130.
- "La région du Nord-Est du Cambodge et son art." Ibid., pp. 131-141.
- "L'Asram Maha Rosei." *Arts et Archéologie khmers*, 1924, vol. 2. fasc. 2. pp. 141-146.
- "L'Art hindou au Cambodge." *Arts et Archéologie khmers*, 1924. vol. 2, fasc. 1, pp. 81-93.
- "Essai sur le Buddha khmèr." Ibid, pp. 93-112.
- "Sur les origines de l'Art khmèr." *Mercure de France*, 1-xii-1924, vol. 176, N° 365, pp. 382-404.
- "Les influences grecques au Cambodge et l'art pré khmèr." Paris, *L'Art Vivant*, 1925.
- "Sur la route d'Angkor : le Prasat Phum Prasat." Saigon, *Extrême-Asie*, déc. 1925, N° 14, vol. 12, pp. 493-494.
- "Introduction à l'étude des arts khmèrs." *Arts et Archéologie khmers*, 1925, vol. 2. fasc. 2, pp. 167-234.
- "La femme dans la sculpture khmère ancienne." Paris, *Revue des Arts asiatiques*, 1925, vol. 2, fasc. 1, pp. 35-41
- "La fin d'Angkor." Saigon, *Extrême-Asie*, Sept. 1925.
- "Note sur la sculpture khmère ancienne." Hanoï, *Études asiatiques*, École Française d'Extrême-Orient, 1925. vol. I, pp. 297-314.
- "A propos d'art hindou et d'art khmèr." *Arts et Archéologie khmers*, 1926, vol. 2, fasc. 3, pp. 329-348.
- "Les collections khmères du Musée Albert Sarraut." *Ars Asiatica*, XVI, Paris, G. Van Oest, 1931.

- "Les Temples inconnus du Cambodge." Paris, *Toute la terre*, June 1931.
- *Angkor, Les Villes d'Art célèbres*. Paris. Laurens, 1932 (English translation).
- "Troisième recherche sur les Cambodgiens." *Bulletin de l'Ecole Française d'Extrême-Orient*, Hanoi, 1935, vol. 35, pp. 159-206.
- "Une merveilleuse cité khmère. Banteai Chhma, ville ancienne du Cambodge." Paris, *L'Illustration*, April 3, 1937, N° 4909, pp. 352-357.
- "Les Monuments khmers sont-ils des tombeaux?" Saigon. Bulletin de la Société des Eudes Indochinoises.1941, N.S., vol. 16. N°1.pp. 121-126.

Publications on the Indigenous Arts of Cambodia

- "La Convalescence des Arts cambodgiens." Hanoï, *Revue Indochinoise*, Imprimerie d'Extrême-Orient, 2e sem. 1918, p. 207; 1er sem. 1919, pp. 871-890, 22 p. ill. p. 16, fig. 21.
- "L'agonie des Arts cambodgiens." Hanoï, *Revue Indochinoise*, 2e sem. 1918, p.207.
- "Question d'art indigène." Hué, *Bulletin des Amis du Vieux-Hué*, Oct.-Dec. déc. 1920, pp. 444-452.
- "Étude sur la psychologie de l'artisan cambodgien." *Arts et Archéologie khmers*, 1921, vol. 1, fasc. 2, pp. 125-137.
- "Seconde étude sur la psychologie de l'artisan cambodgien." *Arts et Archéologie khmers*, 1921, vol. 1. fasc. 2, pp. 205-220.
- "Royal Dancers of Cambodia." *Asia*, 1922, vol. 22, N° 1, pp. 47-55, 74-75.
- "Soixante-seize dessins cambodgiens tracés par l'oknha Tep Nimit Mak et l'oknha Reachna Prasor Mao, Arts et Archéologie khmers." Paris: *Société d'Edition Géographique, Maritime et Coloniale*, 1923. 331-386 p.
- "The Oldest Living Monarch." *Asia*,1923. vol. 23. pp. 587-589.
- "La reprise des arts khmèrs." *La Revue de Paris*, Nov. 15, 1925. pp. 395-422.
- "Avec les danseuses royales du Cambodge." Mercure de France, May 1, 1928, pp. 536-565.
- "La mort de S.M. Sisowath." *L'Illustration*, Oct. 1927.
- "Les cérémonies d'incinérations de S.M. Sisowath." *L'Illustration*, April 1928. 86è année, n°4443. Samedi 28 Avril 1928. pp. 410-415.
- "Die Kunst der Kambodschanischen tànzerinn." Munich, *Atlantis*, Jan.-Mar. 1929, vol. 1,pp. 10-16.
- "Die Tanzerinnen des Konigs." [Miscellanea], p 16. 2 plates (1 col.) *Atlantis*, Jan 1929.
- "Le théâtre et la danse au Cambodge." Paris, *Journal Asiatique*, Jan.-Mar. 1929. vol. 214, pp. 125-143. (See Appendix for English translation)
- "Contemporary Cambodian art studied in the Light of the Past Forms." Boston, *Eastern Art*, 1930. vol. 2, pp. 127-141.
- "La Direction des Arts cambodgiens et l'École des Arts cambodgiens." Saigon, *Extrême-Asie*, March 1930, N° 45, pp. 119-127.
- "La fin d'un art." Paris, *Revue des Arts Asiatiques*, 1929-1930, vol. 6, fasc. 3., pp. 176-186; p. 184 et 251, fasc. 4, pp. 244-254.

- "La fin d'une tradition d'art : les pagodes cambodgiennes et le ciment armé." *L'Illustration*, January 11, 1930, vol. 175, pp. 50-53.
- "De Pagode en Pagode." Paris. *Toute la Terre*, July 1931.
- "L'Orfèvrerie cambodgienne à l'Exposition Coloniale." Paris, *La Perle*, 1931.
- "Rapport sur les arts indigènes au Cambodge." Congrès International et Intercolonial de la Société Indigène, Paris. 1931.
- "L'Enseignement et la mise en pratique des Arts indigènes au Cambodge." *Bulletin de Académie des Sciences Coloniales*, Paris, 1931.
- "Les Arts indigènes au Cambodge." *Exp. int. des Arts et Techniques*, Indochine Française, Paris, 1937.
- "Les Arts indigènes au Cambodge." 10th *Congress of the Far-Eastern Association of Tropical Medicine*, Hanoi, 1938, pp. 161-181.

Narratives

- "Propos sur la maison coloniale." Saigon, *Extrême-Asie*, 3° trim. 1926, pp. 2-10; March 1927, pp. 307-366.
- "Le Singe qui montre la Lanterne magique." Saigon, *Extrême-Asie*, Feb. 1928, pp. 347-366; mars 1928, pp. 435-450; avril 1928, pp. 499-505; mai 1928, pp. 546-554.
- "C'est une idylle...." Paris, *Mercure de France*, July 1929.
- *La Mode masculine aux colonies*. Paris : Adam, 1931.
- "Nos boys." Saigon, *Extrême-Asie*, August 1931, N° 55, pp. 69-76.

182   *Water and Light*

The last two photos of George with his cat, taken by daughter Nicole, circa 1942.

George Groslier Awards

Kent Davis

George Groslier earned many professional honors during his life, which was sadly cut short by his death under Japanese torture while imprisoned during their World War II occupation of Cambodia. This article lists many of his awards while adding details and representative photos.

In communications with colonial historian and archivist Joel Montague, he remarked that "Groslier is a bit of an oddity" for the following reasons:

Groslier earned his awards over an extended period. He was only 18 when he earned his first recognitions in France in 1905. King Sihanouk of Cambodia presented his final award in 1943/44—shortly before his untimely death—when Groslier was 57 years old. In Montague's words "this shows amazing dedication and productivity over an entire lifetime."

1. Unlike many specialists, who excel in a single field, Groslier was recognized for a broad range of talents and contributions: charitable activities, painting, writing, exposition planning, service to France, Cambodia, Laos and Annam, etc.

2. His awards include some of the highest honors offered by the countries of France and French Indochina, as well as various organizations.

3. Groslier chose to become a native of his birth country of Cambodia. He was not an "outsider" looking in, as were most other scholars, writers and archæologists working in French Indochina. They sought,

and secured, their honors as friends (sometimes sycophants) of colonial governors and bureaucrats. Groslier, on the other hand, labored to create institutions that supported pure knowledge and art, and those institutions continued beyond his lifetime. The National Museum of Cambodia and the School of Fine Arts, both of which Groslier opened through his work, stand today as testament to his dedication.

One more piece of empirical evidence supports Montague's keen insights. The Groslier family archives in Europe and the United States have more than one hundred photos of the man. Unlike other politicians and power-seekers of the era George does not appear in *any* photo wearing or displaying *any* of his honors.

When asked to comment on this Montague stated, "Groslier was not one of the short timers, the amateurs and hangers-on, who sought decorations. I suspect Groslier may have chosen to not to mention his many well-deserved decorations to keep hidden the fact that that the awarding of these baubles was often a bit random. These things (the medals) were important to many people, but not to him."

The inference is that art and service to France, and to Cambodia and its Khmer heritage alone were the true rewards for this great man.

George Groslier Awards

֍

1905	Orphelinat des Arts (Peinture) – Médaille de Bronze
1905	L'Enseignement Moderne (1° Prix de Diction de Paris) – Médaille de Bronze
1907	Prix de Rome (Peinture) – Second Grand Prize
1909	L'Exposition artistique du Régiment du Génie (Peinture) – Médaille de Bronze.
1911-1914	L'Ordre Royal du Cambodge (H. M. King Sisowath) – Chevalier
1911-1914	Ordre Royal du Munisaraphon
1911-1914	Médaille d'Or du Roi (Cambodge, H. M. King Sisowath)
1911-1914	Ordre du Million d'Éléphants et du Parasol blanc (Laos, H. M. King Sisavang Vong) – Chevalier
1912 (Dec 7)	Ordre du Khim-Khanh (Annam) – Chevalier
1913	La Société de Géographie Commercial (Section d'Angers) – Médaille de vermeil
1925	La Société de Géographie de Paris – Médaille Dupleix
1926 (May 22)	Ordre national de la Légion d'honneur – Chevalier
1929	Le prix de littérature coloniale – *Retour à l'Argile* (*Return to Clay*)
1931	L'Exposition Coloniale de Paris – Diplôma d'Honneur
1931	L'Exposition Coloniale de Paris – Médaille de vermeil
1932	L'Académie des Sciences Coloniales de Paris – Médaille de Bronze
1934 (May 28)	Officier de l'Etoile d'Anjouan (Comores)
1939	Mérite Social – Chevalier
1939 (26 May)	Dragon d'Annam – Officier
1943-1944	L'Ordre Royal du Cambodge (H. M. Norodom Sihanouk) – Commandeur

֍

GROSLIER Award Examples

Following Groslier's murder his actual awards, along with almost all of his personal papers and possessions, disappeared. The following images are representative of a number of his awards, but are not necessarily identical.

Orphelinat des Arts students in 1905, the year of Groslier's award.

Orphelinat des Arts

The Orphanage of the Arts is an educational institution founded in 1880 by French actress Marie Laurent to benefit orphaned children of architects, painters, sculptors, dramatic artists, musicians, writers, journalists and men of letters, regardless of religious affiliation. The 1912 bronze medal pictured here was awarded seven years after Groslier's award. The foundation operates today as Les Enfants des Arts [www.enfants-des-arts.org].

L'Ordre Royal du Cambodge
(H.M. Sisowath)

Founded on February 8, 1864 by King Norodom, the Royal Order of Cambodia recognized and rewarded outstanding civil and military service. Its centerpiece displays the royal shield of Cambodia as seen in the 1899 example here. One of the oldest French colonial awards, it was first awarded by the King of Cambodia, and later was awarded jointly by both the King of Cambodia and the President of the French Republic. Groslier received the rank of Chevalier (Knight) circa 1911-1914, and was elevated to the rank of Commandeur (Commander) by King Sihanouk circa 1943-1944. Though abandoned by the Khmer Rouge government in 1975, the order was restored by royal decree on October 5, 1995.

Ordre Royal du Munisaraphon

In February 1905, King Sisowath created this Royal Order to recognize Cambodians and foreigners who had distinguished themselves in the fields of education, literature, science and history. When Groslier received his award there was only one class. This was expanded to three classes in 1948 and to five classes in 1961. Though abandoned by the Khmer Rouge government in 1975, the order was restored by royal decree on October 5, 1995.

Médaille d'Or du Roi (Cambodge, H.M. Sisowath)

The Gold Medal of the King was presented by King Sisowath, who reigned from February 28, 1906 until August 9, 1927. The 1911 issue shown here matches the year of Groslier's award.

Ordre du Million d'Éléphants et du Parasol blanc

The Royal Order of Million Elephants and the White Parasol is an order of Laos, established in 1909 by King Sisavang Vong to reward exceptional military and civilian service. When Groslier received his medal there was only one class. This was expanded to four classes in 1927 and five classes in 1936. The award ended with the end of the monarchy in Laos on December 1, 1975.

The undated medal shown features Erawan, the three-headed white elephant symbol of Laos, with a gold wreath around a stylized green peacock tail below. At the top is a seven-tiered royal white umbrella and a red and gold ribbon inscribed "Lan Sang Hom Khao Luang Prabang" or "The Million Elephants and the White Parasol of Luang Prabang."

Ordre du Khim-Khanh (Annam)

One of the highest orders under the Empire of Vietnam, the Order of Khim-Khanh was given to senior civil and military mandarins in recognition of outstanding service. The creation date of this ancient Royal Order of the Emperors of Annam is unclear. Following Chinese artistic styles it consisted of two precious metal plaques (resembling a gong) hammered with stylized dragon designs, then soldered together and suspended from a gold chain. Below is an embroidered (auspicious) bat shape with brightly colored beads, sometimes made from coral and pearl, on silk and gold thread. Note that the image here is a modern reproduction.

High level awards were complimented by extraordinary presentation cases made from gold, gilded silver or silver with hammered images of auspicious mythological animals including dragons, turtles and Phoenix. The box lid shown shows the highest rank, as determined by the dragon with five claws. Lower ranking awards featured three-clawed dragons.

Prior to 1887 it had two classes but Emperor Đồng Khánh (1864-1889) added two new classes for a total of four: 1st class, or "Great Khim Khanh" consisting of a gold plaque decorated with precious stones; 2nd Class or "Medium Khim Khanh" with a gold plated plaque; 3rd class, or "Lower Khim Khanh" with a silver plaque; and 4th Class or "Little Khim Khanh" with a bronze plaque.

President Bảo Đại, who served as the last emperor from 1926-1945, continued the tradition, but it later came to resemble a European medal and the large plaque was eliminated. Upon the fall of the Republic of Vietnam in 1973 the order ceased to exist.

La Société de Géographie Commercial (Section d'Angers) - Médaille de vermeil

Médaille Dupleix de la Société de Géographie de Paris

In 1821, 217 of the greatest explorers and scientists of the era gathered in Paris to found the Geographic Society of Paris [www.socgeo.org]. Dedicated to promoting exploration throughout the world the group's members have included renowned writers (such as Jules Verne and Anatole France), French presidents (67 to date) as well as geographers, cartographers, explorers and a variety of other celebrities. The foundation has awarded prizes in 55 categories. The Médaille Dupleix, designed by French medalist Louis-Alexandre Bottée (1852–1941), was a literary award named for Governor Joseph Marquis Dupleix (1697-1763), who sought to claim India as a French colony but was defeated by the British. This later inspired France to expand its influence in French Indochina, including its efforts to restore and study the cultural legacies of the Khmer Empire surrounding Angkor, a duty that became the focal point of George Groslier's life.

Ordre national de la Légion d'Honneur

Established by Napoleon Bonaparte on May 19, 1802 the National Order of the Legion of Honour is the highest decoration in France. It is awarded in five degrees of increasing distinction: *Chevalier* (Knight), *Officier* (Officer), *Commandeur* (Commander), *Grand Officier* (Grand Officer) and *Grand Croix* (Grand Cross).

The organization maintains extensive archives on award recipients and has confirmed Groslier's recognition. Their website [www.legiondhonneur.fr] contains a wealth of information in French and English.

L'Exposition Coloniale de Paris

At the height of French colonialism, the country hosted the 1931 Colonial Exposition in Paris. The huge fair at the Palais de la Porte Dorée presented products and achievements from all of France's overseas communities in Africa, the Middle East, Asia, Oceania and the Americas. It ran from May 6th to November 15th with an estimated 8 million visitors attending.

Cambodian art and architecture took the center stage with a spectacular, full-size replica of the central towers of Angkor Wat, but all French colonies, countries and protectorates had dedicated sections and pavilions to promote their arts, products and cultures.

George Groslier arrived in France on January 9, 1931 to prepare for the Expo's opening. His wife Suzanne preceded him, securing an apartment at 25 rue Émile-Desvaux in Paris, about 6km north of the Expo site. Groslier's years of effort to revitalize the production of Cambodian arts and crafts paid off handsomely; more items were sold there than in the best prior year for all the shops in Phnom Penh.

For his participation, Groslier was awarded a Diploma of Honor (*Diplôma d'Honneur*) and Gilded Silver Medal (*Médaille de Vermeil*) like the example above. In the center of the medal's face is a bust of Marianne, the proud and determined woman wearing a Phrygian cap who is a symbol of Republican France and its ideals of liberty, equality and fraternity. On either side are busts of indigenous people from the French colonies. The obverse shows a few of the colonial pavilions, with the model of Angkor Wat in the center.

L'Académie des Sciences Coloniales de Paris

Established in 1922, the Academy of Colonial Science promoted geographical and historical studies in the French colonies of Africa, Latin America, Asia and Oceania. George Groslier's mentor, Albert Sarraut, presided over the official opening ceremony at the Sorbonne on May 18, 1923. The organization's purpose was described with four verbs: "to know, to understand, to respect, to love" ("*savoir, comprendre, respecter, aimer*"). French sculptor and goldsmith Jean-Bernard Descomps (1872–1948) designed the medal seen here. In 1957 the organization changed its name to the Academy of Overseas Sciences (L'Académie des sciences d'outre-mer) and continues its educational mission today. [www.academieoutremer.fr]

L'Etoile d'Anjouan (Comores)

Established in 1874, the Order of the Star of Anjouan is an honorary order of the Comoro Islands (l'Union des Comores), an archipelago of volcanic islands situated off the south-east coast of Africa, to the east of Mozambique and north-west of Madagascar. In 1892 the islands became a French colony under Sultan Mohamed Saïd Omar and the award was recognized by the French government in 1896. Like the Legion of Honor it is divided into four classes and members are inducted with a minimum requirement of five years of public service or eight years of professional activity.

Mérite Social

Established in France in 1936 under the Ministry of Labor, the Order of Social Merit replaced two previous honors: the Medal of Mutual Aid (*Médaille des Secours mutuels*) of 1852; and the Medal of Honor (*Médaille d'Honneur*) of 1858. It was awarded to reward individuals for selfless dedication to helping the welfare of others. The order was ended in 1964 but surviving members retain the right to wear the decoration.

L'Ordre imperial du Dragon d'Annam

Like the Order of Khim-Khanh (above) the Imperial Order of the Dragon of Annam was decreed by Emperor Đồng Khánh in 1884 and established in 1886 to reward exceptional service to the country, which had become a French Protectorate in 1883. Both the emperor and the French government held the right to give the award, which was structured in five classes like the Legion of Honor. The award was discontinued upon the creation of the Republic of Vietnam in 1955.

194 *Water and Light*

Twelfth-Century Musicians and Dancers. This female ensemble could be one of the earliest representations of "chanters" behind the female musicians. [Photo Michael Greenhalgh.]

Bayon Orchestra with Dancers. Again, note the harp-like instrument that has since disappeared from Southeast Asian ensembles. [Photo Michael Greenhalgh.]

Sakrava – The Moon Songs

Kent Davis

The Khmer people of Cambodia have always had a sacred relationship with nature. Seasonal monsoons transformed a dry land to a wet one, with Himalayan floodwaters then depositing rich soil throughout major land areas near the Mekong River and Tonle Sap Lake. The people thanked their gods for the land's abundance of plants and fish, and used a lunar calendar to track the seasons. For this reason the moon has always played a starring role in their local festivals.

While annotating the first English translation of *Water and Light*—George Groslier's personal account of his Mekong travels in 1929—I sought to find a simple explanation for one unique Khmer word he used: *Sakrava*. The word proved more obscure, and the investigation more interesting, than expected.

In Groslier's 1928 novel, *Return to Clay* (*Le Retour à l'argile*), he referred to "Sakrava songs, which were salutes to the moon." In *Water and Light* we again encounter Groslier using the term:

> For three nights the court singers, all female, salute the moon with the songs of Sakrava, and for the three days framed by those sacred nights there are pirogue races. Thus one of the kingdom's most beautiful feasts: the Water Festival.

Despite myriad scholars commenting on Khmer culture, dance, festivals and religious beliefs for the past 150 years Groslier is among only a few Westerners to even mention Sakrava songs.

Groslier's first-hand descriptions suggest that the songs:

1. were associated with festivals held during the full moon, particularly the November water festival,
2. were sung to salute the moon, and
3. were sung by female members of the royal court, specifically for the king as he stayed on his royal barge to officiate.

But when and where did the Sakrava songs originate? How exactly are they associated with royalty? What is their meaning and relevance in the context of Cambodian culture? These were the questions I set out to answer.

First, I contacted Cambodian scholar Solang Uk who, with his wife Beling, published an original translation of Chinese diplomat Zhou Daguan's impressions of Cambodia in the 13th century: *Record of Cambodia's Land & Customs*. His familiarity with Khmer language and culture immediately offered some answers.

According to Uk, the Khmer word can be transliterated as 'Sakavat' (the 't' is mute). There is no equivalent to "r" in the word and he does not know why this letter has been inserted into Western transliterations. The term is derived from the Pali words: *saka* (own) + *vada* (speech). Sakrava songs consist of questions and replies, sung during the royal rituals when the king goes to spend the night in his floating house on the Mekong during the Water Festival. Musicologists refer to this as the "call and response" style of music.

Based on a personal communication with scholar Chanroeun Pa, Uk adds that the word 'Sakrava' can be used in the introduction of a political critique or editorial, but it is more commonly associated with the traditional Khmer Mohori style of music. Mohori (sometimes transliterated at Mohaori) is a Khmer musical style originating from the royal courts of Angkor. Mohori music blends the complex melodies of as many as twelve different instruments with poetic lyrics. Ancient bas-relief carvings at Angkor show this music performed by all-female ensembles. Today, both genders take part in performances at most religious and traditional ceremonies in Cambodia, with the exception of funerals.

The investigation expanded with two more key pieces of evidence. First, I found that Roland Meyer, a contemporary of Groslier, gave even more detailed

19th Century Engraving of Cambodian female band (*Land of the White Elephant*, 1874).

descriptions of Sakrava songs in his fictionalized historical novel, *Saramani*. His relevant extracts appear in the next section in translation.

Most significant, is a manuscript of a Sakrava song actually written by King Sisowath in Khmer. Born in 1840, King Sisowath I reigned in Cambodia from 1904 until his death in 1927, making this a key primary source. Solang Uk has generously provided a full translation from the original Khmer, with annotations, in the third section of this article.

Finally, as the resources expanded, it seemed logical to ask a contemporary scholar to comment on these songs within the context of Cambodian mythology, music and dance. I am grateful to Paul Cravath, author of *Earth in Flower: The Divine Mystery of the Cambodian Dance Drama*, for contributing research and ideas that eloquently link the Sakrava "moon songs" to the timeless relationship between the moon and the Khmer people.

Original cover of Roland Meyer's 1919 edition of *Saramani Danseuse Khmer*.

Sakrava Songs in *Saramani*

Kent Davis

In his historical novel, *Saramani, Danseuse Khmèr*, French author Roland Théodore Emile Meyer gives us the earliest Western descriptions of Sakrava songs. Born in Moscow on July 10, 1889, Meyer's parents moved to Paris where, after his education, he enrolled in the Indochinese colonial service in 1908 at the age of 19.

After serving for three months in Saigon as a cabinet aide to Governor-General Paul Beau, Meyer was transferred to Cambodia in 1909. There his life was forever changed as he immersed himself in the history, language, religion and lifestyle of the modern descendants of the ancient Khmers. The 23 year old George Groslier arrived shortly thereafter in 1910 to follow a similar course.

Both young men joined the newly formed Angkor Society for Conservation of the Ancient Monuments of Indochina,[1] a group whose members shaped the way the world would see Cambodia in our modern era. These men included Jean Commaille, first conservator of the Angkor site; Henri Marchal, who assumed Commaille's duties when Jean was murdered by robbers; and Charles Gravelle, the well-connected director of Cambodia's branch of the Bank of Indochina.

Significantly, three members—Gravelle, Meyer and Groslier—were avid admirers of the exclusively female tradition of Cambodian court dance, performed by an elite group of women kept sequestered in the royal palace. Gravelle helped Groslier gain research access to dancers and the court enabling him

---

[1] La Société d'Angkor pour la conservation des monuments anciens d'Indochine.

to complete the first study of the sacred dance. He also wrote the preface for Groslier's book, *Danseuses Cambodgiennes – Anciennes et Modernes*, published in Paris in 1913. The book's only color plate is Groslier's painting of the royal dancer Ratt Poss[2] performing under the full moon; she became Gravelle's wife in 1923.

Meyer was also smitten by the mysterious royal dancers. He became an adept Khmer linguist and published the first Khmer-French language primer. Unlike most colonials, Meyer chose to assimilate with the indigenous culture surrounding him, learning the local language, customs, religion and even setting up his home among the natives outside the French quarter of the town. Meyer was a perfect example of a Frenchman who "went native," much to the discomfort of some of his fellow colonials.

During his first ten years in Cambodia Meyer wrote copiously, but kept his work to himself. His theme revolved around the tale of a seemingly forbidden East-West romance between a royal dancer in the king's harem named Saramani, and a French boy who came to Indochina to seek his destiny. The boy, like Meyer himself, "went native" and adopted the Khmer name Komlah, which means *bachelor*. Through Saramani and her family, Meyer (writing as Komlah) relates a detailed picture of love and life in colonial Cambodia.

As it turned out, most of his story was based on truth. Meyer did, in fact, marry a former royal dancer by the name of Saramani. It is now clear that she and her friends gave him considerable inside information about the secret life of women inside the palace. The book grew to a massive work of more than 180,000 words exploring many controversial events in the guise of "fiction." In 1919, he finally published it in Saigon as the epic novel, *Saramani Danseuse Khmèr*, with dramatic results.

Meyer's accounts of colonial lust, capitalistic greed and royal decadence were upsetting to some, to say the least. His graphic account upset the royal family as well as many colonial officials. For his bold act Meyer was immediately transferred out of Cambodia and would never work there again. While Meyer continued to advance in the ranks of colonial service his former wife, Saramani, remained in Cambodia with their children until her death.

---

2   See George Groslier's 1912 painting, *Danseuse dorée (Rôle religieux)*, on p. 92 of this book.

In cooperation with the descendants of Roland Meyer and Saramani, DatAsia Press is preparing an English translation of his epic book, as well as a detailed biography of the author himself.

ಬ⚘ಇ

The extracts below appear in *Saramani, Danseuse Khmèr*, "Chapter V: The Palace of the Four Faces." Page numbers are from the original 1919 edition. Translation to English by Pedro Rodríguez. Annotated with the help of Solang Uk. In keeping with Meyer's original, Sakrava is spelled *sakkrava*.

ಬ⚘ಇ

In the Royal Palace – Upon the death of King Norodom on April 24, 1904 King Sisowath assumed the throne. Here Saramani reminisces about her childhood in her rural village south of Phnom Penh (p. 95).

This was the hour when the two adolescents would sit at the steep edge of the Kompong[3] on the upturned hull of some pirogue laid out under the trees. The liquid space stretched out at their feet, limitless but for the faint fires of the huts at Lovéa Em,[4] level with the horizon. The white royal launch, anchored midstream, faced the king's floating house, which, rocked by the waves, resounded at times with the divine melodies of the *mohaori*[5] and the celestial songs of the *sakkrava*.

The Mékoula Salon of the Royal Palace – Meyer's name for the private living area of the king where dancers from the royal troupe would attend to him (p. 108).

"The dishes, I noted, were prepared now in the Siamese, now in the Chinese, and sometimes even in the Annamite or French style. Other women whom the king enjoyed would dine seated on the floor around a large cloth spread in the middle of the salon. Often, very late at night, the king, dressed like a woman in a sarong and lace sash, would sit amid the girls and sing *choeurs de sakkrava* with them. His male voice would rise and at times overpower

---

3   A Khmer word of Malay origin meaning small village.
4   A farming community about 20km downstream from Phnom Penh on the Mekong River in Kandal Province.
5   More commonly transliterated as Mohori or mohori today. For a detailed explanation see Solang Uk's description in the following section.

the women's high-pitched song, and a crowd of mandarins and dancers would gather outside to listen to these harmonious concerts.

The Mékoula Salon of the Royal Palace – (p. 123)

Opium duty, for me the most tedious, took up an entire twenty-four-hour stretch of my week every week. I was getting skinnier and skinnier for lack of rest and sleep, but I would still do more than was asked of me and would sometimes sing with the women specially assigned to the music and choruses of *mohaori* and *sakkrava*.

ಲ⊛ಐ

Siem Reap – The next passage describes the king's visit after reclaiming this northern Cambodian province from the Siamese in 1907 (p. 145).

" 'Ah, the little Kèw-Phi[6] are coming to greet us,' said the king emerging onto the prow of his junk. And the little Kèw-Phi, the girls of the village of Siem Reap, were indeed coming to meet us.[7]

"They were sitting in long dugouts lacquered in black and gold and rowing furiously with their light paddles, vying to be the fastest. As they got nearer we were able to make out their round, powdered faces, the flowers dangling from their ears. They had the faces of country folk dressed up in their Sunday best, and their national song, warbled by a hundred panting young chests, rolled over the limpid, sonorous *bèng*,[8] to the rapture of our senses:

" 'Sisters! The pond is filled with linglekak flowers![9]
" 'Our skiff lacks nothing but silver paddles!
" 'Kèw Phi oy Simala![10]
" 'Thiampeï, Thiainpa, Bopha, Mahahang!'[11]

---

6 A possible interpretation reads Meyer's first word as "Kèv," meaning "dear" in Khmer. The second word "Phi" is uncertain but clearly refers to the girls of the village.
7 From Phnom Penh to Siem Reap by water is roughly 230 km, indicating the significance of the king's royal visit to this northern city.
8 A Khmer word for a body of water, here the Tonlé Sap (alternately *boeng*).
9 Alternate transliteration *lingleak*, which is wild basil with purple flowers (*Clinopodium vulgare*).
10 "Oy" is an conversational word to indicate friendliness. "Simala" is remembering. A possible translation is "Sweet memories of our dear sisters."
11 These Khmer words are the names of the girls: Thiampeï, the fragrant frangipani flower (*Plumeria rubra*); Thiainpa, the fragrant champak flower (*Michelia champaca*); Bopha means flower in Khmer, and is a popular girl's name; Mahahang means Great Phoenix.

PHNOM-PENH
Les Musiciennes de la Princesse Akhanari

"Our women answered the little foreigners in chorus from Princess Akhanari's[12] junk:

    " 'Oh lovely blackbird, whose soft warbling
    " 'Comes muffled to my bank
    " 'Over the tides of the bewitching gulf!

    " 'On a guava tree, loquacious pretty blackbird,
    " 'Why hide what everyone knows?
    " 'Why hide my love for you?

    " 'My voice strives for banter with you
    " 'To glimpse the limitless grace in your teeth,
    " 'To see you smile and smile again!

    " 'And in silence my doleful eye measures out
    " 'The vast ocean that between us lies,
    " 'And which keeps our two hearts from soaring!'

---

12 Princess (*Preah Angk Achas*) Akkhanari (1850–circa 1909) was the 29th wife (second rank) of King Norodom I (1834–1904). She was the daughter of a Siamese prince who served as a Minister to the King of Siam. The princess maintained a troupe of royal dancers and musicians, and apparently a junk to transport them. Her name appears on postcards, like the hand-tinted antique example here by renowned French photographer Pierre Dieulefils. During the funerary rituals for her husband she was responsible for preparing the daily offerings. [Sources: www.royalark.net and *Finale: the royal cremations of Norodom and Norodom Sihanouk, kings of Cambodia* by Jim Mizerski, 2013.]

And voices rang out now from all the pirogues, carried along by the breeze. The languid song of the Malayan oarsmen mixed in with the deep voices of the Khmer, who improvised from boat to boat the love hymns of the *sakkrava*. Human voices drowned out the clap of the oars on the lagoons, and suddenly, as dry land approached in the dim evening light, a Siamese orchestra, hidden at the foot of the Phnom Krom[13] hill, greeted the king's arrival amid his new subjects.[14] The strange harmony was our lullaby until deep into the night.

ഓ⊛ഌ

The Water Festival, Phnom Penh – The passage below describes the festivities held in October 1908 (pp. 164-165).

His Majesty's launch, anchored before the *Phè*, the floating house, along with all the junks and the mast, came alight with signals to their very top. The boats belonged to the capital's great dignitaries and formed a cortege in order of precedence. Each carried a lit altar, which was topped with an animal image made of paper and lit from within. Into the dark of the night this fantastical flock of luminous beasts emerged, with floating pagodas ablaze and reflected in the depths of the impetuous river, into the abysmal depths of the Piphopnéat,[15] to the glory of the Buddha's fourth tooth.[16]

Fireworks flashed from every direction; rockets, bombs, and suns fell to the water with a howl; the flotilla advanced like a vision in a dream between the starry night and waves flecked with fire and foam.

Many women, finding the floating house crowded, had stepped down into the little-dragon junk and the other boats moored to the north of the royal pontoon; I was among these. They gave us firecrackers and rockets, which we lit at will, crying with fright. Then, as the hour approached for me to take up my daily service to the king, I went to join my companions and took a seat on the balcony, which was rocking in the raging current.

---

13 Located 12km southwest of Siem Reap, this 140 m. tall hill is the southernmost of three sacred mountaintop temples built in Angkorean times. The other sites are Phnom Bakheng and Phnom Bok.
14 "New subjects" because of the recent transfer of control from Siam to Cambodia.
15 Probable translation is Supreme Leader of the World (*piphop* = world, *neat* = supreme chief.
16 Relics of the Buddha's body are kept in shrines throughout the Buddhist world.

Siamese theatrical performance. [*The Boy Travellers in the Far East.* T. Knox, 1881]

It was then that far off to the west rose the full moon of Kadék,[17] cold and white over the dark river, in the black winter night...

The king went out for a moment to contemplate the spectacle of celebration, then went back into his apartment and called for his dinner. The Siamese orchestra played its opening tune, and all the women, ravishingly dressed and seated in the great parlor, which was open to the chill north wind, intoned the love songs of *sakkrava*. Desperate laments and calls of distress issued from the choirs, the miraculous voices blending in an inimitable harmony. Now the king was smoking in his room, among his pretty servants, rocked by the rolling waters, fanned by the winter breeze, charmed by the modulations of the celestial *sakkrava!*

The women fell silent to munch on cakes and fill their cups with heady drink in the great lit parlor, where tables abounded with sweets. We ate and smoked at our leisure, seated on the mats and the planks or with our backs against the wooden balcony, our eyes fixed on the Great River of our Cambodia, on the

---

17   Also called Kārttika.

moon we were celebrating, and we were happy, chilled to the bone, ready to sing some more to generate some warmth!

The deep voices of the men, royal singers gathered on a junk, rose in turn, responding, as our voices had fallen silent. At intervals the rhythm of tambourines and drums dominated their male accents. Then the choirs of men and women sang out from all the mandarin junks and traded an infinity of poetic inspirations, interspersed by reprises of the Siamese *piphat*[18] and of our own monotones, slowly chimed out over the currents.

The king emerged once more onto the great terrace and beheld the incomparable moon, the river of his kingdom, the women of his court. He smiled at them and, seeing me sing, approached me: "So you sing as well, and work like the others, you who I was told was lazy," he said, lowering his veiled gaze to me. Then he went off, made a tour of the balcony, and ordered the servants to bring the *ambok*[19] cake.

It came in great quantities, this national *ambok*, this preferred sweet for the cold months. One consumes it all a-shiver beneath sashes of lace, while admiring the celebratory moon in the icy wind of the month of Kadék! The king's *ambok* was made of the finest green rice, roasted to taste and as appetizing as can be. I ground it in my teeth until my jaw was sore with fatigue, then drank one of those excellent sweet and intoxicating French liqueurs, which warm the blood and steady the voice, especially when combined with a good cigar.

I sang all night, while the king dozed. The wives of mandarins had come aboard the floating house and sat nearby, to keep us company and chat between reprises. Rueng kept an eye on me. She was jealous to see me speak with other women. She offered me candies, and her insistence annoyed me.

The love songs made their way around the flotilla, from junk to junk, until at last they returned to us. The moon passed over our heads, then declined toward the occident. The dawn cannon thundered behind us, and its echo rolled over the waters while grey morning snuffed out the stars and rendered the night's river pale.

---

18 A classical Cambodian or Thai musical ensemble with wind and percussion instruments.
19 Traditional Cambodian dessert made from rice and served in cakes.

An unforgettable hour of poignant melancholy! The night of love was over. One after another the mandarins' junks detached themselves from the floating house. They sent their farewells and were carried off by the current, to battle the limpid, purified waves of the great lakes downstream. In the cold gusts of dawn the boats laden with male and female singers unknown to us bemoaned the sadness of separation. The harmony of the *piphat* clattered like hail on the dew- and sea-slicked keys. Our impassioned voices endeavored to survive and keep singing the ancient love lament, to hold down our sobs.

I more than anyone else felt the irresistible beauty of that farewell scene. Tears welled in my eyes at the sight of the foreign boats that for three nights had shared our ardent hymns and now were floating away from us in song. Our voices followed in their wake, the orient was donning long pink sashes, and on the Great River, green and limitless, the *Phè*, rocked by waves in retreat, rang out with the final notes of the choirs of *sakkrava*!

The festivities were at an end, but the king, finding himself comfortable, decided to stay for a while in his floating residence. The women, exhausted by three nights' vigil, returned to the palace to rest. I joined one of their groups and fell asleep as soon as I entered my room, never waking until sundown.

208 *Water and Light*

His Majesty King Sisowath of Cambodia who reigned April 27, 1904 to August 9, 1927

Model Sakrava Lyrics by H.M. King Sisowath

Solang Uk

The 14th day of the lunar month of Kartika marks the annual beginning of the Bonh Om Touk, or the Water Festival. On the 15th (full moon) people make flat rice (*ambok*) from freshly harvested paddy and one hears rice-pounding in every village during the evening hours in preparation for the ceremony of offerings to the moon. Every family and monastery throughout the nation performs this ritual; a literal translation from Khmer is "festival of saluting the moon". Finally, the first day of the waning moon of Kartika signals the last day of festivities. After boat races on the Tonlé Sap River, the king ceremonially cuts a rope stretched across the river, symbolically releasing waters from the north to flow south to the sea.

Cambodia's former King Sihanouk himself wrote and sang a Sakrava song using the melody of a modern popular love song. The words 'moon' and 'Kartika' are mentioned only once in his lyrics but the style of contemporary performances has changed considerably since the early 20th century accounts we are dealing with here.

Perhaps the best primary source for understanding Sakrava songs is to consult the lyrics of a song written by HM King Sisowath, who ruled Cambodia from 1904 until his death in 1927. As the son of King Ang Duong (King Ang Duong himself was a very good poet) born in Battambang in 1840, King

Sisowath grew up steeped in Cambodian traditions so his interpretation of this style of song is particularly relevant.

Below, I offer a translation of HM Sisowath's Sakrava with a caveat that the syntax has changed considerably in English to make it grammatically coherent. The original lyrics in Khmer use redundant words and synonyms to satisfy strict rhyming rules of this style. Still, I hope that readers gain more insights into Khmer culture through this historic composition.

Sakrava's Seven Word Structure

The Sakrava poem is a "Seven word" type of composition (there are at least ten more, five being the most common). The structure of the "Seven Word" poem is as follows ("S" represents a syllable, superscripted numbered "R" represents rhymed syllables). e.g.:

Stanza 1.

SSSSSSS   SSSSSSR^1
SSSSSSR^1 SSSSSSR^2.
SSSSSSS   SSSSSSR^2
SSSSSSR^2 SSSSSSR^3.

Stanza 2.

SSSSSS   SSSSSSR^1
SSSSSSR^1 SSSSSSR^2.
SSSSSSS   SSSSSSR^2
SSSSSSR^2 SSSSSSR^3.

Stanza 3. etc...

Note: In this poem R^3 is always the same word, "oej", a Khmer particle used to express affection.

To achieve rhymes with R^3 I have taken the liberty of modifying word orders from Khmer to English and used the word "all" to suit the translation.

The text is arranged similar to the Khmer pattern, with faithful locations for the "period" punctuation. Below, the original Khmer document appears on the left with my original translation on the right.

ಐ✿ಌ

បែបពាក្យស្រុក

ព្រះករុណា

១. សក្រវាបង្គំព្រះទេវត្តា ដាពិនសោឡ្យសត្រៃត្រីស្តា
ដៀតខ្ញុំត្រែបត្រងក្នុងខេមរា រក្សារាស្ត្ររដ្ឋក្នុងបូរី ។
នឲ្យវបានប្រាំមួយឆ្នាំដាក់ ព្រះទ័យស្ដោះស៊ុំត្រនឹកពោសី
ច្រៀងស្ងាំថ្ងាត់ថ្ងាយក្នុងរាត្រី សូមសិរីសុទ្ធទាំងអស់អើយ ។

២. សក្រវាបង្គំព្រះជននស្រី ដែលទ្រង់ប្រណីព្រះបាទា
ទ្រង់ដាសំដឹកល្អក្នុងគត្តា ច្រោះនាម៉ប្ឋាថ្ងាយបង្គំ ។
រាស្រ្តរដ្ឋខេមរាមានចិត្តស៊ូត្រ ឧទ្ទាក់សិរីក្ដីសុខុំ
ពុទួបានដែលនៅកំពូលភ្នំ បង្គំសូមសុទ្ធទាំងអស់អើយ ។

Model Lyrics of Sakrava

His Majesty

Stanza 1.

Sakrava, (I) salute Lord Indra,	The King of 33 *devata*,
Because I rule Cambodia	And protect my subjects in the kingdom.
Now five years have passed,	With truthful loyalty I think of Indra,
Sing *lam*[A] to salute in the night	To beg for happiness and prosperity to all.

Stanza 2.

Sakrava, we salute Buddha	Who with compassion left his Foot-Print
Preserved in water	To bless all fish[B] that venerate.[C]
The faithful Cambodian populace	Bow peacefully to salute
Buddha's foot[D] on the mountain	To beg for happiness to all.

A Song with fast beat.

B The Khmer word trey, as spelled here, can mean "fish" or be a Buddhist term for "three pinnacle world." As the lyrics say "worship in water", trey probably means fish because the song is for the Water Festival in the Tonle Sap fishing season.

C The original Khmer word bangkum means to salute or venerate. Used alone, it is an abstract idea to venerate God or Buddha. The bow of obeisance to the Buddha or the king with one's head touching the floor is kraab bangkum.

D The original Khmer text uses *pada*, a word for a sacred foot such as that of the Buddha or king.

๒

៣ សក្រវាបន្តិចុទូទាទ
ដែលទ្រង់ដានទុក្ខឱ្យអស់ត្រី
គ្រប់វង់ទាំងអស់កំស្រែស្រល
សូមឲ្យសាន្តសុខទាំងអស់ញា

ដែលទ្រង់លួណ្ណតមានបារមី
សិរីបន្តិកុងតក្គា ។
ទូលថ្វាយថ្វាយវរគ្គា
ទីយាយុយឺនសានសុខទអើយ ។

៤ សក្រវាព្រះចន្ទរៀងរស្មី
ពពកមកបិទអស់តរា
តែដែលអាត្រាត្រវយោដាត់
ដនាអរលន់ប្រាកដស្ដែង

អន់អាប់រស្មីពុំឆ្លេះថ្វា
ចន្ទថ្វាទ្រង់រស្មីបំព្រោង ។
ពពកសាត់ភ្លឺឆ្លះទែង
សច្ឆាយដោយសែងព្រះចន្ទអើយ ។

៥ សក្រវាប្រាព្ធូវយប់ទី ១
មន្ត្រីធំទូបងនា ។
របណាតែងតាមបណ្ដាសក្ដី
អគ្គិសូរីភ្លឺសំពោង

ព្រះចៅបមត្រូវយតំភោរា
ច្រើបល្ហ្វាសភ្លឺព្រាតព្រោង ។
កឋំល់បងឆ្នាក់សណ្ដោងយោង
ព្រាតព្រោងថ្វាយព្រះចន្ទមអើយ ។

៦ សក្រវាផ្ទៃវលយកន្លោង
ពន្លឺភ្លឺផ្ទៃកឆ្លុះរស្មី
សក្រវាគ្រប់វង់បន្តិផ្ទង់
ដិនស្រីមុងពស្យពុក្ខា

ច្រើប្រាតព្រោងក្នុងរាត្រី
ត្រូវនឹងរស្មីសែងផ្កា ។
ដល់អង្គពុទូទ១ព្រះធម្មា
វគ្គាគោរពសូមសុខទអើយ ។

៧ សក្រវាគំរប់យប់ទីតីរ
ស្នេបមានព្រះទ័យត្រដាក់ថ្វា
ឧទ្ទិស្យថ្វាយព្រះទន្តធាតុ
ចាឧ្យដង្ឋនាតផ្ដោះថ្វាយទៅ

ទ្រង់បាត់ពិធីតាំងពីការ
របណាច្រើបភ្លឺសន្ដៅ ។
ដល់ព្រះមុនីនាថបីតតង់នៅ
សូមផ្ដូវសម្រើចនិព្ពានអើយ ។

Stanza 3

Sakrava, (I) salute Buddha's Foot	That is beautiful and powerful
That He had printed for all fish	To graciously salute in water.
All circles unanimously agree	To salute Buddha
Begging for happiness,	Peace and longevity to all.

Stanza 4.

Sakrava, the moon, normally bright,	Is dim and not clear.
The clouds cover all the stars,	Then, the moon appears, somewhat bright.
At midnight when the wind blows	All the clouds away
And the moon shines bright	To the delight of all.

Stanza 5.

Sakrava, so begins the first night	With His Majesty, the leader of the kingdom
And ministers of all ranks gathered,	Many light boats shine everywhere.
Boats decorated according to ranks	Are tied with ropes to tug boats;
As offering to the Venerable Canine[E]	Electric lamps that shine overall.

Stanza 6.

Sakrava, the season of floating the candles,[F]	Decorated light boats shine in the night
Sparkling bright	Matching the light from the moon.
Sakrava, people of all circles bow salute	Buddha's Foot the Dharma,
The crown of Buddha's Clan,	We venerate and beg for good health to all.

Stanza 7.

Sakrava, fulfilling the second night,	His Majesty prepares the offering ceremony
In high spirit,	He decorates the scintillating light boats.
He offers the relic of Buddha's Tooth	To the holy king of scholars
Who resides in the kingdom of Naga	As sure way to Nirvana all.

E Referring to a sacred relic of the Buddha, in this case a tooth.

F For the Water Festival, folded banana leaves create floating candle-holders.

๓

៨ សក្រវាគ្រប់វង់បង្គំផ្គង់ ដល់អង្គពុទទៅព្រះជិនស្រី
ព្រមទាំងសារិកទង់ទន្តី ព្រះធម៌ប្រាប្បីហ៊ឺឮហួតពាន់ ។
ដួរតរង្វវទីកចុះស្រតស្រក ព្យាបកបង្គំព្រះសោភណ
ដែលចិតនៅថានទីឡាប់ពាន់ សូមវន្ទអញ្ជលីបង្គំអើយ ។

៩ សក្រវាព្រះច័ន្ទពេញបូរមីម៉្យ ពន្លឺស្មើឆ្លះមេឃា
ព្រះច័ន្ទឌួបព្រះចមភារា គ្របគ្រងប្រជាក្នុងបូរី ។
តរារៀងរាយចោមច័ន្ទ គួរនាំងដាមុខមន្ត្រី
ចោមដុចវិរិរក្បត្រធិបតី ថ្កុំថ្កើងបារមីតាត់ពេកអើយ ។

១០ សក្រវារប់យប់ទីពីរ ទង់បាត់ពីធីថ្វាយព្រះវៃ
ចំរៀងច្រៀងហោតាមក្រសៃ ក្នុងដំណាក់ដែរវីដលសៃ ។
តាំងអុចប្រទីបលយកគ្មោង ព្រាតព្រោងពន្លឺភ្លឺល្អព្រៃ
ថ្វាយព្រះបង្គមកេរវតសៃ ដាមហ៊ុយកុំពូលត្រៃភពអើយ ។

១១ សក្រវាយោងនៅភ្លាត់ សង្វើមត្រដាក់តាត់ប្រមាណ
អ្នកបកអ្នកច្រៀងរាល់ប្រាណ កុំបង្ខំទានមុខងារខួន ។
ស្រាលជ្រើសរើសរកពាក្យឲ្យខ្ពស់ ឲ្យបានពីរោះស្រស់ដាប់ផ្ទួន
បកប្រាប់អ្នកច្រៀងមានខែមធ្ងន់ គ្រប់ខួនកុំឆ្នេសច្រហេសអើយ ។

១២ សក្រវាគំរប់គ្រប់ ៣ ថ្ងៃ បង្គំសរាល់យត្រៃត្រីង្ស្វ
ព្រមទាំងព្រហ្មាឯនេស្តា ទាំងទេពកញ្ញាថាស្វេតស្រី ។
ព្រមទាំងព្រះបាទពួរវង្ស ដែលទង់ដាច់ទុក្ខឱរស់ត្រី
បង្គំប្រណម្យដាច្រគ្រី ប្រណីបាគទុក្ខដាសុខអើយ ។

Stanza 8.

Sakrava, people of all circles carefully salute	The Holy Buddha's Foot
And all his disciples,	And 84,000 Dharma.[G]
It is now low water season,	Narrators who reside in region of thousand sands[H]
Salute His magnificent Majesty	With ten fingers all.[I]

Stanza 9.

Sakrava, the full moon,	Its light brightens the whole sky,
The moon is like the King	Governing the country.
All stars around the moon	Are like ministers
Of the King's entourage	With magnificent power overall.

Stanza 10.

Sakrava, fulfilling the second night,	The King initiates the Moon Festival;
The songs are sung in order	In the floating palace.
He lights the boats and float the candles	Showing the most beautiful sight,
As offering to the Buddha's crystal Canine	That is the pinnacle of three domains of existence all.

Stanza 11.

Sakrava, as the (north) wind blows,	The dew is very cold,
All narrators and singers	Shall not forget their duties.
To select noble words	That are always melodious rhymes,
Not to neglect anything	When telling the singers all.

Stanza 12.

Sakrava, fulfilling the three nights,	We venerate Lord Indra
And the powerful Lord Brahma	As well as all the goddesses in heaven.
We also venerate Buddha's Foot print	That he had imprinted for all fish
To worship regularly	To rid of misfortune and achieve happiness all.

G Refering to the 84,000 teachings of the Buddhist Triptaka.

H The meaning of this reference is unknown.

I Bringing both hands and all ten fingers together, palm to palm, to salute in the Khmer style called sampeah.

៩

១៣ សក្រវាគំរប់យប់ទី ៣
ទុង់តែងប្រទីបឥន្ធរបណា
ព្រះទ័យស្ម័គ្រស្មោះឆ្ពោះថ្វាយដល់
ជិតជានភូមិន្ទស្តេចនាគនាថ

អំម្ពាស់សិរសីទ្រង់ផ្ទះថ្វា
តាមយសសព្ទភ្ងូវព្រោងព្រាត ។
មន្ទូលមន្ទីរព្រះទន្តធាតុ
ដែលតាំងអភិវឌ្ឍសព្វថ្ងៃអើយ ។

១៤ សក្រវាគំរប់យប់ ៣ ច្បាស់
តារារាយចោមដុំអន្ធ
រស្មីព្រះចន្ទភ្លឺសព្យស់
ស្រមោលបែងចាំងក្នុងគន្ធា

ព្រះចន្ទទ្រចះស្រឡះហួន់
ឆ្លោះត្រង់លើឧលយលើវេហា ។
តរាកំស្រស់ ៗ ផ្កុំបច្ឆា
មុទ្ទទស្សនាតាន់ពេកអើយ ។

១៥ សក្រវាធបុត្រីរសុទ្ធីត្រប់
ងាត្រួយកំពូលលើសិរសា
បុត្រមួយផ្ទិចត្រួយធ្វើឧពនូក
សក្រវាក់ផ្ទៀងត្រួទំនង

ជ្រែងថ្វាយគោរពព្រះបិតា
មេត្តាប្រណីមិនឲ្យឆ្ងង ។
បុត្រជ្រិកជានសុខទាំងរាប់រង
មិនហានវ៉ាឡងត្រប់ឈ្មាអើយ ។

១៦ សក្រវាច់ត្តាវារិទ្ធ
ព្រះចន្ទទ្រង់ឧរលួចចំញ្ញេង
តរាហៃហាមអមព្រះអន្ធ
ងាទីសោមស្យស្រស់ចំគ្នា

បារមីយេញពិតព្រាជនីស្តែង
រស្មីភ្លឺទេឧទ្ទិសា ។
ត្រចះត្រង់ពន្ធឹថ្វា
សរណាជនានុជនអើយ ។

១៧ សក្រវាព្រះពាយឆាត់ពតពក
អណ្តែតលើឧលយដោយមេឃា
អាស្រូវពពកប្រៃពេក
ភ្នានទីឈប់ស្ថាក់បន្ថ្លងនាន

សាត់មកពូនពិតប៉ះក្លា
មុទ្ទទូរទេឧាតនប្រមាណ ។
គួរឲ្យវិវែតកណ្តាលឋាន
ព្រះពាយប៉ះប្រាគ្នាឈប់អើយ ។

Stanza 13.

Sakrava, fulfilling the three nights,	His Majesty with serenity,
Organizes the decoration of boat lights	According to (minister's) ranks, that shine everywhere.
With veneration the King offers	The relic of Buddha's Canine
To the King of Naga	Who worships it to this day all.

Stanza 14.

Sakrava, really completes the three days,	The moon is full and sparkling
The stars shine all around Her Majesty	In procession in the sky.
The moon rays shine pure white,	All stars are also bright,
Shadows reflect in water,	As worthy magnificent sight to all.

Stanza 15.

Sakrava, the King's perfect prince	Offers his singing to his august Father,
Who is the pinnacle of respect	Begging for his forgiveness.
A son is like a beloved heart,	Who finds peace under father's protection,
Sakrava is sung correctly.	And dare not miss any word at all.

Stanza 16.

Sakrava, the glory of the moon	Is really obvious,
The moon moves gracefully	Its light shines in all directions.
The stars escort Her Majesty	With their sparkling light
That gives heartfelt satisfaction	To everybody and all.

Stanza 17.

Sakrava, the wind blows all the clouds	That drift and pile up together,
Shifting, moving in the sky,	Causing great suffering.
It is a pity for the clouds	That seem lonely in the sky
Without a place to pause for a rest	Because the wind keeps pushing the time all.

១៨ សត្រវព្រះពាយរវើយ   ដួនដើយមកពីទិសឧត្តរា
    ត្រដាំត់សប្បាយក្នុងកាយា   ដោយត្រជាក់ត្រសេមសល់ ។
    ព្រះគុណព្រះពាយច្រៃពោក   វិវេកក្នុងចិត្តឥតឆ្ងឹមឆិល់
    ឲ្យបានសោមនស្សរស់កន្ដល់   ដោយដល់ព្រះពាយរាមមកឪើយ ។

១៩ សត្រវព្រះច័ន្ទបរត្រៀងផ្ទៃ   ទាបទេទៅទិសបច្ឆិមា
    រស្មីភ្លឺបែងសែងសង្ហា   ធុះមហាបណ្ណាល័យល់សព្វជាន ។
    បណ្តាមហាជនឥតទាំងឡាយ   សប្បាយសោមនស្សស្រស់ត្រប់ប្រាណ
    លុះព្រះច័ន្ទបរផុតផ្ដាន   រីឪាក្នុងចិត្តពន់ពេកឪើយ ។

Stanza 18.

Sakrava, the cool wind blows	Gently from the north
Bringing a happy cool feeling	Because of the cool dry wind.
The very kindness of the wind	Brings unequal peace and tranquillity
And happiness without worry	Thanks to the goodness of the wind all.

Stanza 19.

Sakrava, the moon moves lower	Towards the western horizon
Its rays shine clear white in heavens	Illuminating all domains.
People of all walks of life	Are joyously satisfied;
As the moon disappears in the horizon	Deep unhappiness sets in all.

Solang Uk

Born in Tuk Meas, Cambodia, Solang Uk completed his university studies in the USA before beginning his career as a research scientist with CIBA-Geigy. After retiring in 1998, Uk began pursuing his lifelong interest; the ancient history of Cambodia.

In 2010, he released *Record of Cambodia's Land & Customs*, the first original translation of Chinese diplomat Zhou Daguan's impressions of Angkor in the 13th century by a Cambodian, assisted by his wife Eeling, a native Chinese speaker. An expanded edition is now in preparation with foreword by mathematician and author Amir Aczel (*Finding Zero*). In 2013, Uk released *Women's Wiles - Cambodian Legends Collected by G. H. Monod*, the first English translation of these early 20th century folktales.

The Lunar Origins of the Khmer People

Paul Cravath

Since the dawn of recorded history, the Khmer people are among the rare races on earth who have retained a strong association with lunar mythology. Is it possible that Sakrava songs—sung annually during lunar festivals—hearken back to ancient times when the moon, mythologically speaking, completely balanced other forces? To best answer this question we need to know what the Cambodian people traditionally felt about both the moon and the king who wrote in its praise. And we want to know why this ritual has survived into modern times.

For Cambodians, the natural function of the moon has always been to provide water, which in a monsoon culture meant fertility. Khmer-speaking people have long believed that the moon "gives out the rain which fertilizes the rice fields; it stimulates the riches of the earth, the abundance of the monsoons, the prosperity of all beings."[1] Moreover, in the historical period, early inscriptions—carved with some difficulty in stone—usually mention the moon phase in which such and such royal event occurred: the fifteen days of the waxing moon, in the light of a full moon, and so on. From this we may conclude that at least from the time of Angkor (802-1431), the moon was a significant marker of time.

---

1   Poree-Maspero, Eveline and Solange Bernard-Thierry. "La lune, croyances, et rites du Cambodge." In *La lune, myths et rites*, (Paris: Editions du Seuil, 1962), p. 263.

Full moon over Angkor Wat. [Photo: KTY Toutatis/S. Lamoureux]

Thus we see that both time and the kingdom's fertility were connected to the moon, certainly by the ninth century and probably from time immemorial.

When Jayavarman II lay the foundations of Angkor in 802, he institutionalized the force which was to balance the moon and its regenerative control of water, namely the king himself. The story of Angkor and its greatness is one of balance between the forces of water and monarchy; the rites which placed a strong monarch at Angkor's center in 802 established a balance that would empower the kingdom for the next five hundred years and remain in the Khmer mind until the present. This balance between water (the moon) and monarch—in other words between the Feminine and Masculine principles—lies at the heart of Angkor's greatness and is fundamental to the Cambodian world view. Sakrava traditions that have survived until modern times still seem to echo this sacred relationship.

The king's floating house. [Montague]

This concern with Feminine and Masculine balance is highly influenced by Erich Neumann (a student of Carl Jung) who noted that "the Feminine is preponderant over the Masculine in early mankind"[2] but cautions that "'early mankind' and 'matriarchal' [Feminine] stage are not archaeological or historical entities, but psychological realities whose fateful power is still alive in the psychic depths of present-day man."[3] While we cannot claim that the power of the moon was ever "preponderant" over the power of the king in Cambodia, we can say that there has always been a balance between them, a clear and active tension, a celebratory respect. And the moon, in the Cambodian mind, is always synonymous with water.

And what exactly were they celebrating for three nights at the full moon every November? In his study of Cambodian court dance, the author has written that

> the heart of Cambodia and the nucleus of its Angkor civilization is one of the natural wonders of the planet: a river that changes direction twice a year. When the monsoon rains raise the level of the Mekong River to a sufficient height,

---

2 Neumann, Erich. *The Great Mother*, (New York: Pantheon, 1955), p. 57.
3 Ibid., p. 43.

"Tinan bacok", the royal sampan. [Montague]

the waters of its lesser tributary, the Tonlé Sap River, are driven back upstream. Standing at the point where the two rivers meet, one can actually see the Tonlé Sap hesitate and then reverse its flow upcountry, propelled by the Mekong flood. When the monsoon rains have ceased, the Mekong eventually recedes, and at a certain level, the Tonlé Sap again turns and empties downstream. Today, at the point where the two rivers meet, stands the Royal Palace surrounded by the city of Phnom Penh....[4]

This latter is the event that was celebrated annually at the full moon in November when the king and his dancers appeared on the royal houseboat where the king had temporarily moved his residence to be central to all river-oriented rituals and contests.[5]

Known as the Bonh Om Touk to Cambodians, three notable foreigners provided eyewitness details of the Water Festival, or *Fete des eaux*, events in early 20th century accounts, but only Meyer and Groslier (both quoted

---

4 Cravath, Paul. *Earth in Flower: The Divine Mystery of the Cambodian Dance Drama* (Holmes Beach, FL: DatAsia, 2007), p. 37.
5 Ibid., 146-7.

previously) noted the Sakrava songs by name. Groslier prefaced his Sakrava mention with this broader explanation of the festival itself, saying that

> Every year at November's full moon, when the current reverses itself, a cord is stretched across the Tonlé Sap, and there is a festival. With a great cortege in tow, the king rides out to the cord on his floating house and cuts it. With this symbolic gesture he releases the waters, eliminating the barrier that had held them captive, and thus allows them to rush off to the sea. For three nights the court singers, all female, salute the moon with the songs of Sakrava, and for the three days framed by those sacred nights there are pirogue races. Thus one of the kingdom's most beautiful feasts: the water festival.[6]

This offers additional confirmation that the king presided over the festivities for all three nights, a fact not necessarily contradicted by a more dramatic account of the event by one of the few westerners ever to take formal instruction in Khmer classical dance. In 1937, Belgian artist Xenia Zarina wrote that

> in the evening after the regatta, there is a display of fireworks on the water; and then, out of the darkness over the river, appears a sight straight from the land of legends: the royal dancers, gleaming in their golden, jeweled costumes, dancing on a floating platform. They drift past the royal barge, past the pavilions on the riverbanks crowded with spectators, and disappear again into the darkness and distance. Only the tinkling, rippling music that accompanied them comes floating back to us. So brief, so lovely, so intangible, the passing of the Royal Ballet, apparently dancing on the water, seemed a mirage—an imagined vision.[7]

Traditionally, the Water Festival, was the only view the general public ever had of the king's dancers.

Structure of a Sakrava

According to eyewitnesses, and the actual Sakrava song written by King Sisowath, "His Majesty, the leader of the kingdom" (stanza 5) attended the festivities for three nights and presided over a kind of call-and-response music that rose intermittently throughout the night. The songs were all in honor of the moon though clearly "the moon is like the king / Governing the country" (stanza 9). Sometimes the songs were more earthy but always ambiguously

---

6   Groslier, George. *Water and Light* (Holmes Beach, FL: DatAsia, 2015), p. 122.
7   Xenia Zarina, "Royal Cambodian Dances," *Classic Dances of the Orient* (New York: Crown, 1967), p. 69.

concerned both the moon and the Feminine. Precisely how the king transmitted a written Sakrava to the women who attended him is not known. Nor do we know how other boats came to have a Sakrava to sing. What we do know is that the Sakrava were songs to the moon, sung by a people who respected the moon as the source of all fertility.

Sakrava songs were also known in Thailand where, in 1918, Prince Damrong Rajanubhab (1862-1943) wrote a preface to "*A Collection of Sakrava— Songs Improvised on Certain Occasions in the Presence of H.M. King Chulalongkorn*. There is no indication, however, that these songs were sung to the moon and may have simply degenerated into love songs.

In 1913 the Cambodians began construction of a new pavilion on the periphery of the palace grounds. It was to be used for performances of dance and other royal rituals. It was named Preah Thineang Chan Chhaya, and today is still called Chanchhaya. This concern for respecting the moon as a symbol of the Feminine—visible in the Cambodian world both in the past and present— suggests strongly that the Khmer people have always been as concerned with the moon as with the sun and that in their balance lay the power of Angkor and the calmness of today.

Paul Cravath

Dr. Paul Cravath is a scholar, actor and theatrical director with extensive Asian theater research experience. In 1975, he was granted unprecedented access to the teachers, dancers and archives of the Royal Cambodian Ballet in Phnom Penh. His resulting study, *Earth in Flower: The Divine Mystery of the Cambodian Dance Drama*, received the Kirayama Prize for Notable Book in 2008. From 1987-2011 Cravath was Professor of Theatre at the University of Hawaii-LCC.

The game of Thirty-six Beasts at play in Cambodia.
Le Petit Moniteur Illustré (7 Juillet 1889).

The Game of Thirty-six Beasts

Kent Davis

While obscure to Westerners, variations of this gambling game have been familiar to Asians for centuries wherever Chinese people have emigrated throughout the world.

George Groslier, ever a keen observer of Asian culture, includes an amusing mention of the game on September 30, 1929 in his journal of travels on the Cambodian Mekong:

> "For the Chinaman[1] does arrive one day. He might be up to his belly in water or lolling his tongue with thirst, but he passes through. In passing, he buys the harvest before it is reaped, paying in advance, getting a good price, dazzling the Cambodian. The following day the Chinaman returns and invites his vendor to play a round of "bacoun" or "thirty-six beasts." Everyone is happy. Life is beautiful. Guitars and flutes madly resound in the huts. The Chinaman leaves town with the money for the harvest, having won it back from the Cambodian. He shall return two months later to collect the harvest, but by then nobody will want to play.[2]

More commonly known as Hua Huoy or Chee Fah it's actually a cross between a guessing game and a lottery. While the word *huay* is still associated with gambling in Khmer, in the Thai and Lao languages it remains synonymous for certain games of chance.[3] The game's simplicity and the visual

---

[1] See fn. 39 on p. 57 of *Water and Light* regarding the translation of this archaic term.
[2] *Water and Light*. DatAsia Press, 2015, p 59.
[3] Note that English transliteration of these Asian words is an imperfect art with many variations: huay, huoy, huai, huoy hua, hua huo, hua hui, etc.

nature of its play transcend literacy, language and culture, accounting for its timeless popularity.

Mystical and Mythological Origins

The game originated during the Han dynasty, which reigned in China from 206 BC–220 AD, and revolves around thirty-six mythical persons incarnated from previous lives as animals (see chart). Each character has a unique history revealing their background, profession, relationships with other characters in the group, and their fate, including who they were born as in the *next* incarnation.

The thirty-six characters are grouped in the following nine classes: Highest Degree or Scholars (4); Generals (5); Traders (7); Taoist Priests (2); Ladies (4); "Happy-lot" (4); Monks (4); Beggars (5); and Nun (1).

Each character is also associated with a particular part of the human body, as well as with certain symbols and ideas that manifest in dreams. The resulting hierarchy is thus related to dream interpretation for the purpose of choosing one's bet in the game.

The game information above is distilled from an 1885 article by C. W. Sneyd Kynnersley who assembled "some description of its origin and of the way in which it is carried on here [that] may prove not altogether uninteresting."[4] The sample of character profiles and their dream associations below certainly live up to his promise.

> 1.– [King] Thai Peng was, in a former state of existence, a dragon. He served in the Chow Kingdom under King Hooi Lian till it was conquered by the Chinese, when he escaped, and having raised an army under Generals Kun San (No. 9) and Chi Koh (No. 11), he proclaimed himself King, but he afterwards led such a dissolute life that Kun San put an end to his existence. Kun Giok (No. 22) was his sister.
>
> Thai Peng was born again as Guan Kui (No. 18). Stake on Thai Peng, Guan Kui, Kong Beng and the 5 dragons[5] when you dream the coronation of a sovereign, cub, or an execution

಄❀಄

---

[4] Kynnersley, C. W. Sneyd. 1885. "A Description Of The Chinese Lottery Known As Hua-Hoey". *Journal of the Straits Branch of the Royal Asiatic Society.* (16): 203-250.

[5] Kynnersley only described three characters as dragons in former lives (Thai Peng, Pan Kwi and Kang Su) so it is unclear who the other two dragons were.

8.— Cham Khoi was a white fish. He took the first military and literary degree and became judge of three provinces. He and his whole family, more than 300 in number, were slain by the Chinese.

Cham Khoi was born again as Chi Koh (No. 11). Stake on Cham Khoi, Sam Wei, Chi Koh and Hong Chun when you dream of a white fish, a buffalo, a gantang[6] of white rice, or 36 pigs.

ೞ ✿ ೞ

12. — Pit Taik was a mouse. Although very powerful, he remained a ferryman till Kun San (No. 9) appointed him the sixth General under King Thai Peng (No. 1).

Pit Taik was born again as Hok Sun (No. 16). Stake on Pit Taik, Guat Poh, Hok Sun and Chi Taik when you dream of a blossom, a tiger, people in a boat, a mouse eating rice, demanding money, eating tortoise, finding an article of value on the road, letting go a snake, or two brothers quarrelling.

ೞ ✿ ೞ

21. — Beng Chu was once a fish (usually called "The Stone"). She was the daughter of Guat Poh (No. 18) and the wife of Pan Kwi (No. 15) and the mother of Hong Chun (No. 6). She was a lady of the highest rank. The whole family was killed by the Chinese.

Beng Chu was born again as Guat Poh. Stake on Beng Chu, Guat Poh, Kong Beng and Hoey Kwan when you dream of anything red, spectacles, a women reading, wearing a gown, coming out of a door, or looking into a glass.

ೞ ✿ ೞ

24. — Hap Tong was the name of a spirit-shop kept by two sisters-in-law Sit and Kiu. Chi Koh (No. 11) tried to force them to marry him and they jumped into a well and were drowned. They had previously existed as pigeons.

Hap Tong was born again as Siang Chiow (No. 23). Stake on Hap Tong, Hap Hai, Kin Kwan and Cheng Li when you dream of drinking milk and sleeping, an elder brother's wife and his younger sister walking together, a woman selling spirits, two persons under one covering, women drinking together, or two sisters marrying at the same time.

---

6 In Malaysia, a gantang of rough rice weighs about 2.54 kilograms.

We can comfortably infer that these characters lived in violent times, appreciated complex relationships (over multiple lifetimes), and that potential gamblers had bizarre, and oddly specific, dreams.

Kynnersley's article also includes drawings of antique Chinese cards featuring the historical figures and their animal counterparts, a diagram showing the correlation with body parts, and a sample gambling card used to record wagers.

In 1901, Léon Charpentier published *Sur la loterie Hua-Hoey. Jeu des Trente-six bêtes*, which was essentially a French translation of Kynnersley's account.[7]

	Animal	Person		Animal	Person
1	Dragon	*Thai Peng*	19	Sheep (or Deer)	*Guan Kiat*
2	Monkey	*Sam Wei*	20	Deer (or Goat)	*Kiat Pin*
3	White Horse	*Kong Beng*	21	Fish ("The Stone")	*Beng Chu*
4	Sea Hawk	*Kiu Kwan*	22	Butterfly	*Kun Giok*
5	Dragon ("The Shell")	*Pan Kwi*	23	Swallow	*Siang Chiow*
6	Peacock	*Hong Chun*	24	Pigeon	*Hap Tong*
7	Goose	*Eng Seng*	25	Bee (or Wasp)	*Mow Lim*
8	White fish	*Cham Khoi*	26	Elephant	*Yu Li*
9	Tiger	*Kun San*	27	Frog	*Hap Hai*
10	Pig	*Cheng Sun*	28	Duck (or Tortoise)	*Hoey Kwan*
11	Lion (or Earthworm)	*Chi Koh*	29	Dog (or White Cat)	*Chi Taik*
12	Mouse	*Pit Taik*	30	Eel	*Thian Liang*
13	Tortoise (or Rabbit)	*Guat Poh*	31	Stork	*Cheng Hun*
14	Buffalo	*Han Hun*	32	Snake	*Ban Kim*
15	Dragon (or Alligator)	*Kang Su*	33	Turtle (or Carp)	*Cheng Li*
16	White Dog	*Hok Sun*	34	Fox (or Ghost)	*An Su*
17	Spider	*Cheng Guan*	35	Wild Cat	*Thian Sin*
18	Prawn (or Lobster)	*Guan Kui*	36	Cock	*Jit San*

This chart follows the numerical assignments described by C. W. Sneyd Kynnersley in his 1885 article. Note that numerical associations for the characters varied depending on the time and place of play.

---

7 Reissued in Paris in 1920 by the Société anonyme d'édition.

"Thirty-six Beasts" in 1888 French Indochina

More than forty years before Groslier's opening observations, the game had already caught the attention of Western readers. The following 1888 article from the *Tuapeka Times* expands on the concept:

> The visit to Paris of M. Constans, Governor General of the French Colonies in the Far East, has led to much discussion about the gambling system which is in vogue out there.[8] The favourite play of the Annamites and Cambodians is called that of the "Thirty-six Animals," and it is said that King Norodom has realised out of it a nice little sum of £20,000 in the space of two years.
>
> One firm has the monopoly of this Far-Eastern pari-mutual, or 'general lottery,' which is never controlled, and is as a matter of fact, connived at by the authorities. Men go about for three months in the year calling on the natives to stake their money on the 'animals' which are really painted or sculptured figures of lions, tigers, elephants, crocodiles, or buffaloes, each representing a piastre, or about four shillings.
>
> The 'animal' that has been backed most heavily is always bound to win, and an official goes through the villages with its head on a stick. The winner receives thirty-four times the value of his bet.
>
> Another popular game is the 'Bacouan,' which is played night and day. The croupier has before him a square tablet, with the first four numbers of the numeration table at its corners. Under a cup he places a lot of little brass coins, and the 'punter' then selects his number. A croupier withdraws the cup, and counts the brass coins in fours. If there are thirty-one of them No. 1 gains; if forty-two the winning number is two, and so on.
>
> This game is popular, not only among natives, but among the French officers and soldiers. Attempts have been made to put it down, but to no purpose. The most inveterate 'Bacouan' player is that merry monarch King Norodom himself, who takes a hand with his meanest subjects in the streets and invariably fleeces them. When his Majesty loses he, it is said, so far forgets his dignity as to divest himself of all his clothes, including his shirt, to dance about the streets, and to demean himself like a veritable King of the Cannibal Islands.

---

8   Jean Antoine Ernest Constans (1833-1913) served in French Indochina from 16 November, 1887 to April, 1888.

Detailed Description of "Thirty-six Beasts" in 1892

In 1892, Bruce Herald gave this expanded description of the game in the *New Zealand News*:

> The "Thirty six Beasts" and "Bacouan" are the two gambling games in Indochina and almost throughout the whole extreme East, where they are assuming proportions of so demoralizing a character that the French Government has found it necessary to control and limit their action in countries under its protectorate by cancelling the concession granted to certain speculators.
>
> The "Thirty-six Beasts" is the favorite game, and is played as follows:
>
> On the ground-floor of a building of a rectangular form there is a spacious hall containing a specified number of baskets, and in the basement there are counterfeit representations in cardboard of 36 animals of different species, and there it is that the croupier officiates.
>
> He is either an intelligent Chinese, or Siamese, or Japanese, or Annamite, or Cambodian, according to the country where the game is played, for it should be known that it is popular, not only throughout Asia, including Persia and Afghanistan, but even in certain parts of British India.
>
> This croupier is in communication only with the person who "farms" the game, and is employed exclusively by him.
>
> Early in the morning, affixed to frames placed at different spots in the town, are portions of artificial animals, such as pieces of horn, of hide, of sinew, of plumage, and fish-bone, etc., each denoting the nature of the animal fixed upon as the winning one for the day. It is a conundrum which the players have to solve. People crowd in front of these frames, each one forming his own opinion, which he is prepared to back, in regard to the animal a fragment of which is submitted to his inspection.
>
> The Asiatic who believes he has made a right guess enters the hall and stakes his money on the animal of his choice. In front of the house there is a mast which reaches down to the basement, and to which are affixed a cord and pulley, which the croupier manipulates.
>
> At five minutes to 12 PM he draws to the top of the mast one of the above-mentioned baskets, containing the counterfeit winning animal, and punctually on the stroke of 12 he pulls the cord, when the four sides of the basket open down and the animal is disclosed, much to the delight of the few winners, who at once claim thirty times the amount of their stakes.

Accepting wagers for the thirty-six animal lottery in an Annamite village. Circa 1930.

As one can see, this game bears but little resemblance to roulette. It lacks the combinations characteristic of the latter game; for example, it offers no even chance — it is either winning thirty times the amount staked or losing.

The natives are very mistrustful, and, according to the statement of Europeans who have witnessed the playing in the extreme East, they keep a keen watch on the croupier, stand close to him for hours, following his movements with lynx-eyed attention, and minutely inspecting, after the game has been played, the basket which contained the winning animal. But with all their watchfulness they cannot prevent the "farmer" of the games from cheating.

Certain animals have many points of resemblance between them; now, we will suppose that there is exhibited inside the frame a piece of wolf's skin; this skin is very like the skin of either a dog, a fox, or a jackal.

If the "farmer" sees that a good deal has been staked on the wolf, by a secret sign conveyed to the croupier in the basement he signals to him to send up one of the other animals bearing a resemblance to it, and the trick is played.

"Bacouan" is much played throughout the whole of Indochina. It is attractive, as many Europeans have discovered to their cost. It is interdicted in Cochin China, but is nevertheless considerably played there clandestinely.

The game of Thirty-six Beasts at play in Cambodia.
Le Petit Moniteur Illustré (7 Juillet 1889).

In its combinations it is not unlike roulette and *trente-et-quarante*. This is how it is played:

Figures one, two, three, and four are traced on a table and as soon as the players have staked on these numbers the croupier places an untold number or Chinese sapeques — small copper money — in a bowl in front of him. He then quickly takes out a handful, which he places on the table. Using a long thin rod for the purpose, he counts the sapeques four by four, being closely watched by the players during the operation. It they are not all even numbers there remains either one, two, or three sapeques. Players who have staked on number one either even or odd money, if chance favors them, get their stakes doubled, and those who have punted on a combination analogous to that of roulette, get either twice, thrice, or four times the amount they have staked.

It frequently happens in Cambodia, where people of all classes are inveterate gamblers, the game of bacouan is played on parole, and so it is that the unlucky punter often incurs liabilities which compel him to part with all his belongings, including even the sale of his wife and children, in order to pay his gambling debts and continue to indulge in his favorite pastime.

Cambodia is under the protectorate of the French Government. The conditions of the treaty between the two countries in regard to the suppression in March, 1888, of the games hitherto legalized have not been strictly observed, and now MM. Vandelet and Faraut, the original concessionaires, claim from the State an indemnity of 800,000 francs, on account of their premature interdiction previous to 1889, which was the limit of the concession.

For a time these games were entirely under the control of King Norodom, who, it is said, took the liveliest interest in them, for they were not only an important source of revenue to him, but they afforded him frequent relaxation. He mixed freely with his people in the gambling hall, dressed in the style in vogue during the reign of George IV, blue dress coat and brass buttons, with tails down to his heels, Nankeen continuations[9], silk stockings, and pumps. He always distributed his winnings among the unlucky players, and paid up unflinchingly whenever he lost, but in this case he reserved the expression of his annoyance at losing for the ladies of his harem, who have a lively time of it when Norodom is in a bad humour. He is sure to have some fault to find with one or the other of them, and then he administers a slight castigation with a small, thin cane, lightly applied to their fair shoulders.

In Cambodia, the French Government has successively allowed and disallowed the playing at these games, either capriciously or to suit the political interests of France. For two years, from January 1, 1885, up to December 1, 1886, it controlled their financial position, deriving profit there-from, and being in direct communication with the concessionaires. On grounds of expediency, it is now definitely opposed to their continuance.

---

9   Nankeen is a kind of pale, yellowish, lightweight cotton cloth, but it is the "continuations" that make this description interesting. Euphemistically known as "inexpressibles" in the 19th century, these tight, form-fitting trousers accentuated a man's features to the point that they left very little to the imagination.

"Thirty-six Beasts" in the French Fiction of Myriam Harry

In reviewing French novels of the period only one mention of the game was found. In 1913, Myriam Harry blended fact and fiction in her book, *Petites épouses: O ma petite fleur d'Annam!*:

> "Your *congaïe*[10] is deliciously droll," said Bertold. "Mine is calmer, but also more sculptural."
>
> "Yes," replied Alain. "What with the dazzling light and those flexible stems behind them, they make quite the lovely Indochinese group... Look at them: Thi-Moï looks like a nice little marmoset in a dress, and Préa-Préa looks like a lovely Hindu ephebe...[11] Why is her head shaved? It's a shame."
>
> "Because, my friend, she is a woman of the top caste. In Cambodia only the daughters of pariahs have full heads of hair... It seemed frightful to me at first, but I've grown accustomed to it... After all, the men wear chignons. Spend a while in this funny country and nothing will surprise you anymore."
>
> "How did you meet her?"
>
> "I won her from King Norodom in a game of thirty-six beasts... She was slave wife to one of his ministers, who for some reason took to hating her. I was living just a few paces from his harem, and almost every night I'd hear a child's lament, moans that would send a chill through me despite the forty-degree heat. With a few cigars and an old Kodak I managed to buy off the eunuch, who told me her name, and the following day I asked the king for her. I did it without ulterior motive, but I was nonetheless disappointed when, instead of an odalisque[12] or even a little girl, out stepped this sort of lad I didn't know what to do with. To the girl I in fact preferred the bear that the king bestowed along with her, for her protection; the king was the bear's benefactor.
>
> "She was only ten years old at the time; she's twenty now. And, with our European ideas and all, I was not without misgivings, as you might imagine..."[13]

---

10 Also spelled *congai* (plural *congaies*), this is simply the Vietnamese word for "young girl," however in colonial context it took on the meaning of a temporary or hired wife.
11 In ancient Greece, a male coming of age.
12 Concubine.
13 Originally published in Paris by Calmann-Levy. Translation from French by Pedro Rodríguez.

The Continuing Cons and Controversy

Like all vices, government authorities and "upright citizens" sought to control and tax the game wherever it appeared, or to eliminate it entirely. Readers can consult Kynnersley for descriptions of the elaborate ways the game was rigged to cheat players, as well as techniques of clandestine operation where it was suppressed by the law.

In Penang in 1885 a group of citizens led by Gho Aik Gho petitioned the local governor to put a stop to it because it had

> brought distress and in some cases dire destitution to whole families, men, married and unmarried women, minors, servants, as well as persona holding responsible positions in mercantile such as clerks cashiers, bill-collectors, etc., whose only mode of living is to be gained through their honesty to their employers, and an upright rendering of a just account.

Specifically

> That the clerks employed in the mercantile services are seduced to try and make a fortune by "Wha Hoey." After trying times after times [sic] with mercantile money, which they may have in charge and continually losing at last they find themselves indicted before a Court of a Criminal jurisdiction and thereby convicted and imprisoned for embezzlement causing disgrace to their friends who may have stood surety for them and giving sorrow to their families.

We can certainly see how this was a problem. Yet, the game goes on and is still played around the world today in various permutations.

Though online resources are often ephemeral, one website must be recommended: [http://perso.numericable.fr/cheefah/]. There you will (hopefully) find a wealth of fascinating modern and historical information with hundreds of images.

In closing, if you dream of a rich man, much money, collecting rent, a pair of gold flowers, a tortoise, a slave burning a coffin, *or* putting out a light... run, don't walk, to your nearest Hua Hoey betting parlor to wager on Ban Kim (No. 32). If the prophecies hold true you will not be disappointed.

Eaux
et
Lumières

Journal de route sur le Mékong cambodgien

George GROSLIER

1931

Préface

Je ne crois pas inutile de dire au lecteur dans quelles conditions fut écrit ce journal. Appelé par mes fonctions à inspecter les pagodes du Cambodge, j'ai commencé par celles qui s'élèvent en bordure du Mékong. Je savais que j'en trouverais là, sur près de deux mille kilomètres de rives, le plus grand nombre, car au Cambodge, comme dans la plupart des pays du monde, c'est le long des fleuves que la population est la plus dense et la vie la plus pittoresque.

J'ai donc navigué près de deux mois, à deux époques différentes, ce qui m'a permis de voir le fleuve sous ses deux aspects les plus caractéristiques : en septembre-octobre, lorsque ses eaux furieuses inondent des provinces entières ; en février-mars, alors que ces mêmes eaux baissent au point qu'elles ne livrent plus passage, en certains endroits, qu'à des pirogues. Il est bien évident que la vie et l'aspect des berges se trouvent complètement modifiés par un tel phénomène et que, si j'ai pu les saisir ici et là, j'aurai conjuré, en partie, la monotonie que risquent de dégager des notes écrites sur un seul sujet.

Jusqu'ici, rien de complet n'a été publié sur le Mékong cambodgien et je ne crois pas, d'ailleurs, qu'aucun Européen l'ait parcouru systématiquement comme je viens de le faire, ni plus commodément, ni plus lentement, conduit à s'y arrêter et à débarquer, certains jours, jusqu'à trente fois. Peut-être puis-je dire encore que semblable tournée, effectuée par un observateur en humeur d'écrire, ne sera pas refaite de sitôt, à supposer qu'on la refasse un jour :

on voyage de moins en moins en chaloupe, le pays se couvre de routes, aussi est-ce en automobile qu'on y circule à présent. Enfin le Cambodge original est tellement bouleversé par les influences occidentales que, bientôt, tout voyage, même au rythme lent d'une rame, sera bien décevant.

Généralement, c'est le touriste qui traverse un pays pour la première fois qui écrit des notes de voyage. Je dois donc m'excuser ici de n'avoir rédigé ces cahiers qu'après avoir parcouru en tous sens le Cambodge et y avoir vécu pendant plus de quinze ans.

Ce premier aveu me conduit à en faire un second. Je signalerai que ces notes, contrairement à la coutume, ne sont pas publiées telles que je les ai écrites, ni dans l'ordre où elles le furent ; qu'ainsi, elles ne contiennent pas exactement ce que j'ai vu au cours de ma navigation ; enfin que je me suis laissé aller jusqu'à y ajouter certaines choses qui n'existaient ni au moment ni au lieu que je décrivais.

Pendant cette croisière de quelques semaines, mes quinze années de vie cambodgienne bougeaient derrière ma plume. Aussi, quand un souvenir vivace, naturellement sollicité par l'heure nouvelle, s'offrait à moi, je l'ai laissé passer. Ce fut irrésistible. Or, malgré ce mélange d'impressions antérieures et de visions recueillies dans l'heure même, j'ai pu, par un dernier travail, et de sélection et de groupement, ramener à deux cents pages une synthèse qui en comptait plus de six cents — et ce, par respect pour le lecteur.

Ce fut bien, en effet, par respect pour le lecteur éventuel que j'ai procédé de la sorte. Etait-ce pour moi que j'écrivais ? Non. Il fallait donc que je fisse un récit compréhensible à l'homme qui jamais n'a vu le Cambodge et ne le verra jamais. N'ayant, pour choisir et filtrer, l'ignorance de celui qui débarque — ignorance qui n'est autre que celle du lecteur demeuré chez lui — j'ai pensé que malgré l'étrangeté des tableaux que je peignais, je devais leur donner des contours et des couleurs accessibles à celui qui les regarderait d'entre les bras de son fauteuil. Et voilà expliqués ce groupement, cette sélection de mes notes, auxquels je viens de faire allusion.

Je souhaite qu'en certaines occasions ce lecteur, vers lequel je me suis avancé le plus que j'ai pu, voudra bien faire aussi quelques pas à ma rencontre ; et qu'il s'efforcera de bien me comprendre, lorsqu'il sera tenté de me mal juger. Ne se pourrait-il pas, en effet, dans plus d'un cas, que ce ne soit pas ma maladresse seule qui nous sépare, mais encore le sujet même de mon livre ?

Premier Partie

Hautes Eaux

21 septembre — 20 octobre, 1929

21 septembre 1929.

J'écris au niveau de l'eau. Elle gémit, se retourne en conque au bord de ma page. Et ma page se termine, en haut, par un avant de chaloupe avec une ancre qui, vue d'en bas, accroche les nuages.

Le fleuve descend dans le ciel. Il en est rempli. Par endroits, l'eau s'aplatit, se fige, paraît glaciale. Au-delà, le courant s'arrête d'un coup de rein sur une barre, rebrousse chemin un instant, dans un tourbillon de vagues courtes que le vent émousse, relève ou couche comme une main promenée au hasard sur une toison. Et ce n'est que lorsqu'on voit ces vagues par transparence, qu'on s'aperçoit que ce fleuve de nacre et d'acier roule une eau fangeuse pleine d'ocre et de lie de vin.

Phnom-Penh, étendue dans le soleil levant, m'est apparue, au moment de sombrer, une écharpe étroite agitée pour mon départ, mais mollement, où les toits du Palais royal et la flèche de la Pagode d'argent, avec leurs tuiles jaunes et vertes, luisaient en paillettes.

Et puis, d'heure en heure, le temps changea et chaque tournant du fleuve se couvrit d'un ciel différent. On baissait les toiles contre le soleil et, là-bas, la pluie pendait en frange sous une draperie de nuages ardoise — saison des grains. La crue atteint son plus haut niveau. Sur la route immense du Mékong qui s'étale à sa rencontre, la mousson glisse, ininterrompue depuis les confins de l'océan Indien, par bourrasques rythmées, telle une respiration sereine et prodigieuse.

Plus de berge. Le fleuve a escaladé les cinq mètres d'où le dominait le bas pays. Il s'étale jusqu'à tous les horizons, jusqu'au plancher des cases. Les bananiers n'ont plus de tronc, les arbres flottent. On circule en pirogue entre des maisons où les poules, les chiens et les serpents, ne trouvant plus assez de terre où se poser, se réfugient avec les habitants. Les charrettes inutiles, noyées, ne dressent au-dessus de l'eau que la pointe de leurs timons pour respirer. Les bœufs s'immobilisent sur des estrades d'où ils ne peuvent plus partir, statues pitoyables auxquelles on apporte à manger des plantes aquatiques. Sur un radeau fait de trois troncs de bananiers, une truie et ses porcelets somnolent. Le radeau est amarré à une case et un petit toit de paillote le recouvre. Lorsque nous nous arrêtons, la chaloupe traîne son mètre de tirant d'eau dans les jardins, entre des sapotilliers et des citronniers, et nous l'amarrons, en nous baissant, à l'enfourchure des arbres, là où commencent à nicher les oiseaux.

La pagode s'élève à moins de cent mètres, mais l'eau m'en sépare. Des enfants, noyés jusqu'aux épaules, poussent une pirogue où je descends et je vois des petits poissons gris filer sur les marches d'un perron bâti à cinq mètres au-dessus du niveau moyen du fleuve.

L'aire sacrée est un îlot recouvert presque entièrement par le sanctuaire et sur le peu de terre boueuse qui reste autour du péristyle, le bétail s'est réfugié. Je traverse cette bouverie et, à l'intérieur du temple, je cherche l'autel entre des piles de sacs de maïs. Le Dieu trône parmi les épis vermillon échappés de ces sacs, dans la chaude odeur de fumier qui entre par les fenêtres et la plainte chuchotée de l'eau.

Les cellules des bonzes, parmi les arbres, sont autant de sampans amarrés. Des passerelles faites de bambous tendus sur des chevalets branlent de l'une à l'autre. Une cocoteraie aiguise ses palmes sur le ciel étamé et plonge sa colonnade dans une eau noire et visqueuse. Vers la gauche, la sala grouille et bruit d'une population campée où des bonzes, devant leur repas, dans leurs robes jaunes, me rappellent les épis de maïs du sanctuaire. Tirant sur leurs cordes, réunies flanc à flanc, en « mains de bananes », des pirogues bercent les reflets de l'eau dont elles sont pleines et troublent ceux qui les portent.

❧❦❧

Il fallut chercher la pagode d'Ansrei Sat, en face de la précédente, sur l'autre rive invisible du fleuve, entre les arbres, et, lorsque nous y fûmes, entre ces arbres et les eaux.

Nous ne vîmes d'abord que son reflet, sous nos pieds, au sein du fleuve, et qu'un serpent d'eau, filant avec rapidité, déchira de sa tête redressée. Puis, descendu de la chaloupe dans la pirogue, regardant de plus bas entre des branches obscures, je découvris la façade et le toit effilé doubler l'image humide, s'en dégager dans une réalité aérienne, moins concrète, moins lourde et moins luisante. Et devant ces deux pagodes jointes socle à socle, offertes à moi comme une dame de pique, une file de faux cotonniers tendait en portée de musique ses lignes de branches.

Sur un lopin de terre resté à sec, un long préau contenait dans son ombre une chose admirable. Ça s'allongeait, laqué noir, frappé de décors d'or, ventre en l'air, dans une courbe d'arc détendu (mais qui vibre encore d'avoir décoché sa flèche) avec des flancs gras de quartier de fruit : une pirogue de course mise au sec, à l'abri du soleil, de la pluie — inaccessible à l'immensité de l'eau qui l'attendait. En passant, je ne pus m'empêcher de caresser le beau pur-sang qu'on maintenait immobile sous son calfatage neuf, qu'on préservait de la fatigue et de l'usure en vue des grandes fêtes nautiques qui auront lieu le mois prochain.

Nuit du 21 au 22 septembre 1929.

Je n'avais pas pris garde au site, lorsque nous nous y arrêtâmes — et maintenant, il fait nuit, une nuit dont une doublure de nuages absorbe la clarté. Ma lampe posée sur l'avant, près de l'ancre, le plus loin possible de moi à cause des insectes, éclaire l'arbre où nous sommes amarrés, des branches blanchâtres de tamarinier et un pointillé de petites feuilles. Au-delà, quoique je cherche, rien, un gouffre obscur, mais, en fait, un village que je ne vois pas.

Derrière moi, le fleuve. Je l'entends. J'entends cette nuit liquide, c'est tout. Je sais bien où elle commence, parbleu ! Là, sous mes pieds. Mais où finit-elle ? Ah ! là-bas, à ce feu unique, piqué sur l'autre rive que je sais par ma carte à deux kilomètres de moi. C'est donc à ce point d'or — comme il est haut et comme il brille, si loin ! — que les deux nuits où je suis suspendu se rejoignent, l'une qui tente de s'évader de la terre et l'autre qui s'y appuie.

Et je me retourne vers le rivage qui me retient si près, invisible, et qui flotte sur le bruit de l'eau. Or, peu à peu, je me familiarise avec ce bruit, distingue ceux dont il est rempli et les situe dans l'espace. Au nord-est, ce frôlement sur de l'étoffe empesée, avec des arrêts, c'est sûrement des feuilles de bananiers qui battent l'eau courante : oui, une bananeraie est là, ses troncs noyés. À ma droite, des souffles et des écrasements de vase dénoncent des buffles, la berge doit donc s'éloigner jusqu'à leur enclos et l'eau aussitôt s'affaler. Je la suis sur trois plans différents et jusqu'à ce que des voix humaines, un instant réveillées, construisent la première case du village. Peu après, un tam-tam me donne l'heure — celle de la dernière prière du jour — et place en même temps, dans un pan de ténèbres où je tâtonnais en vain, abandonné par une eau trop lointaine et muette, la pagode. Enfin, je ferme le demi-horizon que je viens de tirer du néant, sur un ressac qui ne peut clapoter ainsi qu'entre des pirogues amarrées. D'ailleurs, j'entends, de temps à autre, leurs hanches s'entrechoquer.

Maintenant, je le vois comme en plein jour, le village que m'a restitué le fleuve en le moulant de son susurrement. Croyez-vous que si une sapotille dans un petit choc à peine perceptible, ou une goyave plus dure, ou une pesante pamplemousse faisant rejaillir l'eau, oui, que si un de ces fruits était tombé, je ne l'eusse point reconnu ?

Oui, il est là, tel que je le vois, l'invisible village sonore, concret. Il n'y avait rien. Je ne vois rien. Il est venu arbre par arbre, parcelle par parcelle, au fil du courant, assembler son puzzle autour de ma cabine, dans l'ordre où chaque petite vague me le dénonça, s'éclairant, se précisant dans mon esprit derrière mes yeux aveugles et à mesure que mes oreilles le saisirent.

Et puis, la pluie arrive qui crépite sur les feuillages. Je n'avais estimé jusqu'ici que des distances et n'avançais qu'horizontalement. Maintenant, la pluie chante les hauteurs, trace le profil des frondaisons. Je l'écoute modeler les feuillages. Il me manquait ces grands arbres, un peu à gauche des buffles. Et ce picotement au ras de l'eau me montre des herbes où je croyais bien qu'il n'y avait rien, herbes flottantes que le fleuve transportait clandestinement, comme un contrebandier.

22 septembre.

À l'aube, j'ai contrôlé la vision nocturne de mes oreilles. Tout était bien à la place qu'elles m'avaient révélée. Mes yeux revirent le profil des arbres que la pluie avait dessiné. Sauf les indigènes qui surgissaient de leur sommeil, un métier à tisser sur une véranda, des violets luisants d'aubergines, une charrue suspendue à un arbuste, tout me réapparaissait. Le jour n'ajoutait que du subreptice et de l'inutile. Il montrait dans une égale indifférence et avec les mêmes soins ce que l'orage et le fleuve et la nuit avaient choisi, simplifié et assujetti à ma seule présence.

La pagode de Kâs Kèo semble arrachée de l'inondation par une main gigantesque, entraînant avec elle des racines pleines de boue et des mottes de terre. Les sacs de maïs n'encombrent pas le sanctuaire, mais remplissent des greniers sur pilotis, disséminés dans le monastère. Son grand mât — ce mât qui annonce de loin toute pagode et qui porte à sa pointe l'oiseau Hamsa sous un quintuple parasol — son mât, affouillé par l'eau, penche. Il tombera s'il veut, les bonzes n'en ont cure. Manguiers, aréquiers, cocotiers, eux aussi, tiennent par miracle dans une boue visqueuse où l'on s'enfonce jusqu'au-dessus des chevilles. Des chiens squelettiques, affamés, sans force, et qui ne peuvent aboyer tant ils sont épuisés, se traînent dans cette boue qui suce leurs pattes. Ils titubent, restent immobiles pour souiller et repartent plus mornes, laissant traîner leurs arrière-trains.

C'est le matin. Et malgré des pirogues qui arrivent jusqu'au perron du temple, pleines de victuailles pour les bonzes et conduites par des femmes aux beaux vêtements, cet îlot présente un aspect de délivrance encore menacée avec quelque chose d'ignoble que je ne peux définir.

Arrivée à la pagode de Tuk Khléang, modeste, harmonieuse avec un beau fronton où Vishnou chevauche l'oiseau Garuda dans un décor de flammes ; ces reliefs sous un vieil or et s'enlevant d'un fond de clinquant vert émeraude. L'art opulent d'avant l'influence occidentale. Pas de cloisons, ni de murailles sous ce toit que ses formes fuyantes et ses courbes allègent et maintiennent dans l'air aussi bien que les colonnes sur lesquelles il se pose. Les élèves de l'école de pagode gueulent les lettres de l'alphabet avec des voix acides qu'ils forcent pour faire croire qu'ils travaillent, malgré cet événement qu'est l'arrivée d'un Français, et surtout à cause de cet événement. Ah ! rassurez-vous, petits garçons ! Je ne suis pas l'Inspecteur d'Académie.

Le chef de monastère me conseille d'aller à une autre pagode, tout près, là. Avec une précision qui semble la fixer à un quart de degré près, son doigt me montre la plaine liquide où je ne vois que des arbres sans tronc, semblables à des choux-fleurs. Allons donc où ce doigt clairvoyant me commande d'aller.

Redrapant sa toge, le bonze jette des ordres vigoureux, monosyllabiques, poignées de grains qui lèvent aussitôt : « Une pirogue ! Une claie ! Une natte ! Les enfants de l'école pour pagayer ! » Et la pirogue glisse à mes pieds. Je m'assois au centre. Devant moi, neuf enfants de dix à douze ans, torses nus, sautent deux par deux et instinctivement par rangs de taille, le plus petit, seul, en tête, accroupi sur la nuque de l'embarcation. Combien y en a-t-il, derrière ? Je n'ose me retourner, car si la pirogue a huit mètres de long, elle n'a pas cinquante centimètres de large. Mon derrière occidental l'occupe d'un bord à l'autre et chaque bord émerge de deux doigts. « Allez ! » dit le bonze, et neuf dos s'inclinent.

Bientôt l'eau se calme. Il semble que l'on touche le fond, mais je n'y connais rien, car les petits pagayeurs poussent soudain des cris et je m'aperçois que cette eau, que je croyais sans courant, frémit. Pour passer le dangereux remous, les enfants font des efforts d'hommes. Ils piochent l'eau de leurs courtes pagaies, les plongent comme des poignards dans ce grand corps traître dont a bientôt raison leur jeunesse astucieuse. Leurs cris découvrent des dents cruelles qui rient en ayant l'air de mordre. Et lorsqu'ils arrivent en eau franche, qu'ils ont lancé la pirogue derrière les deux festons liquides soulevés par notre vitesse, ils s'arrêtent, la pagaie sur le genou. Dans le silence, j'entends qu'ils halètent. Et ils se retournent afin de m'observer. Des faces interrogatrices remplacent les nuques aux cheveux drus qui martelaient, il y a un instant, la cadence précipitée de notre course.

La pirogue tend et distend son arc. Accrochée à l'inondation par les pagaies-poignards, elle gonfle ses flancs et je vois, sous cette respiration, l'eau suinter par des joints mal calfatés. Mes pieds y baignent. Elle est tiède. Elle va et vient. L'écope y flotte, petite pirogue qui navigue dans la grande.

De l'archipel des arbres, notre passage fait fuir des oiseaux aquatiques qui alternent leurs vols inégaux : l'aile lente des échassiers, l'aile hâtive des sarcelles. Deux *Grues antigones* à la tête rubis viennent droit sur nous, leurs cous touchant leurs dos, les pattes raides jointes sous les ventres. Et il tombe de cette estampe japonaise, sur ma main, des gouttes d'eau qu'avaient emportées les oiseaux à leurs plumes, en s'élançant.

Voici la pagode cherchée derrière des arbres démesurés couverts de nids de cormorans, des coupoles de nids. Une queue noire dépassait de chacun. Laissant l'eau éblouissante, j'entre dans l'obscurité du temple. Sur le dallage, au frais, une dizaine de bonzes, les uns à côté des autres, dorment si profondément que mon pas ne les réveille point. Et qu'est-ce qui les réveillerait puisqu'ils n'ont pas fini leur somme, celui du jour après celui de la nuit ; celui de tous les jours après celui de toutes les nuits ?

D'ailleurs, allons-nous-en, cette pagode est ridicule : en béton. J'étais prévenu dès l'entrée par deux soldats français peints en vert, de chaque côté de la porte, et j'avais vu, dans une cellule, un Bouddha couché depuis l'année dernière, badigeonné au ripolin, un bouton de porte en cristal taillé incrusté sur le ventre.

ఆ❀ఎ

On amarre la chaloupe pour la nuit à un arbre mort, près de la pagode de Kâs Noréa. L'hélice s'immobilise dans un fleuve d'argent. Au contraire, entre nous et la berge, l'eau passe de l'ocre au goudron sous des fanes de maïs et des petits cônes d'écume. Des bœufs, sur leur estrade depuis huit jours, regardent le drapeau tricolore qui tombe à notre poupe.

Je demande au chef de village quelques vivres à acheter.

— Ah ! Monsieur, il n'y a rien ici.

— Pas d'œufs ?

— Ce n'est pas la saison et les poules, gênées par l'inondation, ne pondent pas (ce sont des poules mouillées).

— Des concombres ?

— Il n'y en a pas.

— Eh quoi ! Pas un citron, pas une sapotille ? J'en vois sur ces arbres…

— Ils ne sont pas mûrs, monsieur.

— Du poisson, au moins, me direz-vous qu'il n'y a pas d'eau ?

— Pas de poisson non plus ; de l'eau, il y en a trop.

Se moque-t-on de moi ? Non. Comme il y a trop d'eau, m'explique-t-on (quand un Cambodgien donne une explication, il faut s'attendre à tout), comme il y a trop d'eau, il ne reste pas un lopin de terre où trouver des vers pour appâter les nasses.

— Mais le poisson pêché à l'épervier, à cet épervier que je vois sécher, là ?

— Tout petit ce poisson, Monsieur. Et puis c'était ce matin. Depuis, on l'a mangé.

Donc rien de frais à me mettre sous la dent, ce soir, mais on m'informe que, demain matin, il y a une fête à la pagode.

Le chef de la pagode survient. Cérémonial habituel. Je donne ma lettre de service, calligraphiée en français et en cambodgien, signée de Son Altesse Royale le Prince Ministre de l'Intérieur et des Cultes, et revêtue de son sceau pourpre, rond et grand comme une face de jeune fille.

Le vieillard prend la missive, la regarde longtemps, et lorsqu'il me la rend, que je crois qu'il l'a lue, il m'informe qu'il a de mauvais yeux. On appelle un bonze secrétaire qui la lirait bien, mais il a oublié ses lunettes. Un novice part chercher les lunettes. Enfin voilà les lunettes. Mais la nuit est tombée. Alors nous allons au monastère, tout doucement... Qui donc, ici, est pressé ?

Lecture à haute voix de la lettre. On sait enfin ce que je viens faire, qu'on me doit aide et assistance et faciliter par tous les moyens ma mission. Le chef de bonzerie me serre le poignet, m'offre une chaise, me confirme l'absence d'œufs et de vers de terre, parlant de la pénurie de poulets, de poissons et de la misère du peuple. Il me confirme aussi la fête du lendemain. Bonsoir. Je retourne dans ma chaloupe manger une choucroute garnie sortie de sa boîte. Et j'irai demain à la fête.

23 septembre.

La pagode sort du matin et des eaux comme d'un globe de cristal. Un tam-tam jette des appels. Dans le temple, le long de la nef centrale, de vieux dévots déroulent des tapis et des nattes. Une à une, des points cardinaux, couvertes de fidèles, des pirogues petites et grandes glissent vers nous comme des aiguilles dans du brocart. Surtout des femmes, de tous les âges, qui pagayent et gardent leurs pagaies en entrant dans le sanctuaire. Elles les déposent le long d'un bas-côté, afin que de mauvais plaisants ne partent pas avec leurs pirogues pendant qu'elles seront à leurs dévotions — j'entends les femmes, point les pirogues.

Maintenant, sur les tapis, les offrandes s'accumulent en de grands plateaux de cuivre, recouvertes de cônes d'étoffe rouge. D'abord, je ne vois que la polychromie de cette opulente nature-morte, ce qui orne ces offrandes : des bougies qu'on allume et des baguettes d'encens ; des fleurs naturelles et des fleurs en étoffe ; de petits motifs décoratifs ingénieux, faits de feuilles enroulées et tressées de papier découpé. Enfin, je prends garde aux offrandes elles-mêmes.

Ah ! Bouddha inhospitalier ! Des pyramides de bananes ! Pas de citrons dans le pays ? En voici par douzaines, transpercés d'un fin bambou comme des marques de billard, et piqués dans des poignées de riz aggloméré. Les sapotilles ne sont pas mûres, Monsieur ! Celles qui l'étaient, je les vois en effet, à point, dans ces corbeilles. Deux œufs par-ci, cinq par-là : les poules du pays ont, depuis hier soir, pondu. Je croyais que seules les canes pondaient à l'aurore. Des œufs de cane, d'ailleurs, en voilà aussi.

Je compte à mes pieds dix-huit plateaux rangés en colonne de compagnie. Ils contiennent plus de cent tasses, cuvettes, bols pleins de potages de poisson, de currys, de ragoûts de porc à la citronnelle, de soupes de poulet et de riz, de soupes remplies de tout ce que je n'ai pu acheter hier au soir ; des soupes faites avec la misère du pauvre peuple sur laquelle le bonze s'apitoyait. Le centre de cette pagode est un étalage de restaurant, un marché aux fruits, une table de banquet illuminée.

L'air sent l'encens, la bougie, le riz chaud, le tabac, le bétel, l'huile, le poisson cuit. Le Bouddha en ciment, haut de trois mètres, qui domine tant de boustifaille et qui, vu sa taille, doit posséder un fier estomac, ces dix-huit bonzes qui sont venus s'accroupir pour prier comme on se met à table, ont de quoi ripailler durant trois jours, sans respirer.

Chacun parle, religieux, laïcs. Ceux-ci vont, viennent, allument bougies et baguettes, fument, rigolent le cas échéant. On est chez soi. Des enfants jouent. Les retardataires arrivent sans se presser. Tam-tam. Alors, tout à coup, je comprends pourquoi, de la terre recouverte par les eaux, de la disgrâce de la saison et de la pauvreté populaire sont sortis des citrons et des œufs, et pourquoi on a trouvé d'introuvables poissons.

Les femmes d'un côté, les hommes de l'autre ont joint leurs mains, doigts écartés. Et, dans un silence progressif, une voix s'élève, grave, chevrotante, pathétique tant elle est douce et fragile et tant elle accuse de vieillesse et d'usure. Cette voix, ce fantôme de voix psalmodie une stance que tous les hommes répètent. Puis elle reprend, puis le chœur qui gronde.

J'en cherche la source et ne parviens pas à la trouver. Enfin, je vois, là-bas, isolé de la double file des bonzes, sur un matelas de soie amarante, le vieux chef de pagode presque aveugle, accroupi, dans une immobilité de momie, la face cachée par un éventail de plumes. Les plis de sa toge neuve, de soie plus dorée que l'or, portent sa vieille tête desséchée. Il n'est plus vivant, mais sculpté. Rien d'inspiré dans sa pose statique et centenaire. Face invisible, il est là, dans une majesté objective qu'on sent vide : ni lui, ni les fidèles ne comprennent le pali qu'ils récitent. Il est là, enchâssé au cœur même d'une humanité infiniment misérable, qui croit en sa forme, révère sa seule présence, et qui sait, sans le comprendre, y consentant avant de le vouloir, que tout ce qui est à elle de plus précieux appartient d'abord, sans condition, à son clergé. Ainsi le bois coupé, brisé, desséché, brûle sous sa flamme.

24 septembre.

Les eaux, en se retirant, laissent une vase alluvionnaire, pâteuse, extrêmement fine et pure, faite aux trois quarts d'argile. Elle se dérobe sous mes pieds nus, gicle entre mes orteils, parfois à peine supportable tant elle est imbibée de soleil. C'est la terre de la terre qui courut avec l'eau, polissant son grain. Elle devint ainsi la chair pulvérulente du fleuve. Il la faisait mordorée et transparente lorsqu'il la portait. Elle est maintenant noirâtre comme du foie de bête. Marchant sur elle, j'ai la notion puissante de marcher vraiment sur le pays, de m'enfoncer jusqu'aux mollets dans son essence où se mêlent la roche et l'eau de source. Tout le Cambodge est fait de cette vase voyageuse, arrachée à d'autres pays.

Le matin, en certains endroits impollués des rives les plus sauvages, cette argile de potier garde les empreintes des dernières caresses que le fleuve lui fit en se retirant.

Sur ses contours moelleux, ondulations de peau frémissante, un réseau de sillons étroits les effleurant, ont glissé en tous sens et mille fois se recoupent : les traces des vers de terre.

Dans quelques jours à peine, pénétrée par le soleil, cette moelleuse matière, cette brune cervelle arrachée à l'espace, faite de germes et de pourriture, de vie rampante et aquatique, de frai de poisson, de pierres broyées, de plumes d'oiseaux, de bave de batraciens, de feuilles décomposées et d'or, ce magma universel se lèvera dans la lumière et le vent l'emportera. Oui ! Belles palmes de cocotiers et larges feuilles lustrées et festonnées des arbres à pain, le fleuve ira vous rejoindre par sa poussière et les traces qu'y ont laissées mes pas marcheront sur vous !

En attendant, je suis bien sale. J'en ai jusqu'aux genoux de cette vase qui, depuis que j'écris, a séché et où je vais me replonger dans un instant, car une autre pagode est en vue. Je fais ma petite saison de Dax en même temps qu'un pèlerinage. Et quel sport ! Du matin au soir, je passe de la chaloupe dans une pirogue, de la pirogue dans l'eau, de l'eau dans la vase et de la vase dans un sanctuaire.

Le timonier se met à la berge, sous la végétation. Il semble qu'elle est déserte. On appelle. Qui ? — « Une pirogue pour parvenir à la pagode ! ». Et dans cette brousse, toujours une oreille humaine entend, mais personne ne bouge. Il y a là un village, un monastère qui se fichent de ces appels venus du fleuve et qui portent la menace d'un dérangement. Les oreilles n'ont-elles pas perçu un bruit de machine à vapeur ? Nous répétons nos appels et le pilote ajoute : « Administration ».

Enfin, des branches, des herbes, de la boue, de l'eau — jamais je n'ai pu prévoir d'où — une tête noire de serpent surgit, relevée, le corps suit : c'est une pirogue, un homme et ses oreilles, un administré, qui ne pouvait plus ne plus entendre et qui, ayant entendu, ne pouvait pas ne pas obéir.

Tantôt la pirogue est minuscule : où vais-je me mettre ? Là ! Quel équilibre ! Et je passe. Au tour de mes gens. Tantôt la pirogue est très grande. On y est à l'aise. Mais elle a plus de ventre et me laisse alors à un mètre cinquante de la terre ferme, juste assez loin — je l'ai bien remarqué — pour que je ne puisse enjamber la mélasse d'un seul pas.

Mes pieds ramollis se blessent dans les herbes. Insolations sur mes cous-de-pied. Égratignures aux mollets laissées par des chaumes de maïs, hier matin. J'ai les reins douloureux à cause de l'équilibre qu'il faut tenir sur la pirogue en équilibre. Tout va bien, et puis il y a le retour. L'embarcation étant restée en plein soleil, l'eau dont elle est à moitié pleine et qui fatiguerait le piroguier s'il l'écopait, m'échaude, car j'y lave mes pieds insolés et égratignés : sinapisme d'où ils ressortent d'un rose ravissant de crevette. Voilà la chaloupe. Hop ! On regrimpe. La chaudière se prolonge dans ma cabine par $40°$ d'air qui sent l'huile, mais je suis à l'ombre ! En route ! Coup de vent qui me colle une chemise glacée sur le torse. Dans une demi-heure, on recommencera. Sur l'autre rive, un groupe d'arbres domine les autres et il doit bien contenir un toit à tranchant de sabre et où de roucoulants pigeons s'entretiennent avec des clochettes éoliennes.

Mais nous en finirons aujourd'hui même des régions inondées et des pirogues-piloris. Celles que nous croisons, de plus en plus nombreuses, passent chargées de noix de coco, de sacs de patates, de courges ou de voyageurs nonchalants. Les terres s'élèvent de plus en plus doucement, comme un ventre qui aspire. Nous pénétrons dans le grand bras septentrional du fleuve. S'il arrive à un mètre du sommet des berges, il n'a pu les submerger et reste dans son lit.

Les bœufs marchent sur la terre, broutent de l'herbe vivante, et les porcs ne vont plus en radeau. À la hauteur de l'île Dach, j'ai revu une charrette, — cette belle bête qu'on ne rencontre qu'au Cambodge, bête à trois corps, deux de bœufs fauves et un troisième à col de cygne, aux flancs de traîneau, roues gémissantes.

Dans ces régions qui ne souffrent d'aucun excès du Mékong, on trouve du poisson quoiqu'il y ait de l'eau et parce qu'il y a de la terre, conformément à l'explication que j'ai déjà consignée. Ce poisson, on le pêche : on va jusque-là ! Population plus laborieuse.

Depuis trois jours, voici pour la première fois une rive entière hérissée de fers, de glaives froissés entre eux et miroitant. Le soleil se balance dans des éventails : je veux dire des rives couvertes de cocotiers et de palmiers à sucre. Enfin, je viens de voir une route de berge filer sous des pamplemoussiers et, sur cette route, Dieu soit loué ! Un indigène à bicyclette.

Mes pieds vont sécher.

25 septembre.

Il y a, dans l'équipage, un matelot étonnant. Il me sert depuis quatre jours, participe aux manœuvres du bord, porte mon fourniment à chaque débarquement. Je ne vois que lui sous toutes ses faces, dans toutes les postures, et je n'ai pas songé encore à lui demander son nom.

Quand j'ai besoin de lui, je crie : « Eh! » et il répond. Un mufle de contrebandier chinois avec une moustache clairsemée en demi-dôme devant deux morceaux d'écorce de cannelle, ses lèvres. Des yeux injectés de sang. Une peau de cuir bouilli. Je n'ai pu encore définir dans quel sens ses cheveux sont plantés. C'est un Cambodgien dans un maillot à rayures bleues et blanches, puisqu'il est aussi matelot de la flottille du Protectorat. Ah ! la belle brute : l'homme tel que Dieu l'a fait.

Son pied dépasse soudain le toit, jambe et cuisse suivent, celle-ci tatouée d'ardoise, un haillon cache le sexe ; puis le maillot administratif. L'homme descend, plié se déplie, jette le câble à l'eau, puis s'y jette à son tour afin d'aller l'amarrer. Tout à l'heure, il était dans la soute et montait du bois. Il enlève son maillot, le met à sécher près de la machine et me suit, chargé du pied-échelle et de la chambre 18 X 24. Nous revenons. Le maillot est sec mais si chaud quel homme avant de le remettre l'agite dans l'air. Eh! crierai-je cinq minutes après. Bat ! répondra-t-il, laissant le riz froid qu'il mangeait pour baisser la tente. Sur ce, un coup de sifflet du pilote l'appelle sur le toit. Il y grimpe. Aussitôt après, je le vois plumant un poulet que mon cuisinier lui a fourré dans les mains.

Afin de ne pas traverser ma cabine qui sépare l'avant de l'arrière de la chaloupe, Eh! en fait le tour par le toit ou les flancs. C'est un feu follet. Ainsi du matin au soir, Eh! tantôt dans l'air et tantôt dans l'eau, tantôt dans le bois de chauffe et tantôt dans la machine, du réduit où se trouve le fourneau au toit chauffé à blanc où ses pieds, en se posant, sentent, me semble-t-il, la corne brûlée ; tantôt en maillot et tantôt en peau ; les cheveux collés comme ceux d'une coquette à la mode ou dressés en palmeraie, Eh! sert le Gouvernement.

Il faut le voir mettre la table, car il est aussi maître d'hôtel. Quel labeur, que de soins ! Il a rempli de sel et de poivre les deux coquetiers du bord, parce qu'on a oublié la salière et qu'il est ingénieux. Jamais il ne pose un objet où je m'y attendais. Moi, civilisé, je sais en effet où doit aller cet objet. Mais lui, Eh! dès qu'il a pris une fourchette, ne faut-il pas qu'il réfléchisse, mesure son coup, prenne une décision ? La fourchette posée, il éprouve du remords. Ne s'est-il pas trompé ? Alors il parachève son ouvrage et pousse la fourchette deux centimètres plus à gauche. Quand je lui parle, je vois sur sa face deux expressions se mêler : celle de la vache qui regarde son veau et celle du lion qui sent la chair fraîche.

಄❈ೞ

Nous entrons dans la pagode de Prêk Pol vers 13 heures. Au-delà d'une vaste cour à peu près nue et torride, un monstre en béton armé, paré des plus vives couleurs : la pagode neuve. Elle imite dans un art, pâtisserie et manège de chevaux de bois, la pagode ancienne, trop vieille, désaffectée et que l'on voit au Nord, sous son double toit de bois, racée comme une fine jument sous la selle.

Je sais ce qui m'attend dans cette carcasse nouvelle où restent les traces du coffrage et je suis sur le point de repartir, lorsque j'aperçois un petit îlot d'ombre de la largeur de ma main. J'y vais et y trouve blottie une chose merveilleuse.

En quinze ans de voyage au Cambodge, je crois avoir vu des cellules et des cellules de bonzes, de toutes les formes et de toutes les grandeurs, des toujours sales et des jamais propres ; délabrées ou battant neuf avec des persiennes à espagnolettes et des réveille-matin, des monastères-clapiers, des ermitages forains, des prétendues cellules de chef de bonzerie vastes comme des hangars et remplies de bric-à-brac. Mais celle-ci...

Un frangipanier charnu recouvrait un de ses angles. Devant, un arbuste à feuilles vertes dessus, rouge vineux dessous. À droite de l'échelle, une jarre en forme d'olive, large, pesante, vénérable, pleine d'eau de pluie.

Deux toits jumelés couverts de chaume, très aigus, impeccables de proportions. Un fronton sculpté.

La cloison en bois dur est percée d'une porte et d'une fenêtre à glissières, le tout sculpté comme le fronton. Un travail excellent, fin et large à la fois. Deux oiseaux stylisés, face à face, entourés de rinceaux. La fenêtre sous un petit linteau courbe. Et le tout rehaussé d'une vieille enluminure suffisamment vive pour donner de la vie aux reliefs et assez passée pour rendre cette vie chimérique.

Qu'abrite cette châsse unique aux cloisons fleuries, et si petite que, me penchant sur l'eau de la jarre, j'en distingue l'image entière reflétée ? Est-ce une vierge qu'on honore dans ce tabernacle? À la taille d'une princesse qu'un artiste cisela, il y a soixante ans, ce coffret ? L'avancée du chaume l'entoure d'une frange d'ombre qu'éclaire le sol ensoleillé. La bordure ciselée du fronton, toute violette, y est jetée tel un collier triangulaire au cou d'une biche.

On me dit que le chef du monastère loge là. On le hèle. Une voix ensommeillée répond du reliquaire. On crie encore qu'un Français est là. « Administration ! ». Il dormait, le pauvre vieux. Et il paraît. La vierge, la princesse, est âgée de quatre-vingts ans ! Sur ses pommettes décolorées, des paupières tombantes et nacrées. Tout en soie jaune, le vieux prêtre descend par son échelle et je vois les pieds chenus qui en polissent les marches depuis un demi-siècle. Il est grand, solide. Comment peut-il tenir dans ce tabernacle ?

Il me l'apprend aussitôt, car me tirant par la main, il m'y fait monter avec lui, et j'y entre, — assis. Il me montre en premier lieu son diplôme de chevalier de l'Ordre royal du Cambodge, bien encadré, entre des images-réclames japonaises. Cigarette. On cuit. Il ressort toujours en me tirant par la main et ses quatre-vingts ans guident mes quarante.

Il parle incessamment. Son allure est d'un astronome. Il se dandine, sa canne à poignée d'argent sous le bras et tenant sa cigarette comme un vieux gommeux. Il veut m'emmener dans sa pagode, la neuve ! Merci. La voir de loin me suffit et je mens au saint homme en lui disant qu'elle est très belle et ressemble à une gare de France. Se réjouissant dans son cœur, il me reprend la main. Il me tire à travers le village, car il veut m'accompagner jusqu'à la chaloupe. Devant une échoppe, vague restaurant chinois que des saucisses enguirlandent, il s'arrête, me fait entrer. Va-t-il m'offrir un verre, cet original ? Une vieille s'avance, sa sœur qu'il tenait à me faire connaître, en plus de sa cellule sculptée. Elle est mariée à un Chinois qui... Je m'oblige à compter mentalement jusqu'à cent, après quoi je me lève. Cette fois, il me suit, vient jusqu'au bateau, y descend, inspecte ma cabine. Ah ! Plût au ciel qu'elle fût historiée et enluminée comme sa case ! Nous échangeons nos noms sur des papiers et il part, le mien à la main.

Que ce vieillard, dans son tabernacle qui le pare de l'éternelle jeunesse de tout ce qui est beau, meure longtemps après moi !

27 septembre.

La fenêtre de ma cabine coupe la rive en tableaux successifs encadrés de bois verni — ou plutôt en un tableau qui ne change pas dans ses grandes lignes, mais fourmille de détails mouvants. Je gomme, rature, enlève un coin de terre, remplace un village par un autre, cherche si des aréquiers ne feraient pas mieux que des faux cotonniers. Je mets des gens, ou j'en enlève. Je viens d'essayer un couple de pélicans, pesants, avec des allures de caravelles, mais un peu grotesques. Il n'y avait de bien que le vent qui les poussait en retroussant leurs plumes. J'ai aussitôt enlevé les pélicans avant même de les avoir vus se percer le flanc pour nourrir leurs enfants.

Bien entendu, je laisse l'eau qui prend à la base du cadre, s'en éloigne de moins en moins rapide et de plus en plus luisante. Le champ labouré par le courant se transforme en miroir juste assez loin pour refléter la rive. La terre de celle-ci, couleur de pain d'épice, a été coupée en gradins à peu près réguliers par les étapes successives de la décrue. Et voilà ce que je n'ai pas à changer dans mon tableau.

En revanche, grand choix d'embarcations. Les jonques chinoises sous leurs voiles de paille tressée, la poupe relevée en arrière-train de poule, le nez pointu près de l'eau sur laquelle louchent deux yeux peints. Que leur ventre est plein — même lorsqu'elles sont vides ! Des hommes, qui paraissent moucherons sur ces pesantes bêtes, aident cependant de leurs longues rames le vent lorsqu'il mollit. Et, sa voile inutile, la jonque sort des pattes.

Du sampan plus modeste, sous sa cabine en plein cintre, je retiens le gouvernail à profil de soc. Il laisse entre lui et l'arrière de la poupe un croissant de lumière où des herbes flottantes se coincent et font une queue. Des pagayeurs debout poussent l'embarcation, une jambe servant à chacun de balancier. Le dernier tient la barre entre ses orteils.

Quant aux pirogues, j'en dispose à tout moment. Je n'ai pas à y descendre, dans celles-là, et je ne m'en sers que pour la joie de mes yeux. Même au sec, même restées suspendues au flanc de la rive, tandis que les eaux du fleuve baissaient ; même exécutées en modèles réduits, ex-voto déposés sur les autels de certaines pagodes riveraines, elles demeurent aquatiques. Tirées sur la vase, elles y flottent. Leurs poitrines relevées et bombées ne coupent pas l'eau, elles l'écartent et s'en soulèvent un peu afin de l'écarter moins. Elles obéissent mêmement aux femmes, aux petits enfants et aux vieillards parce qu'elles suggèrent aussi bien une idée de parure, de berceau et de cercueil. Elles deviennent une arme effilée sous la poussée d'un fort gaillard.

Moi, balourd, avec mes soixante-dix kilos de chair molle, mon inexpérience, et qui, depuis dix jours, chaque fois que j'y embarque, les sens onduleuses sous mes pieds, risque à chaque coup de les retourner ; moi qui n'ose m'y asseoir que juste au milieu, parce qu'ailleurs je sens bien qu'elles ne me garderaient pas, — j'éprouve, à les voir passer sous des familles entières qui y trouvent leurs aises, des jeteurs d'éperviers, des pêcheurs au carrelet, des monceaux de provisions ; à les voir flotter si stables, pleines d'enfants qui y jouent ; j'éprouve, à les regarder, la perplexité de la poule qui a trouvé une fourchette. Leur susceptibilité à mon égard leur ajoute un prestige de plus. Ce sont de belles inaccessibles, trop sveltes, trop sensibles, qui ne se donnent qu'à ceux qu'elles connaissent et qui les connaissent. Et je ne peux mieux les comparer qu'à leurs sœurs, les filles du Cambodge qu'on voit passer, l'air sérieux, la bouche sévère, le visage dur, cherchant à se cacher et qui, dès qu'on leur dit avec politesse les mots qu'elles comprennent et qui leur plaisent, vous répondent avec confiance et vous offrent aussitôt un sourire plein de charme et de puérilité. Et je rêve au moment où je saurais dire avec politesse, aux pirogues, des propos qui leur plaisent et qu'elles comprennent.

Couronnant les gradins de la berge, assis au dernier rang du cirque, les villages qui n'ont qu'une rue, le fleuve, et l'épaisseur d'une maison, s'étirent, se soudent, chapelet long de cent kilomètres de cases en claies de bambous, sous leurs chaumes et sur pilotis. De-ci de-là s'étale avec lourdeur un toit de tuiles. Chaque porte est un trou noir. Des enfants nus, couleur de terre, en sortent ; ou un homme qui court surveiller sa pirogue que le sillage de notre chaloupe menace d'arracher à son piquet ; ou une femme portant sur la tête une cruche dorée comme un pain, qu'elle remplit au fleuve et qu'elle remonte, lourde et vernie, sur la hanche — deux urnes côte à côte.

Ailleurs, cette femme, ces enfants, cet homme, toujours les mêmes et toujours autres, se baigneront, têtes noires hors de l'eau. Les mystérieuses forces sous-marines de notre hélice les inquiéteront. Le torse musculeux de l'homme émergera, revivifié chargé de l'enfant. Le pagne collant et scintillant autour du corps, la femme fuira vers la berge en faisant de son ventre bouillonner l'eau. Puis, remontée sur terre comme sur un socle, elle ramassera le sarong sec qu'elle y avait laissé et, pudique, droite dans ce cylindre qui l'isole, elle fera tomber à ses pieds le voile ruisselant et s'en dégagera en ondulant — telle une couleuvre qui mue.

☙ ❦ ❧

On perd peu à peu notion de la grandeur du paysage. Il faut voir un bœuf, comparer sa taille à ce qui l'entoure, pour découvrir que la touffe de bambous qui le domine ferait retomber ses dernières gerbes au-dessus d'une maison de cinq étages.

Mais quand, près d'une berge, on se tourne du côté du fleuve, l'autre berge, couchée sur l'horizon, trop mince et trop finement dentelée, n'offre plus aucun repère. Ce n'est que lorsqu'on reconnaît que ce qui ressemble à une feuille et paraît immobile est un sampan dévalant le courant, que l'immensité du paysage se dégage et atteint sa démesure. Or, chaque fois que je suis ainsi rappelé à l'ordre, je n'éprouve pas la sensation que je me remets au point, que j'avais insensiblement étranglé le fleuve, rapetissé ses rives, baissé son ciel. Je vois positivement, d'un seul coup, l'horizon élargir son cercle et le fleuve reprendre la grandeur que je lui avais contestée.

Nous le traversons dix fois par jour, puisque les pagodes jalonnent deux rives que notre navigation zigzagante lace l'une à l'autre, de toit doré en toit doré. Ainsi, chaque fois que nous nous trouvons au milieu du fleuve, sur sa ligne noble, les deux berges à égale distance de nous, de grandeur et de valeur semblables, nous confèrent un équilibre grandiose. Elles se rejoignent devant nous pareillement inclinées et fermant un triangle liquide et aérien, debout sur sa base. Puis, dès que nous approchons de l'une, le triangle se couche, incurve un de ses côtés en demi-cercle. Encore un peu, la terre surgit, se colore, les arbres montrent leurs essences, leurs troncs, leurs branches, les nids épineux des cormorans. J'entends les deux coups de cloche du pilote qui font taire la machine. Trois coups : l'hélice renversée brise l'élan de la chaloupe. La berge tombe sur nous de toute son ombre. Un enfoncement mou, et l'étrave pénètre l'argile — tel un couperet de boucher dans de la viande.

Ici se cache une pagode nouvelle, invisible encore, mais qu'une touffe d'arbres plus grands et plus denses que ceux des environs nous a dénoncée.

On entend un murmure de voix enfantines, celles des jeunes élèves qui, quelque part, derrière ces murs de verdure, dans l'école en plein air, près de l'appentis aux pirogues de course, chantent leur alphabet. La paix monastique s'exhale par les voix de la jeunesse.

Nous contournâmes cet après-midi l'île de la Tortue, qui n'est pas celle des boucaniers, mais une île alluvionnaire, d'une dizaine de kilomètres de tour et qui contient trois pagodes.

Navigation difficile par le Sud. J'entendais la voix du pilote inquiet tomber du ciel, c'est-à-dire de la logette sur le toit de la chaloupe où, seul, sous une tente de soixante centimètres de côté, il domine la route en se racornissant au soleil.

Il hélait les pirogues rencontrées. Sa voix courait sur le fleuve à des distances qui me stupéfient toujours. Elle dressait le piroguier qu'elle attrapait, qui répondait, que je n'entendais pas, mais que je voyais faire un geste dardé vers je ne sais où. Que montrait-il ? Une eau plus claire, un froncement de berge, le tremblement d'une touffe d'herbes ? Je ne voyais rien. Mais le vieux timonier, là-haut, sous sa casquette ornée d'une ancre ; le vieux aux yeux chassieux qui, depuis vingt-cinq ans, vit sur le fleuve, avait saisi le renseignement mystérieux : je sentais le coup de barre. De points dangereux en passes ensablées, des voix et des bras de passants inconnus nous enseignèrent notre route

☙✺❧

28 septembre.

— Eh!

— Bat !

Mon homme jaillit de l'eau et essore sa moustache en la suçant de sa lèvre inférieure. Nous venons de nous réapprovisionner en bois. Il a plongé pour se laver et pris mes souliers pour les laver aussi. À grande eau : il leur a donné cette habitude. Toute cette eau qui vient du Tibet suffit à peine à ce nettoyage tant ils sont boueux.

J'étais revenu de la précédente pagode le pantalon englué jusqu'aux genoux. Il sèche sur la machine. Mes deux paires de souliers aussi, mais à l'avant, suspendues à côté des bouteilles à rafraîchir. Je pars encore une fois les pieds nus et en pyjama : aucun de mes amis collet monté ne me rencontrera dans ces mauvais lieux.

L'opérateur photographe va devant, jeune Annamite déluré qui entend avec prévenance me montrer le chemin. Léger, il passe ; moi, j'enfonce. Eh! suit, portant l'attirail. Un maudit champ de cannes à sucre récoltées s'ouvre devant nous. Une heure de l'après-midi. La boue brûlante et les feuilles sèches des cannes me blessent. On s'arrête.

Voilà Eh! avec un bambou. Il m'en fait un pont mobile. Lorsque je suis au bout, je me pose sur une motte avec la grâce d'un échassier et Eh! pousse le bambou. Nous faisons du cinq cents mètres à l'heure. Je ne suis pas équilibriste. De plus, le bambou roule sous mes pieds. Mais Eh! marche à côté de moi, dans la mélasse jusqu'à la ceinture, le bras levé avec onction, tel M. Loyal aidant une écuyère à descendre du fier coursier. Nous arrivons. Le matériel qu'a déposé Eh! pour faire le sapeur-pontonnier ne suivant pas seul, il part le rechercher, revient.

Dans une heure, lorsque nous serons de nouveau à bord, Eh! aura fait six fois le trajet. Et maintenant, comme il ne peut laver mes chaussures, c'est mes pieds qu'il arrose et frotte avec précaution : on dirait un laveur d'or.

Pendant ce temps et tandis qu'on se remet en route et que nous nous en éloignons à jamais, j'embrasse la maison du marchand de bois. Elle se termine en surplomb sur le fleuve par une terrasse qui se prolonge d'un balcon minuscule où sont rangés des pots chinois. Des faux cotonniers l'encadrent, ainsi qu'un grand tamarin où pendent des nids en forme de quenouilles. Des enfants nus, l'un tient un chat. Une métisse sino-cambodgienne se penche, ce qui couche sur sa nuque une orchidée luisante à triple coque : son chignon. Sous elle, amarrées au même pilotis, trois pirogues s'ouvrent en éventail.

Enfants, femme, éventail s'enfoncent, se brouillent dans les plus lointaines ondulations de notre sillage. Je vois le toit descendre jusqu'au fleuve. Derrière, une gerbe de bambou se lève, darde en tous sens des tiges sèches gainées d'une écorce qui se déchire en triangles de papier noir. D'autres retombent sous leur feuillage, font des arches sur le toit. Et le toit glisse à l'eau. Et le bambou se mêle à d'autres bambous. Et il n'y a plus rien qu'un bruit régulier de machine.

☙❀❧

Aux temps anciens, le Mékong a coupé le Cambodge en quatre quartiers et en a fait son blason. Son grand bras vient de Chine. Un second remonte au Grand Lac chercher le reflet d'Angkor. Les deux autres descendent à la mer. Le nœud est Phnom Penh. Ce travail fut fait en grand, avec apparat. Il est un peu pompier et d'une magnificence monotone.

Le bras supérieur et celui du Sud-Est forment un angle. Voyant cela, le Père des eaux imagina de le fermer et d'en faire un triangle. Il jeta un nouveau bras qui partit de Kompong Chàm et déboucha vers Banam. C'est le Tonlé Touch, le « petit fleuve », qui délimite deux provinces aux noms sonores, Srei Santhor et Sithor Kandal. Elles sont des plus riches. Le Mékong a enfermé dans son triangle le cœur du Cambodge.

Le grand fleuve est trop grand. La civilisation le remonte trop facilement. Trop de marchands installés sur cette avenue et trop de soleil au-dessus. En toute saison, le courant va trop vite, ronge ses coudes, sème des îles où il n'est besoin et rend étrangers les deux pays qu'il sépare.

Mais le Tonlé Touch, fleuve sans source et sans estuaire, près du géant où il naît et où il va se perdre ; le Tonlé Touch, à qui la fin n'apporte rien qu'il n'ait trouvé dans sa naissance, le Tonlé Touch s'avance tout doucement, en se dandinant, sans se soucier de retrouver au plus tôt le tronc tumultueux d'où il s'est évadé. Il fait des grâces, des manières, entre ses berges qui jamais ne s'éloignent l'une de l'autre au-delà de la portée d'une voix d'enfant.

Flânant ainsi, il a trouvé la juste mesure et des proportions contenues qui ne laissent qu'un peu de ciel entre le reflet des arbres vis-à-vis ; un sillon de lumière qui semble être son lit, comme s'il coulait dans le ciel et sans que jamais son vert liquide soit amoindri par son bleu céleste. Il soude le tournant au tournant, revient sur lui-même se regarder couler, reprend du souffle après un étranglement et s'aplatit après s'être creusé. Il se garderait bien de montrer une rive sans l'autre, d'avancer sans ses deux concubines, de les empêcher de bavarder entre elles, ce qui l'obligerait de répondre à chacune. À chaque tournant, il les met côte à côte, afin de les voir ensemble, de choisir celle qu'il va prendre, avant de les séparer de nouveau. Ainsi va-t-il, gentiment, courant brisé, se donnant des airs de petits lacs entourés d'arbres, de vergers et de villages et qui ne communiquent entre eux que par un invisible lien comme les perles d'un collier.

Nous y sommes entrés hier, vers quatre heures. À cette heure et en cette saison, le soleil est déjà bas et se couche comme les poules. Il coulait en biais dans les caprices du fleuve — et dès cinq heures, y passa horizontalement. Je ne sais comment il s'y prenait ou si le Tonlé Touch y mettait de la malice : la terre et l'eau étaient à peine touchées, de sorte que les ombres que rien ne reflétait plus se firent opaques. Les gens et les choses s'y incrustaient, pépins lumineux dans une pulpe olive.

La rive à contre-jour formait écran, cardait ce soleil par ses déchirures et ne le jetait qu'en poignées sur la berge opposée. Des éclats tombaient danser dans l'eau. Sur ce paysage crépi tel un tableau pointilliste, les ventres fauves des bœufs suspendaient des lanternes. Les maisons éclairées n'étaient pas de la même matière que les maisons à l'ombre. Le dessous des arbres, nocturne, impénétrable, se couronnait de coupoles enflammées, — car bientôt le soleil teinta ses projections.

Les manguiers prirent alors la couleur de leurs fruits. Les balustrades des jardins couchèrent des échelles de lumière, devant quoi des enfants nus couraient tout en or, se volatilisaient et ressortaient plus loin. Un seul portait une petite culotte, d'un vert acide : elle tomba ! Le gosse la ramassa et reprit sa course, une grosse émeraude sous le bras. Des oies en marche, d'un blanc glacé sous les bambous, roulèrent tout à coup pareilles à des jaunes d'œuf, puis redevinrent boules de neige. Je vis une pirogue pleine de violettes avec une seule écaille rutilant sur sa tête de serpent. Un pêcheur releva son carrelet vide de poisson, mais rempli de grains de grenades. Je vis... Jamais je ne vis rien de pareil, d'aussi mouvant entre les doigts de Dieu que ce paysage à la fin plus scintillant qu'un corps de poisson et plus somptueux qu'une queue de paon.

Bien entendu, une population dense et curieuse de notre passage pendait en grappes aux échelles des maisons. Les baigneurs qui sortaient de l'eau s'érigeaient en statues sous les péristyles des aréquiers. Un groupe de bavards se découpa une seconde sous un arbre où cent petits points brillaient, des oranges. Nous dépassâmes un vieillard installé sur un radeau de bambous, qu'il convoyait avec le courant, assis sous un petit toit, tel un anachorète dans un ermitage flottant. Comment oublier cet homme couché dans un sampan, une jambe en triangle ? Sans daigner tourner la tête vers nous, il jouait de la guitare.

Par instants, enfin, lorsque je regardais d'entre ces berges qui, par le jeu des lumières, m'apparaissaient l'une cliché négatif, l'autre cliché positif, lorsque je regardais à l'opposé du couchant, les méandres du fleuve ne portaient que des couleurs glacées et déjà crépusculaires. Notre étrave ouvrait la pulpe d'un fruit, l'hélice broyait du clair de lune.

29 septembre.

Je viens de quitter la belle duchesse de Moha Léap. Pas une faute de goût dans son intérieur opulent. Elle est accueillante et digne. Cinquante ans, c'est vieux pour une Cambodgienne ! Mais elle naquit saine et forte, de parents riches qui transmirent leur noblesse et leur héritage à cette fille unique. Retirée dans un monastère qui se modernise, elle n'a rien sacrifié aux temps actuels, ni à l'Occident. C'est d'une pagode que je parle.

On peut la considérer comme une des fleurs de l'art cambodgien du XIXe siècle. Quelques petits détails sont un peu chinoisés — mais le Chinois est installé au Cambodge depuis si longtemps, et le Cambodge lui doit tant, qu'il serait malséant que le seuil du temple lui soit interdit — surtout lorsqu'il y porte son dragon, frère du serpent khmer et les feuilles d'or où il le suspendra.

La pagode de Moha Léap est entourée de cloisons charpentées, vernies intérieurement de vermillon et qui reposent sur une plinthe en céramique ajourée. Soixante colonnes supportent son toit à double bas-côté. Douze mesurent dix mètres de haut et trente-cinq centimètres de diamètre. Elles sont en bois « sockrâm » à dureté et lourdeur de marbre, soigneusement tournées. Ce bois rare a reçu une couche de laque noire. Sur ce fond deux fois précieux, un maître doreur enlumina, il y a trente-trois ans, les soixante colonnes, de bas en haut. Et, comme en architecture khmère, les colonnes vont et travaillent toujours deux à deux, la dentelle dorée change ses motifs de deux colonnes en deux colonnes. Chaque pochoir ne servit ainsi que deux fois — tels une voix et son écho que l'espace engloutit et ne rend jamais.

Lorsque j'entrai dans la nef où le jour ne pénétrait, en rasant le sol, que par la plinthe ajourée, les soixante colonnes, fondant leur laque noire dans la pénombre, disparaissaient. Leur décor subsistait seul. Les spirales, les feuillages, les petits animaux, les nymphes d'or se découpaient dans le vide, sans support, en tubes ajourés. Ils ne montaient plus recevoir une charpente, ils pendaient en guirlandes régulières et s'enfonçaient dans le luisant du dallage. J'entrai dans la nuit, la douce nuit dorée du ciel d'Indra, soutenue par des feuillages incorruptibles et flottants, où les déesses reçoivent et nourrissent les bienheureux. Le rouge des cloisons la rendait plus vivante, retirait à l'or ce que son éclat eût gardé de métallique, le vivifiait et, j'imagine, de la couleur du sang des dieux.

J'ai hésité à dissoudre cette atmosphère, à ouvrir les fenêtres qui porteraient autant de coups de hache dans cette austère féerie, à ce palais de cristal noir et or, auquel il suffisait pour qu'il se dressât en équilibre, au-delà de mes prévisions et de mon jugement, qu'un mince filet de jour y glisse.

Les fenêtres ayant crié sur leurs gonds, le vaisseau qui ne m'avait livré que son âme se réincarna. Une bande luisante, nacrée, glaciale se plaqua sur chaque colonne. Les enluminures redevinrent métalliques sous un plafond qui se révéla entièrement peint et couvert de héros et d'animaux légendaires.

Ah ! qu'il me plaît d'avoir trouvé sur ces bords du Tonlé Touch la plus belle pagode que je connaisse. Dans sa ceinture vermillon, portée par ses soixante géantes sans défaut, enveloppée de dentelle d'or, elle levait son front cornu dans le matin. Le matin baignait sa nuit divine. Et, nonchalante, elle laissait pendre sa traîne dans le plus beau des fleuves.

Quelques kilomètres plus bas, je crois à une gageure en accostant au pied d'une autre pagode. Je ne la connais que trop, celle-là, et viens de fuir trente de ses semblables. Mais, la retrouver là, après avoir respiré un air si pur, m'y cogner, m'y casser le nez, si près de la vieille patricienne ! Après un entretien si mesuré, vraiment sacré, dont chaque mot contenait une sonorité de conque, où chaque parole tombait de lèvres fières et dans une langue si pure, rencontrer cette parvenue, cette métisse qui mange à tous les râteliers, abîme son paysage et fait paraître imbéciles ses enfants !

Elle est panachée de badigeons à la chaux et faite de béton armé depuis son porche jusqu'à ses clochettes. Le ciment, maltraité dans des moules émoussés, imite tout ce qui était naguère en bois sculpté et doré.

Il l'imite ? Je suis indulgent. Comment voulez-vous qu'un moule digère et rende intact du bois fleuri, du bois vivant d'où les dieux, en ronde bosse, se dégagent parmi des rinceaux en flammes ! Et ici, sur cette décoration à vigueur d'éponge, cette triperie de crosses entrelacées, ce vermicelle trop cuit, les couleurs inouïes d'un badigeon affreux s'en sont venues remplacer la feuille d'or. Trois piastres de poudre de couleur crue passée au balai remplacent trois cents piastres de métal incorruptible, laminé si fin que le souffle du doreur suffisait à l'appliquer. Trois piastres de barbouillage que trois orages délavent, au lieu de trois cents piastres de lumière que trente ans de servitudes rendent plus profonde et dont la patine est une parure de plus.

Le porche nous prévient à lui seul. Il est flanqué de deux soldats français, grandeur naturelle, s'il vous plaît, moustachus, la veste pincée d'une martingale dans le dos. Un melon sur le haut du crâne, ils montrent les dents et tiennent un fusil. Depuis huit jours, j'ai rencontré aux portes de ces pagodes plus de soldats français que n'en comporte la garnison de Phnom Penh. Ces statues pourraient être amusantes : il ne faut pas avoir de préjugés. L'idée de flanquer l'entrée des temples de deux statues de gardiens menaçants date de mille ans et les sanctuaires angkoriens furent ainsi gardés par des *dvarapalas*. Et ma foi, qu'aujourd'hui les *dvarapalas* soient des soldats français... Mais c'est qu'ils sont idiots, ces pantins ! D'un grotesque triste, sans verve, sans rancune, même !

Le reste du portique est du même jus, avec des petits miroirs ronds, réclames serties dans le béton. Dix mètres plus loin, la maison du chef de monastère porte un fronton et ce fronton — me croira-t-on ? — une pendule en plâtre avec son balancier. Cet exquis motif échappé de nos cheminées il y a trente ans, et devenu, on le voit, spécifiquement cambodgien, se retrouve dans le décor plâtreux du faîtage de cette maison : il est six heures.

L'intérieur de la pagode, inachevé, porte encore les traces du coffrage. On croit entendre siffler le train qui va entrer dans cette gare. Derrière l'autel, surmonté de fers dressés et entrelacés qui attendent la chair pleine de cailloutis du Bouddha prochain, sont rangés les barils de ciment vides. Les balustres de la véranda, répétés à l'infini dans un moule qui ne joignait plus, sont rangés en registres comme des bouteilles. Ils ont déjà reçu leur badigeon, ce qui remplit les bouteilles de dentifrice. Elles sèchent. Le dentifrice se décompose et fait grincer des dents.

Depuis trois ans, les cinquante bonzes de ce monastère s'acharnent sur cette horreur, ayant déjà reçu dix-huit mille piastres des fidèles du diocèse. Il en faut encore dix mille pour terminer l'œuvre. Depuis six mois, les travaux sont suspendus. Soyons sans crainte, on trouvera les dix mille piastres.

Du péristyle de cette usine, je regarde, à cent mètres de là, la vieille pagode désaffectée. Elle pourrit au soleil, sous son vieil or, dans son bois vénérable que la paresse des hommes n'a pas voulu aider, sous ses plaies que pas une main miséricordieuse n'a pansées — la remplacée, la dédaignée, la vieille et loyale épouse, sous ses bijoux.

Ainsi, sur tous les points du pays, les vieux sanctuaires laissent la place au béton armé, avec quoi les nouveaux constructeurs tentent de les imiter. Ils ajoutent ainsi à leur incohérence. On peut accepter une nouvelle pagode en béton armé : mais alors qu'elle ne copie pas l'ancienne ! L'église du Raincy, bravo ! Mais refaire la Sainte-Chapelle en ciment armé...

Cette évolution n'est pas seulement puérile, elle est destructrice. D'abord, lorsque le monastère n'a pas assez d'argent pour accoucher de son édifice nouveau, il s'exerce sur le vieux. Les frontons en bois sont remplacés par des frontons en ciment. Là-dessous, la charpente flanche, mais au moins une partie de l'édifice est à la page et sort du moule. Ainsi des bandeaux sculptés, ainsi des antéfixes. On est si fier, c'est si facile que, non content de remplacer, on ajoute par-ci par-là un petit lion, une petite console, un petit soldat français, un réveille-matin. Et les bonzes épanouis regardent toute la journée ce vieil arbre qui, sur le tard, se met à produire des artichauts, des pommes, des lanternes, des poissons et dont le frémissant feuillage se remplit de ciment.

On n'assiste pas seulement à cette métamorphose. Il y a partout la destruction pure et simple du vieux sanctuaire jugé inapte à recevoir la greffe. Ses poutres sculptées deviennent des passerelles dans les échafaudages du monstre qui sort de terre. Afin de ne pas perdre le précieux cailloutis, on l'entoure d'une épaisse clôture de bois. Approchons. Sur cette clôture, des animaux sculptés sautent dans des arbres, des héros mythologiques, tête en bas... Qu'est-ce ? Ne cherchez pas. Ces bas-reliefs ont cent ans. Ils proviennent de la pagode désaffectée. Le vert Rama dont la flèche ne manque jamais son but, est devenu gardien de chantier. Quant à ce qui ne peut plus servir, quoi que ce soit — on le laisse aux termites.

Mais entrons dans la pagode vétuste ou récente nous reposer un peu. C'est là que nous trouverons enfin, et conservés à l'abri par l'exercice même du culte, les ex-voto traditionnels, les vieilles chaises à prêcher, les pupitres, les petits mâts votifs, les vitrines construites à l'image de la pagode, les porte-luminaires. Sera-ce en ciment aussi ? Non : on ne sait plus. C'est décomposé, entassé, déboîté, calamiteux. Encore des réveille-matins sans aiguilles, des carafes en verre trouble. Des bocaux où nous mettons, en France, nos cornichons, remplacent ici les élégantes urnes cinéraires d'art local et, remplis de petits ossements, s'alignent ingénument. Et puis des lampes. Un musée de lampes, des lampes-suspension louis-philippardes à globes, à abat-jour, sans globes ni abat-jour, des lampes à pied avec leurs pieds signés : « Manufacture française d'Armes et Cycles de Saint-Étienne », des lampes à ressort détraquées, des lanternes tempêtes, des photophores, des lanternes de chef de gare, des lampes à huïle, à essence, à gaz d'essence, à pétrole et à acétylène. Au pied du Bouddha, voici la touque qui contient le pétrole ; à côté de cette statuette siamoise en métal estampé, la bouteille de bière où l'on a mis l'essence. On verrait bien la boîte qui renferme le carbure, mais le chef de bonzerie la cache chez lui, parce que les gamins lui chipent sa « pierre à lampe » pour faire des feux follets avec leur salive et une allumette. La lampisterie offre encore des fleurs en papier, en étoffe, sous des globes, des tissus déguenillés et des guirlandes de toile d'araignées intactes qui pendent, des bandeaux chinois, des parapluies, des images coloriées sous verre, imprimées en Allemagne, d'après des modèles hindous, importées du Siam par des Chinois qui les vendent aux Cambodgiens, des pots pleins de sable où l'on plante les baguettes d'encens, des, des, des...

Voilà donc ce que nous, Européens, vendons à ces artistes.

30 septembre.

— Eh !

— Bat !

La finesse d'oreilles de cet homme est incroyable. Il était à l'arrière de la chaloupe. J'ai dit Eh ! dans un soupir : Bat ! En dix jours, il resta une seule fois sans me répondre, hier : il était saoul !

Nous avions fait escale à Kompong Chàm, un des plus importants centres du Cambodge, et j'avais donné congé l'après-midi à l'équipage. Je le vis partir. Eh ! n'avait pas son maillot marin, mais une de ces petites vestes... Dédaignant le prestige de l'uniforme, il s'était mis en civil, quoi ! Ils me revinrent tous ivres jusqu'aux oreilles, le pilote en tête, pilotant.

J'appelai donc Eh ! Il ne répondit pas, il vint, en ciment armé comme une pagode, la bouche entr'ouverte dans un sourire de dieu, les yeux voyant plus loin qu'ils ne regardaient et à travers une béatitude qui les recouvrait d'une taie. La garnison du bord sur le toit de la chaloupe rigolait, interpellait les gens des rives. Le pilote devait manœuvrer la roue avec ses pieds, ce qui ne m'inquiétait pas, car un Cambodgien fait ce qu'il veut avec ses pieds. J'avais plus de crainte qu'il ne prît des hauts fonds pour des abîmes et fantaisie de couper à travers la campagne.

Eh ! arriva donc. Je ne sais plus pourquoi je l'avais appelé. Je vis ses dents noires. D'abord je crus que c'était encore ses lèvres. Or, il riait. Jamais je ne l'avais vu rire. Il riait en me regardant. C'est à cela que je compris surtout qu'il était ivre. Je lui dis alors de foutre le camp ! Il me fit un salut militaire. Le bras levé me montra que l'homme portait sur le flanc un singe dansant tatoué qu'une cicatrice coupait en deux d'un trait livide.

La chaloupe tituba jusqu'à l'étape, ô Rimbaud !

En deux journées nous descendîmes et remontâmes le Tonlé Touch, puis à Kompong Chàm, reprîmes le grand fleuve. Il fêta notre retour d'un orage nocturne. À partir de 23 heures, sous un ciel terrible, la rive reçut des coups de soleil fulgurants. Nous y étions blottis et le vent venant du large, nous poussant en plein travers, nous y appuyait. Le flanc bâbord de la chaloupe se moulait dans la rive détrempée. L'autre, offert à toute la largeur du fleuve, recevait un flot court, un courant dévié et une pluie torrentielle. Malgré les toiles baissées sur les persiennes, l'eau entrait et j'avais froid. L'équipage, blotti à l'arrière, cuvait son alcool de riz et dormait comme un seul homme. Le fleuve gonflant son dos, ou le monstre d'Hippolyte nous eût enlevés et déposés sur la berge, — j'aurais été seul à m'en apercevoir.

༄ ✥ ༅

Le pays du Tonlé Touch, les rives des provinces de Kompong Chàm et de Kraché où nous arriverons après-demain sont chinois autant que cambodgiens. Le Chinois y fait tout, le Cambodgien rien — ou plutôt si : du riz, du maïs qu'il vend au Chinois. Il fait encore le *couli* et le piroguier du Chinois. Entre temps, il se repose. Enfin il se fait Chinois aussi, en mettant ses plus belles filles dans le lit de l'immigré. C'est une vieille histoire qui dure certainement depuis huit siècles, probablement depuis vingt. Voici :

Le Chinois arrive, bel homme musclé, clair de peau, travailleur et courageux, bon garçon, marchand de tout ce qui se vend, entrepreneur, commissionnaire, cuisinier ambulant, acheteur de peaux, d'oiseaux, de riz, de tout ce qui s'achète, tâcheron, maraîcher, menuisier, maçon, spécialiste de béton armé, fermier de pêcheries, tenancier de jeux clandestins, colporteur, distillateur, usurier. Il est capable de faire tout cela. Il y a pensé tandis qu'il venait de Chine, *couli*, dans la cale d'une jonque de mer. Et, en débarquant, il était prêt.

En quelques mois, il sait la langue. S'il ne la sait pas, il la parle couramment avec ses gestes, son sourire, en montrant la pacotille qu'il transporte dans un ballot ; puis, sur ses doigts, le prix qu'il la vend. Peu après, il possède une charrette ou un sampan pour porter son ballot. Quelques mois de plus, il s'arrête en un point du sol. S'il y a déjà un village, c'est tant mieux. S'il n'y a pas de village, il en viendra un. Une maison ne tarde pas à s'élever. Des claies de bambous autour de douze mètres carrés de terre battue. Quatre touques à essence vides dont le propriétaire a remplacé un côté par une feuille de verre : ce sont les vitrines. Cette installation est à peine terminée que le sampan a fait un petit plus gros que lui, capable de transporter cinquante sacs de riz — ou cinq cents kilos de quelque chose de transportable. Les rameurs des deux embarcations sont cambodgiens, engagés pour dette, c'est-à-dire que le Chinois leur a prêté, à chacun, cinquante piastres qu'ils ne pourront jamais rendre sous forme d'argent. Ils s'acquittent en travail estimé 0 $ 10 par jour — alors que, s'ils étaient libres, le même Chinois serait obligé de les payer 0 $ 50. Il est vrai qu'il y a les intérêts de son prêt. Et d'ailleurs, tout le monde est content.

Parmi sa clientèle, le Chinois n'a pas tardé à remarquer une fille de dix-sept ans, noire de peau, aux cheveux drus, riche de deux oranges mûres, de deux chevillets d'argent et d'un sarong de coton. Même si le père n'a pas quelque dette à l'égard du Chinois, il lui donne la fille. Le Chinois enlève les chevillets de la petite, signe qu'elle n'est plus à marier, et les remplace par deux bracelets d'or, signe qu'elle est sa femme ; ce qu'il prouve en la faisant aussitôt enceinte. Qu'elle épouse un Cambodgien rustaud, plus noir qu'elle, bon tout au plus à faire un bonze, un piroguier, le débiteur de quelque Chinois, quand le Chinois lui-même frappe à sa porte ? Non. Ainsi a-t-elle fait le beau mariage.

Dès lors, elle enfantera annuellement de beaux enfants, aux corps plus clairs et plus élégants que le sien. Les fils aideront le père à la boutique. Les filles porteront le chignon des grand-mères paternelles qu'elles ne connaîtront jamais et métisseront leurs costumes en enfilant, sous la longue veste khmère, le pantalon chinois. Cette génération se partagera entre la lignée paternelle et la souche maternelle, tantôt éclaircissant son teint davantage et tantôt l'obscurcissant de nouveau. Puis le dosage des deux sangs se fixera.

Telle est cette vieille race sino-cambodgienne qui peuple à peu près exclusivement toutes les régions prospères, commodes, bien accessibles du Cambodge. Le Cambodgien contemplatif, rêveur, musicien, bavard, bon et désintéressé fait confiance à ses marchands. À lui les hautes et dures régions, les rizières qu'il cultive, le reste du pays lointain et dépeuplé. Il s'y confine entre sa pagode et sa case et, en fin de compte, le temps qu'il ne passe pas à servir le bonze, il l'emploie à attendre le Chinois.

Celui-ci arrive un jour, de l'eau jusqu'au ventre ou la langue pendante de soif. Il passe. En passant, il achète les récoltes sur pied et les paye d'avance, ce qui lui permet de les acquérir à bon prix et de laisser le Cambodgien ébloui. Le lendemain, le Chinois repasse et invite son vendeur de la veille à une petite partie de « bacouan » ou de « trente-six bêtes ». Tout le monde est en joie, la vie est belle, les guitares et les flûtes sont folles dans les cases. Le Chinois repart avec l'argent de la récolte que le Cambodgien a perdu au jeu. Et la récolte, il reviendra deux mois après la rechercher. Mais alors, personne ne jouera.

De Kompong Chàm à Kraché, le fleuve est chinois. Mais au fait, ne vient-il pas de Chine aussi, le fleuve ? Toutes ces chaloupes ? Armateurs et équipage chinois. Stung Trang, Krauchmar, Chlong, Kraché — ces grands marchés riverains ? Population, boutiques, commerce, chinois et sino-cambodgiens. Chinoises, ces jonques énormes qui engloutissent par tonnes, à toutes les époques propices, les produits du sol. Bref, le Cambodge n'est que chair inerte sur un solide et souple squelette chinois et sino-cambodgien.

D'ailleurs, autant le Cambodgien déteste l'Annamite, il aime le Chinois. Lors de troubles, quand une bande de paysans ivres se met en route pour quelque pillage, on voit bien, par-ci par-là, flamber une boutique chinoise et le propriétaire avec, s'il n'a pas pris la fuite à temps. À ces occasions qui ne se renouvellent pas deux fois en dix ans, le Cambodgien semble s'apercevoir que le Chinois le soigne comme le meilleur ami qu'on cocufie. Mais, le lendemain, tout le monde fraternise.

Car le Chinois prend possession du sol pacifiquement. Il n'impose rien, n'appelle personne. Il traite les affaires conformément aux us et coutumes : c'est bien lui qui, depuis dix siècles, dirige ces us et coutumes, à petits coups de pouce insensibles — mais personne n'y fait attention. Il dote les pagodes et rend ainsi au pays une partie de l'argent qu'il y gagne. Il accepte le travail que le Cambodgien ne veut pas faire. En un mot, il est là. Il est là chaque fois qu'il le faut, patient, les mains diligentes et le ventre extensible.

Je n'oublierai jamais qu'il y a quinze ans, parti de Stung Trèng, j'arrivai après huit jours de marche sur le Nord-Ouest, dans une région déserte, au pied de la chaîne des Dangrèk qui sépare le Cambodge du Siam. Je touchai au dernier village septentrional du pays sans avoir vu âme qui vive depuis deux jours. Il y avait là une vingtaine de cases. J'allais m'écrier en descendant de cheval : j'arrive au bout du monde ! Les nuages couronnaient, à un millier de mètres de hauteur, les monts solitaires. Au-dessous, un Chinois trônait dans sa boutique et ma sueur se glaça ; une voix chantait : « Ah ! je ris de me voir si belle en ce miroir ! ».

Le phonographe du Chinois.

1er octobre 1929.

M ais c'est qu'ils vivent entourés de femmes, toute la journée, ces bonzes ! Il est vrai que nous sommes en semaine sainte. Ah ! je sais bien que c'est à peu près toujours la même chose. Elles arrivent à toute heure, ces femmes, à pied, en pirogue, en charrette, chargées d'offrandes de toutes couleurs, des plus beaux fruits, de feuilles de bétel sans tare, de plateaux couverts de bols pleins de soupes soignées et de cigarettes et de bouteilles de limonade — de tout ce qui se mâche, se suce, se respire, fait plaisir aux yeux et à l'estomac.

Les jeunes canéphores mettent leurs plus beaux atours, des écharpes teintes par la *Badische Anilin Fabrik* de Ludwigshafen et des bracelets qu'on voit déjà sur les bas-reliefs d'Angkor. Elles suivent les vieilles en file. Il en arrive de trois lieues à la ronde. Elles s'entassent dans la sala pour la demi-journée, puis de là passent dans la maison du chef de bonzerie, après s'être lavé les pieds. Quelques-unes font le ménage du monastère et sont aux petits soins pour les anachorètes. Je renifle des parfums de santal et d'autres moins orthodoxes qui jaspent de relents humains et de cuisine une atmosphère d'encens. Un troupeau de métisses chinoises vient de partir, une bande de Cambodgiennes le remplace, grises, sales, tremblantes de prières et de vieillesse, avec, parmi elles, fleurs piquées dans ce buisson poussiéreux, des jeunes filles.

Au pied de l'autel, le chef du monastère, consulaire, couvert du pollen de sa toge, assis dans sa chaise sacerdotale au dossier évasé, entouré de quatre novices, lit son kampi d'une voix de grelot. Un gamin l'évente à grands coups d'éventails isolés, avec les gestes de lui lancer des pierres. Il lit, s'arrête pour cracher, se reposer, mâcher une chique de bétel, je veux dire sucer une chique, car il n'a pas de dents. Un novice écrase, au préalable, la chique dans un tube de cuivre en poussant un piston dont la poignée est un coquillage.

Ainsi se déroule débonnairement le sermon, avec des intermèdes, au-dessus de la foule recueillie, sous le roucoulement des pigeons. Des chiens se battent à côté en poussant des cris de rage affreux. Du haut de la sala, un fidèle jette dans le tas un des trois cailloux d'un foyer qui, bien ajusté, fait un bruit mou en tombant dans la meute. La prière reprend. Les pigeons n'ont pas cessé de roucouler. Heures familiales et populaires, naïves, où le mysticisme se fait bon enfant.

Devant le prédicant, je vois étaler, sur une natte et du linge blanc, des paquets de bougies et d'encens, du tabac pour la chique, des sous et des piastres métalliques dans une coupe — la future pagode en béton — des tranches de cannes à sucre, du sucre de palmier, des fleurs de sucre, des gâteaux sucrés, toute une sucrerie que suceront les vieilles chères lèvres, après les oraisons.

D'un côté les femmes, de l'autre les hommes et des gamins des deux côtés. Les hommes sont empesés, portent des fronts tendus, des mines affairées et, pleins de précautions, déplacent de droite à gauche ou de gauche à droite un cornet de bétel. Ils le déplacent afin qu'il fasse mieux là où ils le mettent, rehausse la plantureuse nature morte dont ils escomptent bien que les bonzes leur repasseront la moitié. Enfin, nous voyons des Cambodgiens au travail et se débattant au milieu des soucis et des difficultés de la vie ! Ils sucent leurs grosses cigarettes comme des tétines de biberon, réajustent, à chaque geste, leurs écharpes. Lorsqu'une vieille femme, autoritaire, leur jette un ordre ou un avis, à travers la sala, ils prennent un petit air de s'en ficher et l'exécutent en se dandinant.

Cette assemblée permanente de tout un peuple et de son clergé, autour de victuailles, entre des colonnes polies, sous un toit étincelant, dans une atmosphère d'encens et de fermentation, la bonne chaleur de l'ombre, au cours d'un temps qui n'est limité que par le tam-tam monastique ; cette réunion quotidienne d'oisifs de tous âges dont les plus jeunes, par-dessus les épaules drapées de jaune et tandis que les vieilles clabaudent, choisissent les pucelles qu'ils sauront bien, ensuite, retrouver ; tout ce riz cuit et cru accumulé en petites coupes ; cette convention millénaire passée entre les deux moitiés d'un peuple afin que l'une travaille en vue de nourrir la seconde qui n'a d'autre mission que de prier pour tous — et puis, ces dix mille religieux qui ont fait vœu de pauvreté et se drapent de soie ; vœu de solitude et qui vivent dans une population toujours mouvante à leur pied ; vœu de mendicité et qu'on sert comme des princes ; vœu d'abstinence et qui s'épanouissent entourés de victuailles et de confiseries ; vœu de renoncement (car tout désir engendre la douleur) et qui se suspendent comme des fruits à un arbre filtrant pour eux sa sève la plus succulente ; vœu d'humilité et à qui l'on ne parle qu'à genoux et mains jointes ; le long d'un fleuve, ce peuple, ces bonzes, contents et solidaires les uns des autres depuis vingt siècles, heureux et confiants, — je m'abuse peut-être, mais voilà qui n'est pas ordinaire et me semble prêter à la méditation.

༄

J'ai envie ce soir, après ma page d'écriture, de m'offrir une petite douceur. Neuf heures. Mon café était bon. La chaloupe somnole accrochée à un arbre et j'ai un flacon de curaçao. Je l'avais oublié.

— Eh !

— Bat !

Il ne dormait pas, l'animal. Je lui demande un verre à liqueur. Je n'en ai pas emporté, mais je pense que le matériel administratif du bord en comporte une couple. Non, pas de verre à liqueur. Eh! revient avec le coquetier. Ce coquetier en porcelaine fait d'ailleurs bien l'affaire. Eh! ne me le sert-il pas à chaque repas, en guise de salière ? Au fait, où a-t-il mis le sel ? Il me le montre sur le coin de la table. M'imaginé-je qu'il l'eût jeté ? Et je déguste mon curaçao.

— Eh !

— Bat !

— Fini.

Il prend le coquetier. Penché sur le fleuve, il le lave, l'essuie avec le bas de son maillot de matelot, puis repousse le tas de sel dans ce coquetier qui, de verre à liqueur, redevient salière, sous un index torsadé dont l'ongle est un fragment d'écorce.

Et je songe : Eh! me servira-t-il ce coquetier si d'aventure je veux manger des œufs à la coque ?

2 octobre.

Je viens d'assister à la mort d'un arbre, en plein soleil et en pleine eau — comme un arbre d'ici se doit : épilogue d'une lutte qui durait depuis une trentaine d'années, peut-être, entre le fleuve et lui. Celui-là, deux mois par an, remontait se rouler au pied de l'arbre, faire des grâces de vieux serpent hypocrite ; puis il redescendait lentement, ayant rongé un peu de terre.

Quel nom botanique donner à cet arbre ? Trois mètres de tour de taille, une coupole d'ombre sous des roches de feuillages à travers quoi le soleil, depuis longtemps, ne passait plus. Ce grand niais à tête trop lourde penchait déjà hors de la berge. Les deux tiers de ses racines étaient à nu, en plein air, lavées, ossements décharnés et blanchâtres, crypte à cent colonnes capricantes entre lesquelles chaque crue était venue clapoter avec un bruit de rames.

Pendant ce temps et sous son poids de plus en plus terrible, l'arbre avait lancé du côté opposé, en terre ferme, des câbles de détresse, rectilignes et qui saillaient comme des veines. Manœuvre inutile : il aurait fallu qu'il les lançât de son tronc et de ses branches, en biais, comme des étais et des haubans de grand mât. Mais il n'avait pas tant d'astuce ce pauvre géant ! Il comptait sur ses oiseaux pour le maintenir debout ? Il ne pouvait pas, non plus, se reculer, n'est-ce pas, ni supplier le fleuve de lui laisser sa terre. Et d'ailleurs, dans sa confiance végétale, imprévoyant des malfaçons de Dieu, prenait-il garde à la poignée d'avenir que lui enlevait chaque flot passant ?

Aussi, quand vint le temps où il se sentit chanceler, il était trop tard. Nous allions partir : le matelot qui avait dénoué notre câble remontait à bord. À cent mètres derrière nous, j'entendis le grondement de dix éclatements successifs, un arpège abominable. Je regardai. Le grand corps décrivait un arc de cercle, sa frondaison sifflante comme de la vapeur. Le fleuve le reçut dans une reculade de vagues qui nous rattrapèrent et soulevèrent la chaloupe. Des racines atrocement tendues dans une résistance inutile, craquaient encore. Une épaisse poussière rouge montait du sol et de la poussière d'eau retombait sur des flots déjà renouvelés, étrangers au drame, et qui prenaient le mort pour une petite île de verdure.

೮⊕ೞ

Comment expliquer la diversité de l'accueil que je trouve dans les villages ou les bonzeries ? Ici, j'ai l'impression que chacun me donnerait sa femme si je la demandais, et là, que si le monastère possédait des fusils, je serais descendu, tout coup portant, dès qu'on m'apercevrait. Ces deux accueils supposés, Dieu merci !, marquent les deux extrêmes entre lesquels je ne sais jamais dans quel sens la réception qui m'attend se déroulera et sans que je puisse établir une corrélation entre la nature de cette réception, la densité de la population, sa richesse, son éloignement ou l'air du temps.

Le *mê-srok* (chef de village) de Kompong Réap voit arriver la chaloupe, saute dans son sampan et fiche le camp, plus rapide qu'un cormoran. La nuit tombe, laissant le village obscur. Nous appelons : il est mort depuis cent ans, ce village ! Nous nous installons par nos propres moyens. Une heure après, ce même village a pris conscience que nous nous passons de lui et restons dans notre coquille, que l'animal n'est pas méchant ; une torche s'allume dans chaque case et le village devient une constellation.

Le lendemain, nous abordons à Viléa sans rien demander. Je n'ai pas fini de me débarbouiller que j'entends un brouhaha sur la berge. Viléa est le siège du Gouverneur de la province. Il est là avec sa suite et vient me recevoir. Sa veste de soie sort de l'armoire. En cinq minutes, il a réuni le *mê-srok*, le *chantop*, un secrétaire, des gardes. Vingt curieux non convoqués sont là aussi. On se congratule. Je profite de l'occasion pour demander à acheter — je précise acheter — trois poulets : et le *mêsrok* part en courant ; une douzaine d'œufs : départ accéléré du *chantop* ; du poisson, ça n'est plus l'heure, mais on m'en promet pour le lendemain, avant mon départ.

Le Gouverneur m'invite à aller dans sa maison me reposer. Je décline l'invitation avec des paroles fleuries. Il me demande la permission de se retirer. Je la lui donne. Alors commence un supplice inverse de celui de la veille. Un garde arrive chargé d'un panier : cadeau du Gouverneur. Dans ce panier, il y a : une bouteille de cognac, une d'anis, une de byrrh, deux de médoc, deux de bière, deux de limonade, une boîte de fruits japonais et six de sardines de Californie, celles-ci portant sur le couvercle une image de poisson qui ressemble à une baleine. Ce pauvre diable de Gouverneur vient d'acheter ça chez le Chinois pour me l'offrir. Je n'accepte qu'une bouteille de limonade et explique que ce prélèvement me fait plus de plaisir que le tout. Le porteur, confondu, n'ose repartir. Il insiste. Je démontre que la chaloupe, trop petite, coulerait sous cette cargaison. Tout le monde rit, le garde disparaît avec son chargement. Dix minutes après, il revient à la suite d'une assiette de citrons. J'accepte les citrons. Il repart. Encore dix minutes et voilà une cage avec cinq beaux poulets. Combien ? Mais non, voyons, on me les donne : poulets du Gouverneur. Et il faut que j'accepte par une courtoisie égale à celle que ces braves gens dépensent à m'offrir. Je me croyais bonze !

Or, cet après-midi même, je suppliais, dans un autre village, qu'on me vendît un poulet. Chacun répondit qu'il n'y en avait pas. Une vieille sorcière qui lavait je ne sais quoi dans l'eau du fleuve (j'avais l'air de la lui voler, cette eau), me cria comme si elle m'insultait que « cette saison-ci, elle n'avait mangé du poulet qu'une fois ». Dans ce village, j'entendais caqueter les poules. Elles couraient entre les perches à bétel. Des coqs « comme s'il en pleuvait » s'ébattaient jusqu'au bord de l'eau et transperçaient l'air de leurs cris. Je veux bien qu'on me dise qu'il n'y a pas de poisson dans le fleuve parce que je ne peux aller y voir ; mais pas de poulets dans ce village-poulailler !

Je n'ai vu qu'un gamin de douze ans dans la pagode de Kâs Chrèng : il n'avait pas eu le temps de se sauver. Il alla chercher les clés du sanctuaire chez le supérieur qui me fit attendre vingt minutes et ne daigna pas se déranger. De leurs cellules, les bonzes me regardaient quand je ne regardais pas les cellules, et dès que je me tournais vers elles, ils se retiraient des fenêtres. Nous avons épousseté l'autel afin de faire un cliché, monté notre pied-échelle devant le fronton Ouest, personne n'a paru. Ce fut la pagode au bois dormant.

Puis, dix kilomètres plus loin, dans l'île Bey-Pey, la chaloupe encore à cent mètres de la berge, le chef de monastère nous attendait, vieillard majestueux, que je voyais d'en bas, statue romaine plafonnant. La confrérie l'entourait. Il parlait déjà pendant que nous nous amarrions, me souhaitait la bienvenue, commençait l'historique de son misérable ermitage et, tel le vieux bonze Sim que j'éveillais dans sa cellule sculptée, il me prit la main et me fit faire le tour du propriétaire, ingénu, confiant, ayant tant à me dire qu'il semblait m'avoir attendu dans son île depuis sa jeunesse. Je dus monter dans sa case, m'asseoir sur l'unique chaise du couvent, ce que je parvins à faire sans que son pied passât entre les lattes du parquet. Un novice grimpa les douze mètres d'un cocotier d'où il fit tomber des noix pleines de clair de lune. On me donna un panier de goyaves. Adieu ! moines courtois sans peur et sans reproche ! Je m'éloignai. Rangés sur leur berge hospitalière, ils m'honorèrent de leur présence immobile, jusqu'à ce qu'ils ne fussent pas plus gros que des fleurs de jonquille.

2 octobre.

Nous faisons la causette, cette vieille Cambodgienne et moi. Le jour se levait et l'équipage chargeait du bois. Elle passait, vit la chaloupe et, par la fenêtre de la cabine, un Français. Elle s'arrêta.

— Eh ! vieille, lui dis-je, tout va bien dans ta famille ?

Elle répondit avec onction, vint s'accouder au plat bord et contempla ma trousse de toilette. Je lui dis d'où je viens. Sans plus, elle entre. Une veste, blanche naguère, une écharpe écossaise en baudrier et les lobes des oreilles percés par des trous à travers lesquels je vois le jour comme par deux hublots.

Elle va à la pagode, mais ne se presse pas, car les bonzes ne sont pas encore levés à cette heure. Moi aussi, lui dis-je, je vais à la pagode. Je ne fais que ça depuis dix jours. J'ai déjà visité quatre-vingt-quatorze pagodes, ma vieille, et me sens devenir bonze ! Nous rions. Ses rides se gonflent de malice. J'ajoute que je suis fatigué, que je n'ai pas assez dormi : la moitié de la nuit, nous développâmes des clichés. Alors, elle m'invite à me coucher et m'offre de me masser.

Le massage est en grand honneur au Cambodge et les vieilles y excellent. Allait-elle, à la pagode, masser le chef du monastère ? Elle me tape sur le bras, le visage offusqué. Quel âge avez-vous, vieille ? Soixante-huit ans. Et je m'étends. Elle relève les jambes de mon pyjama et ouvre ma veste. Quelques gosses regardent le tableau, de la berge. Eh ! qui venait nettoyer la cabine repart avec son faubert.

Ce fut épouvantable. Cette vieille m'empoigna le ventre et me le tordit comme du linge sale. Elle enfonçait deux doigts, deux morceaux de rotin, entre mes abdominaux, allait saisir je ne sais quelles fibres de la couche profonde et tirait d'un coup sec, en lâchant — tout comme on joue de la lyre.

J'irai jusqu'au bout de ma narration : cette opération avait pour but de libérer, paraît-il, les vents accumulés dans l'abdomen pendant la nuit. Et le muscle que cette vieille anatomiste allait saisir, elle m'en donna le nom : « le muscle du zéphir matinal ». Je traduis littéralement, sauf un mot qui, en français, me paraît trop bref.

Puis deux araignées sèches s'agrippèrent à mes hanches. Je crus hurler lorsqu'elles me séparaient les biceps des humérus ou tiraient sur chacun de mes orteils jusqu'à ce qu'ils craquassent. Comment ce vieux corps pouvait-il déployer tant de force ?

Je lui ai donné vingt sous. Elle les enveloppa dans l'angle de son écharpe en me disant qu'elle allait acheter des affaires avec, pour offrir aux bonzes. Ainsi les bonzes de cette rive auront prélevé une once de ma graisse — à moi aussi.

ঙ ✤ ଓ

En amont de Kompong Chàm, le Mékong exagère tout. Il s'élargit encore, mais la terre plus haute l'encadre mieux, impose à l'esprit une idée de limite, donc de mesure. Les reproches que je lui faisais ces jours derniers tombent et, remontant toujours, dès Stung Trang, nous atteignons à la majesté pleine, définitive, sans rien qui dévaste, ni inquiète. Là, les berges se dressent brusquement à une cinquantaine de mètres, dominent un immense tournant des eaux et leur opposent une membrure de roches d'un rose tragique, au front desquelles une ligne de végétation pose un diadème concave. Puis, de Stung Trang à Kraché, ce n'est qu'une frange de bambous géants, aux formes jaillissantes de geysers ou de gerbes, les tiges serrées dans des poings.

Le courant qui ne peut s'étaler est plus rude qu'en aval, plus capricieux surtout. Nous essuyons des grains. L'eau embarque à l'avant et le vent rebrousse sur les vagues une crinière rousse. Le fleuve tourne : plus un souffle, l'eau se fait mercure à contre-ciel, d'huile verte à contre-rive et jaunit en léchant la terre. On la croirait immobile, si l'on ne voyait passer des troncs morts qui flottent en bombant des dos luisants et rugueux de crocodiles. Un cormoran surpris n'eut pas le temps, ni le courage de s'envoler. Il plongea, fila entre deux eaux et, de-ci de-là, remontait respirer, ne sortant qu'un cou reptilien et un bec mou qu'il tournait en tous sens. Puis, tout à coup, sur cette eau lisse où se dissimulent cependant de puissantes ondulations aplaties par la réverbération, la chaloupe tangue au point que je ne peux plus écrire.

Nous rencontrons des trains de bois dont quelques-uns couvrent plus d'un demi-hectare. Les troncs en grume, descendus un à un du Laos par un flottage de deux mille kilomètres, sont recueillis au Nord du Cambodge après les cataractes de Khône.

Quel étrange métier que celui de ces piroguiers, pêcheurs d'arbres, qui guettent, des rives, le passage de ces amphibies énormes et précieux, animés de l'élan des eaux ! Ils pagaient à leur poursuite, les captent, les enchaînent avec des câbles de rotin — flottants eux aussi — et les ramènent à la berge. Puis, lorsqu'ils ont ainsi rassemblé le monstrueux troupeau, ils jettent de tronc en tronc des jougs de bambou qui les maintiennent parallèles. Le chaotique parquet repart. Il mettra un mois pour atteindre la mer. En un point quelconque, une case de paillote abrite les habitants de ce parterre dont le fond est celui du fleuve, les timoniers de cette plage en dérive, les comptables de cette fortune confiée au fil de l'eaù.

4 octobre.

Encore une fin de jour sur une berge où tout est balancement immobile. Pas une case visible, mais un village présent, derrière des chants de coqs, une poussière de voix humaine, et des draperies de convolvulacées jetées d'arbre en arbre. La planche passerelle, un câble — c'est tout ce qui nous retient à cette terre et à cette heure de tendre argent où le crépuscule vient de s'éteindre.

Des femmes se baignent avec leurs enfants, sous mes yeux d'étranger qui n'existent pas pour elles. N'est-ce pas leur heure depuis qu'elles étaient ces enfants, un instant nécessaire au rythme de leur vie ? Presque toutes métisses sous les coquilles pointues de leurs chignons. La peau claire de quelques-unes, seule matière claire du paysage, en capte toute la lumière. Elles sont venues, suivant la trace laissée par leurs pieds, ce matin ; ont posé leurs cruches d'argile et, sur ces fruits, la veste et le pagne secs qu'elles mettront au sortir de l'eau. Puis elles entrèrent dans le fleuve après avoir remonté leurs sarongs au-dessus des seins. Ainsi, en ce moment, le long de ce fleuve immense, des milliers de femmes se baignent, changent de vêtements sans offrir à l'air plus de nudité que celle de leurs épaules et de leurs jambes.

Mais sur leurs formes, la soie, rendue plus soyeuse et plus étroite par le vernis de l'eau, colle à elles comme la peau. Aussi, malgré la pudeur des baigneuses, ce sont des nudités qui surgissent du fleuve, des nudités laquées, des nudités d'ébène aux épaules d'ivoire et casquées de jais — des nudités aquatiques sous les luisants qui les parcourent et terrestres par leur chair. Elles sentent le lait et le charbon. Leurs seins jeunes ou fanés, écrasés sous le nœud du pagne, elles ne font que des gestes utiles. La turbulence des enfants blanchit le fleuve. Elles émergent alors plus douces dans une tranquillité athénienne, animale et barbare.

Sur la gauche, dans un sampan que vont rejoindre et bercer les vagues repoussées par ces corps, un homme assis, des épaules d'athlète sur une taille d'éphèbe, les pieds traînant dans l'eau et qui doit être un des maris, regarde, sans les voir, les femelles du village. J'observe son immobilité végétale et l'expression repue de son visage. Cette vie si lointaine de moi est en lui depuis des siècles. Je le crois insensible à ce qui m'émeut, mais en regardant mieux, je vois que sa main attentive tient une ligne de fond dont il épie et percevra le plus léger appel.

10-20 octobre.

Rivière de Pursat. — La chaloupe touche par son milieu un lit de sable, tourne sur ce pivot et s'échoue en travers du courant qui la couche. Huit heures du matin. Nous sommes à l'entrée d'un village, à la hauteur de la pagode où le pilote avait mission d'accoster.

Pour les bonzes, le spectacle est de choix, imprévu par surcroît. Assis en ligne, ils considèrent la chaloupe française en posture ridicule. Machine arrière, coup de barre, machine avant pendant une demi-heure, en vain ! Je hèle les bonzes, les prie de faire appeler le chef de village, mais les bonzes sont sourds : il y a beaucoup de bonzes sourds au Cambodge. Un sampan apparaît, poussé par deux rameurs qui nous aperçoivent, et le sampan file vers la berge où les hommes débarquent et disparaissent. Alors Eh! et un autre matelot se jettent à la nage et vont à la recherche du chef de village.

Il arrive en pirogue et je sais bien ce qu'il va me dire : depuis le moment où nous nous sommes échoués, tous les hommes valides du village ont éprouvé la nécessité d'aller voir leurs rizières, même ceux qui n'en ont pas, même ceux qui en revenaient et apprirent qu'au milieu de la rivière une chaloupe française était en difficulté.

Voilà donc le *mê-srok*. Je lui montre mes papiers à sceaux et lui offre une cigarette qu'il met sur son oreille. Puis, je lui suggère qu'une quinzaine d'hommes... Il se lève, m'assurant qu'il va les chercher. Mais non, vieux roublard, reste avec moi et appelle quelqu'un qui viendra à ta voix hiérarchique et connue prendre tes ordres. Nous mettrons, de cette façon, deux heures à réunir nos quinze hommes, mais je sens bien que si je te laissais repartir...

Alors le *mê-srok* interpelle les bonzes. Les bonzes ne sont plus sourds et un novice va au village. Des pirogues apparaissent qui ne font plus demi-tour. Quinze hommes ? Vingt se précipitent, chacun donnant un avis. Ah ! que de bonne volonté ! On lance un câble qui n'est pas assez long pour tous les haleurs qui, maintenant, accourent. Encore un peu, femmes, enfants, vieillards s'y mettraient — et les bonzes ! En cinq minutes la chaloupe est déséchouée. J'offre trois piastres afin que nos sauveteurs achètent des cigarettes. On les refuse. Dans ce pays, l'effort n'est rien, mais l'obtenir...

☼❀☾

Nous quittons le Grand Lac pour aller retrouver le Stung Srèng par la plaine : trois mètres d'eau la recouvrent. Nous naviguons où, dans six mois, des charrettes soulèveront la poussière des pistes. Le pilote cherche sa voie parmi des sommets de buissons et des arbres aux troncs noyés, que l'eau immobile reflète, un peu moins ensoleillés et posés sur des ombres visqueuses. On vire sur place, au gouvernail et à la perche, péniblement, de longues perches que l'équipage arc-bouté plante dans les frondaisons.

Comme une bufflesse harcelée par les mouches, la chaloupe frotte ses flancs aux arbres qui balayent son pont et y jettent des fourmis et des chenilles. De temps à autre, un matelot plonge, coupe-coupe en main, afin de débarrasser l'hélice des plantes sous-marines qui s'y sont enchevêtrées. Et tandis qu'il travaille, entre les temps où il vient reprendre souffle à la surface, le silence est tel que la chaloupe, sa machine morte, semble s'abandonner, découragée d'errer à travers ce monde en suspens et tout provisoire ; où partout l'eau, elle-même étrangère, reste muette, ignorante de sa route, et épaisse comme une gelée.

Enfin, nous tombons sur une jonque épaulée contre des arbres telle une bête au gîte. Ses hôtes mangent. Près d'eux, somnole, la tête sous l'aile, un échassier familier à pattes rouges. Le vivier cylindrique en joncs tressés flotte au bout d'une corde et des nasses sèchent sur le toit de la jonque. Une fumée monte tandis qu'un bouquet d'arbres masque cette vision incompréhensible dans un désert qui semblait ne devoir pas finir, ce cliché de vie flottante et familiale d'hommes qui jamais ne sentent de terre pulvérulente sous leurs pieds.

Mais le cliché reparaît, un autre encore, tout près, et si semblable au premier que nous croyons toujours buter contre la même jonque. Mais non, nous entrons dans les faubourgs de Bak Préa, village d'un millier d'âmes, centre de pêcheurs et de marchands de bois, bûcherons surprenants qui, de leurs sampans, étêtent les arbres et les débitent au gré de la baisse des eaux, de haut en bas.

Une centaine de maisons bâties sur radeaux faits de gros bambous et que des planches ployantes relient, ou des sampans — et voilà le village, ce village ancré à une terre qui n'apparaît jamais, village toujours mobile dans son immobilité.

L'eau y est à la fois ignoble et magnifique, noire comme du café, jaspée de graisse où le soleil enrubanne des roses et des violets métalliques. Elle est couverte de détritus, d'écailles et de tripes de poissons, de cendres, de plantes flottantes ; grouillante d'alevins, de petites crevettes sautillantes, d'insectes et de larves. Des poissons surgissent verticalement du fond, et, l'air et la lumière les renvoyant (tel un mur renvoie des balles élastiques), ils replongent et disparaissent avec une instantanéité d'étincelles. J'ai l'impression qu'ils se sont cognés contre la surface de l'eau où leurs chocs laissent des bulles et d'imperceptibles bruits de déchirure. Ou bien d'autres poissons, en troupe, de biais et parallèles, viennent bâiller. Et leurs bouches rondes font des trous dans l'eau.

Sur les plateformes des cases, les passerelles, par ce village où rien n'est stable, où tout glisse, se dérobe, penche et s'entrechoque ; dans de petites pirogues où le seul passager qui peut y trouver place doit, sans cesse, écoper du pied l'eau qui passe par-dessus bord ; ou encore, dominant une poupe de grosse jonque marchande sans rambarde — des kyrielles d'enfants.

Ceux qui ne savent pas marcher rampent. Qui les surveille ? Les autres. S'il en tombe un, la population est si dense qu'il serait rattrapé, j'imagine, par dix plongeurs, avant d'être noyé. Ici, d'ailleurs, l'enfant sait nager en même temps que marcher. Cette fillette de cinq ans ne pagayera pas mieux, durant sa vie, qu'elle le fait sous mes yeux. Générations d'amphibies.

Entre des planches en chicane, deux mains plongent pour laver une marmite. L'homme ne vit qu'accroupi, les pieds mouillés. Il boit cette eau, il y fait cuire son riz, il s'y soulage ; les chaloupes y font leur vidange d'huiles brûlées et de cendres ; des bêtes mortes y pourrissent ; la terre et la verdure s'y décomposent en bouillie où la rame entre aussi loin qu'on peut la pousser. Et à l'avant d'une pirogue, une jeune fille se lave de cette eau, s'en arrose voluptueusement, sous un vol de corbeaux, bain tiède dans du plasma et de la pourriture.

Et voilà, en émergeant, ces hommes aux corps admirables, ces vieilles femmes nouées qui passèrent là leur vie, des essaims d'enfants, petits équilibristes aux yeux vifs, nés de la fécondité régulière des femmes. Combien en meurt-il ? Beaucoup sans doute. Mais meurt-on ? Voyez : en face du village, sur ces flotteurs de bambou, cette petite maison solitaire et déserte, peinte d'un bleu de ciel avec des rosaces d'un rouge ronflant. Elle est ceinturée de pots chinois où poussent des arbustes soigneusement taillés et piqués de fleurs en papier. Des banderoles d'étoffe la festonnent. Passant auprès, des pagayeurs s'inclinent. C'est un sanctuaire. Il flotte comme un bouquet au front du village infect, vireux — et ses dieux se nourrissent de la même eau.

ಐ❀ಐ

Cette fourmi s'avance sur la main courante. Je la vois par transparence comme une goutte de miel. Le corselet oblique et levant sa tête de chèvre, elle porte, entre ses mandibules, un grain de riz cuit. Elle se hâte, fière comme Artaban. C'est une fourmi rouge : la bête la plus féroce de ces pays. Là où elle tombe et pressent le moindre danger, elle mord aussitôt mais ne fuit pas ; elle plante ses deux mâchoires aiguës, dresse le ventre et, poussant sur ses pattes, elle tire... elle tire... Si l'éléphant et la panthère avaient son courage et son agressivité, il n'existerait plus d'hommes sur la terre.

Elle empoisonne la vie des voyageurs, elle est partout, la sale bête ! En cette saison et dans cette région inondée, les arbres en sont couverts. Naguère, lorsque je relevais dans le Nord du Cambodge le plan des ruines de Bantéai Chhmar, il y en avait tellement que je faillis renoncer à mes recherches. Insinuées sous mes vêtements, elles s'en donnaient à cœur-joie sur ma peau. Oui, j'eusse renoncé, dis-je, si je n'avais trouvé expédient de me mettre à peu près nu. L'ennemi ainsi à découvert, je chargeai un couli de m'épousseter avec un balai de feuilles.

Mais revenons à celle-ci, amazone qui s'est faite ménagère, transporte son grain de riz et qui, sur cette chaloupe emportée, croit retourner vers l'arbre d'où elle tomba. Je lui barre la route du doigt. Elle essaie de le contourner. J'avance, elle file à gauche : encore l'obstacle. Elle se dresse, elle vibre — ça va mal ! Alors, dans sa colère, croyant tenir ma peau, elle serre ses mandibules, et voilà le grain de riz, coupé en deux moitiés, qui lui échappe.

Si le Créateur donne à cette bête, avec le courage, la férocité et l'entêtement, aussi quelque vanité, quelle vexation doit remplir en cet instant son cerveau minuscule ! Deux pichenettes, j'envoie les moitiés du grain dans l'eau. La fourmi tourne, cherche son bien, s'en va. Et je la laisse à sa double humiliation.

ಶಿ✵ಲ

Dernière heure du jour. Nous ne voyons plus assez pour avancer dans le labyrinthe liquide. En cette lumière grise, ah ! la mélancolie des blanches aigrettes, en troupes envolées et qui tendent une écharpe à fleur d'eau. On l'aperçoit, elle se déchire et disparaît au même instant — était-ce une illusion ?

On amarre à un buisson, après l'avoir vigoureusement battu avec des perches, afin d'en faire tomber les reptiles qui, chassés par l'eau, s'y seraient réfugiés. Je me hâte de dîner sans lampe, avant la montée des moustiques, car hier soir, à cette heure, j'en ai connu l'étrange assaut. Autour de ma moustiquaire close avec des épingles de sûreté, l'invisible nuée tendait ses sifflements par milliers qui faisaient rage et s'enchevêtraient. Je me sentais littéralement au centre d'une sphère gazeuse de plusieurs mètres d'épaisseur. Elle m'isolait du monde. Dans cette région noyée, des anophèles exclusivement, l'espèce porteuse de fièvre.

ಶಿ✵ಲ

Nous avons enfin trouvé le lit de la rivière de Kompong Chèn. Aux hautes eaux, le phénomène est le même partout autour du Grand Lac : les rivières au-devant desquelles, sur dix kilomètres, celui-ci lance ses eaux débordantes ; ces rivières n'offrent plus que des deltas de lits étroits et visqueux recouverts par l'inondation. Il faut en suivre cependant les invraisemblables sinuosités, car bientôt les fonds manquent qui nous permettaient jusqu'ici de couper court.

Les eaux boueuses de la rivière et du Lac, se mêlant chacune à bout de course, déposent leurs impuretés, deviennent étonnamment transparentes, mais la végétation qui s'y décompose les teinte encore d'acajou, et l'ombre des feuillages fait de cette eau une matière semblable à de l'écaille.

Après cette première métamorphose, la forêt inondée se clairsème, ses derniers arbres disparaissent. Buissons et roseaux font un paysage triste, écrasé par le soleil, où la chaloupe cherche son chemin à la perche.

Puis le monde, lentement, se reforme. Des herbes révèlent que la terre monte, qu'elle n'est plus qu'à soixante, quarante centimètres. De nouveau, l'horizon change d'aspect avec de grands arbres, ceux-là que jamais l'inondation n'atteint. Le corps flasque de la rivière s'articule. Encore une heure et le sol émerge enfin, noir, gluant, où butent des détritus, car, en même temps, un léger courant se révèle. Ainsi voit-on naître et sortir du chaos cette rivière monstrueuse, alors qu'elle s'y perd.

Désormais, cette illusion de création se fait de plus en plus saisissante. Les berges s'organisent entre lesquelles l'eau maintenue et dont la vitesse augmente se charge de limon. Leur courbe se redresse. La chaloupe vire librement et file à toute vapeur. Les villages se multiplient. Ce matin, à l'estuaire, six mètres à peine séparaient deux invisibles bords ; midi : sur soixante et cent mètres de large, le Stung Chèn galope entre des flancs de terre vive couronnés de manguiers et de vie humaine ! En d'harmonieux tournants où l'on voit, balancé comme un pendule, le soleil changer de rive, les forces mobiles et immobiles s'épousent dans une commune victoire ; et des plages de sable, nées de leurs luttes, bombent des dos éblouissants.

Tandis que ce matin, cherchant l'embouchure de cette rivière en un lac sans bords visibles, je me sentais inquiet, oppressé par le désert qu'elle était encore ; à travers cette forêt sans troncs où plus rien n'était rien de complet, dans je ne sais quelle catastrophe immobilisée où ma vue ne reconnaissait rien d'habituel qui la fixât, — maintenant, entre ces beaux rivages à pic et ces massifs d'arbres qui m'emprisonnent, je me retrouve ineffablement libre. Tout est en si parfait équilibre, et cet équilibre je l'ai vu si normalement s'établir, qu'il me semble que si je continuais à remonter le cours de cette rivière née sous mes yeux, je la verrais désormais se perdre dans la terre et mourir à sa source.

Deuxième Partie

Basses Eaux

15 février 1930.

Après quatre mois d'interruption, j'ai repris ma visite des pagodes riveraines du Mékong. En ayant fini avec le grand fleuve, c'est dans ses deux bras occidentaux que je vais désormais voyager. L'un descend de Phnom Penh à la mer, l'autre des Grands Lacs à Phnom Penh. Les eaux sont à leur plus bas niveau, apaisées, décantées en partie de leurs limons, sans grande transparence pourtant, mais verdissantes au soleil sur les fonds de sable.

Nous partîmes hier soir au lever de la lune dans sa deuxième nuit de plénitude. Phnom Penh, cité chinoise et annamite autant que cambodgienne, fêtait le Dragon, et le cortège lui-même, dragon déroulé, longeait les quais dans un crépitement de pétards et une écaillure de lanternes. Des traînées de la foule se nouaient à des autels portatifs sanglants de carmin, mouillés d'or et flambants. Sur des chars, dans une lumière d'acétylène — camions couverts de rochers et de kiosques élyséens en étoffe — des fillettes chinoises, maintenues par des supports invisibles, dominaient les symboliques et mouvants paysages, l'éclatement des pétards et un grondement de gongs. Elles pénétraient la nuit de leur rutilance, artificielles, immobiles, la figure sans expression et pétrie dans de la porcelaine. On ne les sentait vivantes que lorsqu'au bord d'une opulente manche qui se levait, battait un éventail. Des enfants portaient des fruits lumineux et des animaux mythologiques où une bougie, par transparence, faisait un cœur sautillant entre des côtes de rotins.

J'ai traversé cette presse, cette foule engluée de sueur, de poussière et de lumière, sombre aussi, ces fumées d'huile et de salpêtre, ces légendes, ces odeurs d'essence et cette chaleur humaine, les cris, la pyrotechnie qui éclatait entre des jambes nues, derrière le Dragon ondulant sur ses porteurs et agitant une tête frénétique. J'ai descendu une berge obscure où la chaloupe m'attendait et, quelques minutes après, tandis que s'éloignait cette fête crépitant sous une poussière qui lui faisait un halo de nébuleuse, je suis entré tout d'un coup dans le liquide silence du fleuve.

Dépouillant un rouge opaque, la lune devenait d'un blanc safrané, glaciale et transparente. Les nuages qu'elle transperçait et que sa lumière saturait, l'enveloppaient d'une pulpe où elle s'incrustait, dur noyau. Des reflets tombés d'elle sautillaient sur l'eau, puis s'y enfonçaient en traits sinueux. La fraîcheur me força à fermer ma cabine et à m'envelopper d'une couverture au moment où le fleuve s'embrumait. Et je viens de m'éveiller.

Nous évitons à grand-peine les bancs de sable entre des berges desséchées. Depuis quatre mois, il n'est pas tombé une goutte d'eau. Les arbres dont la crue affouilla les bases, et aux troncs desquels nous nous amarrions aux hautes eaux, nous dominent maintenant de leurs racines lavées, échevelées à cinq mètres au-dessus de nos têtes. Debout par miracle, ils se dressent comme sur une planche de botanique. Ceux qui tombèrent, dépouillés de leurs feuillages, jalonnent le fleuve de monceaux d'ossements. La terre laissée par les eaux, décimètre par décimètre, stratifiée, refécondée, s'affaisse en grands pans. Les éboulements ont ouvert des criques à vif, des alvéoles lustrés et monstrueux ; ou bien se sont colmatés en des pentes où les pieds humains entretiennent des sentes luisantes. Ailleurs, sur ces flancs nouveaux, on voit déjà de jeunes plantations de tabac.

Ainsi, chaque année, avec une rapidité dont on ne se fait pas une idée, le paysage fluvial se recrée entre deux bouleversements. D'abord, la montée des eaux que nous vîmes courir entre les pilotis de ces cases qui dominent aujourd'hui le fleuve de huit mètres. Il recouvrait alors la région à perte de vue. On juchait le bétail sur des estrades. Tout n'était qu'eau mouvante et boue. Et vint un temps où, de jour en jour, l'indigène, inquiet, les yeux fixés sur des repères laissés par les crues précédentes, se préparait à transporter son maigre bien dans sa pirogue et à fuir tandis que des troncs flottants passaient à la vitesse d'un cheval au galop.

Aujourd'hui, la berge réapparue, il ne la reconnaît pas, soit que le courant y ait porté d'énormes coups de hache, soit, au contraire, qu'une plage en amollisse les anciens contours. Un champ de tabac étale déjà ses larges feuilles en un lieu où l'adolescent se souvient que les chaloupes accostaient naguère. Et le fleuve en son nouveau chemin se traîne sans courant, tâtonneur, épuisé. Ses affluents à sec n'y déversent que la végétation qui les tapisse. Où un paquebot pouvait passer, une jonque s'échoue. Mais à peine cet apaisement aura-t-il pris son rythme, des frissons saisiront cette eau et elle reprendra une course et un assaut qui, déjà, se réorganisent à cinq mille kilomètres en amont, sur les pentes du Tibet.

16 février.

Nous accostons une grosse jonque chinoise. Elle nous avait dépassés la nuit, longeant la berge, muette, éteinte, révélée par le seul clapotis de l'eau sous son ventre, tirée par le courant et dirigée à la perche par des hommes invisibles. Ces gens vont la nuit et travaillent le jour. Cette jonque est une épicerie bourrée de marchandises qu'elle vend et remplace à mesure par des marchandises qu'elle achète. Son patron me salue poliment de ce sourire chinois, déclenché par une ficelle et qui plisse le bas du visage en découvrant les dents. Et le sourire reste ainsi, sérieux et appliqué, jusqu'à ce qu'on retire sur la ficelle.

Je ne peux moins faire que de visiter la jonque : il me faut la traverser pour atteindre la terre. L'avant est dégagé en faveur des clients et une bascule occupe le centre. L'entrée du roof, ouverte d'un bord à l'autre, s'encadre de papiers rouges mouchetés d'or et qui portent des caractères de bon augure comme d'étranges insectes épinglés. Sur le linteau, deux yeux peints louchent de chaque côté du matricule et d'une date, 1920.

À l'intérieur qu'éclaire seule l'entrée, voici du carry dans des bouteilles Perrier ; des sacs d'aulx et d'oignons. Sur des rayons, bouteilles de limonade, de bière et de vin de Chine. Les jarres de sauce fermentée sont en rang le long du bordage, sphériques, noires et luisantes comme des boulets de canon. Couffins de vermicelle. L'air sent la saumure et l'huile de bois. Les étiquettes des conserves japonaises et des paquets de pétards, les étuis de josticks, bariolent un peu partout de taches vives la flottante boutique. Des couronnes de fils de fer et des grappes d'outils se suspendent au plafond. Un côté est occupé par de la quincaillerie ; le fond, par de la papeterie dans une vitrine. Deux marches et, sans y pénétrer, je vois le logis du patron, tendu de nattes, sale et brillant, ouvert sur la poupe et au-delà, sur un petit jardin et un fourneau d'argile. Deux pieds humains dépassent d'un corps couché invisible : les orteils rayonnent. Du linge sèche sur la barre monumentale du gouvernail et cette poutre, maintenue par deux bridons, inscrit sur le ciel la courbe allongée d'un dos de jument sous une housse. La voile brun rouge est carguée dans des anneaux de rotin. Le roof est couvert de caisses, de barils de carbure et de peaux. Enfin, à la base du mât, un étonnant poisson de faïence ruisselant d'émail vert jade et rose crevette, fantasque, gorgé d'air et plus humide que s'il sortait du fleuve, tient dans sa bouche un faisceau de bâtonnets d'encens. Je quitte la jonque et le Chinois referme son sourire comme un éventail.

Elle retourne à Chaudoc, appuyant ainsi ses flancs sur chaque pli de rive. Le vent mollit ? L'équipage rame. L'eau baisse ? Des perches remplacent les rames. Les deux yeux saillants de sa proue épient, la nuit, le moindre feu ; le jour, jusqu'au geste d'un enfant. Ainsi, leur échoppe errant, ces hommes trafiquent. Ils l'amarrent ici une heure ou passent un jour au pied d'un village. Ils achètent de l'huile de poisson, des peaux et vendent du pétrole et des cartes à jouer. Ils troquent du fer contre du kapok. Ils ont encore des bracelets de chrysocale et les offrent à des femmes qui se donnent à eux bestialement, en des endroits convenus trois mois à l'avance.

ಸು⊕ಬ

Dans ce pays dur à l'Occidental, les matins et les soirs, une heure durant, compensent ce que les journées ont d'ardent et d'implacable. Tout est si frais, si gai, si délicat au lever du soleil, dans le présage de l'accablement journalier, que le paysage se fait féminin. Le ciel le couvre d'une coupole de cristal où une lumière adorable court et se répercute.

Comment aurai-je le courage de quitter celui-ci, élaboré dans le recueillement nocturne tel un diamant dans du charbon ! Il m'entoure à des distances si harmonieuses que mon regard le parcourt d'un paisible circuit. Un coup de sifflet de la chaloupe, à des intervalles aux beaux rapports, revint trois fois en ce centre miraculeux que nous occupons et glissa avec allégresse sur des eaux pleines de ciel.

La rive, derrière moi à contre-jour, ravinée de canons et de failles qui rompent la stratification d'une coupe géologique, me donne à une échelle infime mais cependant imposante, le cataclysme d'une cordillère. Miné en bas, un pan de terrain a glissé verticalement, conservant son couronnement d'herbe. La lumière naissante atteint, après des millénaires, la grasse matière mise à nu par le glissement. La surface de l'eau est au niveau de la couche d'argile. Au-dessus, monte une surface suintante de sucs où des radicelles tracent un réseau nerveux. Au-dessus encore, des arbres plafonnent à contre-jour. Et cet écran préhistorique, rongé par un halo, me repousse au fleuve.

Au Nord, à deux encablures, un vieux cuirassé est embossé, je veux dire un îlot dont la terre a des reflets d'acier et une proue en éperon. Pas de mâture, mais un équipage d'ajoncs penche sur la massive coque des panaches blancs. Sur l'éperon près de l'eau, un petit autel votif dédié aux génies du courant leur tend un tronc de bananier piqué de boutons de lotus.

Un quart d'horizon glisse sur le fleuve, en amont, si loin et en une ligne si ténue qu'on ne la devinerait pas si le point noir d'une jonque ne révélait l'eau, et sa voile, l'atmosphère. La rive en face, à deux cents mètres, scintille sans une ombre, coupée d'un estuaire à sec qu'un pont enjambe. On distingue des pièces de tuiles neuves sur un vieux toit. Des bœufs, de cette berge à pic, boivent la tête en bas, dressés sur leurs pattes de devant. Une plantation de faux cotonniers aux branches horizontales dépasse la croupe d'une plage compartimentée de champs de tabac et de tomates. Cette plage se termine en pointe, d'un sable pâle que ponctue une colonie d'aigrettes. Derrière ce fuseau, la rive se recule, puis fuit avec le fleuve vers un lointain sans issue où sa terre ocre devient blonde sous une verdure qui s'argente.

Et, puisque j'ai fini mon tour d'horizon, cette partie de l'aval si délicate et presque immatérielle est interrompue par la silhouette sauvage de la rive où j'écris et qui dresse, encore obscur, un praticable coupant comme un soc. Des hérons le survolent qu'a effrayés notre coup de sirène.

☙✺❧

Il y a une dizaine de jours, j'ai eu l'occasion de survoler, moi aussi, cette région, à douze cents mètres, dans un hydravion chargé du relevé cadastral. Après quatre mois d'une saison sèche absolue, je croyais dominer un pays poudreux, desséché, tel qu'il paraît être lorsqu'on y chemine par ses pistes et dans sa poussière rougeâtre. Quel n'a pas été mon étonnement de découvrir bien plus d'eau que de terre, comme si j'avais quitté le Cambodge et survolais un pays tout nouveau et inconnu de moi !

Jusqu'à l'horizon, je ne vis que lagunes, étangs, marais, trous miroitants ; une carte de taches d'eau entre des arroyos à sec ; une mosaïque de marigots, de lagons laissés quatre mois avant par la crue, d'un vert éclatant, d'un gris nacré, ou noirs. Les îles du Bassak (dont je ne vois aujourd'hui en les contournant que les terres émergeantes), montraient leurs assises sous-marines et les sables déposés à leurs pointes leur faisaient des nageoires et des empennages ondulés. L'eau du fleuve, visible seulement dans ses parties profondes, traçait un second lit aux teintes estompées, étonnement sinueux dans un lit plus vaste. En vue oblique, un pan de forêt ressemblait à une pièce d'astrakan où courait l'ombre de l'avion.

À un kilomètre au plus du fleuve, de chaque côté, toute culture cessait, laissant place au pays désert, inculte, rugueux, galeux, dépouillé de poil par grandes plaques rocailleuses que des chapelets d'étangs trouaient encore. Et, abstraction faite du fleuve, rien n'était plus étrange que cette bande de terre cultivée et d'un vert intense, tordant sa mince arabesque à travers l'immense cuve sauvage que nous dominions et dont les bords se perdaient dans des confins d'un gris métallisé. Les villages demeuraient invisibles et seules des plantations d'aréquiers nous les dénonçaient. Ces arbres, minces stipes blancs à plumeaux sombres, vus d'en haut, se piquaient en terre comme des poignées de fléchettes que nous aurions jetées. On ne distinguait que des pirogues se déplaçaient, minces navettes, qu'au miroitement d'une pagaie. Les oiseaux volaient avec leurs ombres au-dessous d'eux. Une traînée de poussière sur une piste suivait une écaille, roof de charrette. Notre vol rectiligne coupa trois méandres du fleuve qui me parut couler de tous côtés comme s'il se tordait visiblement sous mes yeux. Par endroit, des rectangles de rizières s'avançaient jusque sur ses eaux et cessaient si nettement qu'on eût dit que dans l'attente d'un débarquement pompeux, une opulente municipalité avait déroulé des tapis.

17 février.

En m'embarquant l'autre soir à Phnom Penh, je vis un matelot accroupi sur l'appontement et préparer la lampe à acétylène du bord. Il l'insultait en invoquant la vermine du ventre de sa mère sans que je pusse savoir, à travers la pauvre syntaxe cambodgienne, s'il s'agissait de sa mère à lui, matelot, ou de la mère de la lampe. C'était Eh ! — mais un Eh ! méconnaissable.

D'abord, je ne pensais pas le retrouver, une chaloupe de moindre tirant d'eau que celle de ma précédente tournée m'ayant été affectée et chaque chaloupe administrative possédant son équipage. Mais mon homme, ayant su que je repartais, avait demandé de me suivre : justement, son bateau était à la peinture. On se fait, comme ça, dans la vie, des sympathies qui se révèlent quand on y pense le moins. Et je ne cacherai pas que de retrouver cette brute noire engueulant la lampe qui devait m'éclairer ; cet infime bougre qui pouvait flemmarder tandis que séchait son bateau, mais qui s'était arrangé pour m'accompagner — ne me laissa pas insensible.

Ensuite Eh! en quelques mois s'était transformé. Il portait un pantalon blanc, un maillot neuf et, c'est là que les choses se corsent, un béret blanc de marin à passepoil bleu. Ce passepoil, ayant déteint bizarrement, faisait une sorte de chenille autour du béret. Eh! m'apprit que sa femme était morte (d'une maladie dont j'ai cherché en vain le nom dans les lexiques), lui laissant une fille de quatre ans, d'un premier lit, par-dessus le marché. Et on appareilla.

Je vis un autre matelot détacher les câbles, décoller la chaloupe en faisant le grand écart et y sauter à l'instant où je crus qu'il allait se fendre en deux, laisser une de ses moitiés sur l'appontement tandis que nous aurions emporté l'autre — bref, ce que j'avais l'habitude de voir exécuter à Eh! Mais Eh! accroupi à l'avant donnait des ordres. J'appris de la sorte qu'il était passé premier matelot et qu'il dressait un matelot en second. Ainsi, les peuples évoluent sans qu'on y prenne garde et jamais, en me considérant moi-même, je n'eus notion, à un tel degré, de l'infini que quelques mois pouvaient apporter dans la vie d'un homme.

Depuis notre départ, Eh! se tient donc sur le toit de la chaloupe, j'allais écrire la dunette. Je l'appelle, il répond avec la même rapidité mais c'est le second matelot qui vient. Néanmoins, il continue de débarquer avec moi, de porter le matériel photographique. Il sait maintenant ce qu'un rôle de matelot arrivé comporte de noble et de vulgaire. La lampe à acétylène à charger, tendre ma moustiquaire, porter une chambre 18 x 24 en bois verni : voilà ce qui le flattait naguère. Le reste, moins : bon pour le second matelot ! Chacun à son rang !

D'ailleurs cette visite des pagodes qu'il faisait il y a quatre mois dans l'équipage que j'ai dit, n'est plus qu'une promenade. On aborde correctement. Plus de boue, plus de gymnastique sur les pirogues. S'il s'est senti humilié sous ses cuissards de fange et sous sa brousse de cheveux mouillés, il se rattrape bien depuis deux jours. Ah ! ce béret ! Tantôt il barre le front de l'homme et tantôt cascade sur sa nuque. Un débarquement me le montre plat, l'autre bulbeux. À l'entrée des monastères, Eh! s'arrête, pose son fourniment et, respectueux de son dieu et de ses moines, malgré son ascension, il enlève ce béret, le plie en tampon, le fourre dans sa poche et reprend l'attirail.

✣

Bak Nam, le dernier village cambodgien, à l'estuaire d'un arroyo et du Bassak. Cent mètres plus bas, la Cochinchine commence, mais elle est déjà là avec ses cases annamites. Au demeurant, le Chinois domine et l'on ne voit plus que quelques Cambodgiens. Ils ont, à un kilomètre de là, deux pagodes dépenaillées, couvertes de paillotes, mais, dans le village, une belle et riche pagode annamite, basse, bien maçonnée, est installée.

Les berges sont partout percées de fours en série où cuit, dans des cuves hémisphériques recouvertes de feuillage, une étrange mixture. Une odeur écœurante en vient. Des coolies annamites, les vêtements dégoûtants, plongent dans les marmites de longues louches. Au pied de chacune de ces cuisines, un enclos de claies isole un rectangle d'eau courante dans quoi les cuisiniers déversent le contenu de leurs cuillers, une écume jaune sale, grumeleuse, visqueuse. Chaque enclos en est couvert. Par là-dessus, un soleil qui n'épargne rien, des corbeaux, des rapaces pêcheurs. Dans l'eau libre, à travers des moires vireuses étirées et enlacées au long des clayonnages, des escadres de canards circulent, la queue ridiculement frémissante. Enfin, d'énormes pieux où l'on amarre des filets en travers du courant barrent la rivière tous les cent mètres. Ah ! le maudit coin !

Bak Nam n'est qu'une fabrique d'huile de poisson. Il cuit par cent kilos dans ces marmites et c'est l'huile qu'il dégorge qu'on jette dans les réservoirs où, flottante, elle se coagule. On l'y prend, on la recuit et on la met dans des touques dont des jonques chinoises, venues vides, repartent pleines. Huile d'éclairage.

La saison bat son plein. Depuis un mois, le poisson qui convient au jeu est mûr. Dans un mois, il aura fondu dans les bouilleries et, le reste de l'année, il deviendra flamme fumeuse dans les cases du pays. Et tout est si bien ajusté qu'un mois après la disparition de ce poisson, les eaux remonteront, atteindront les fours, les noieront, les désagrégeront, car ils sont creusés dans la terre même des berges. Puis le fleuve redescendra. Les cuisiniers rebâtiront leurs fours, rafistoleront leurs parcs à huile, tendront leurs filets, et les petits poissons, par tonnes frétillantes, sauteront dans les marmites.

Depuis un siècle probablement, chacun est fidèle à ce rendez-vous annuel. Qu'une année, les mères poissons s'arrangent entre elles pour pondre quinze jours plus tard et passent la consigne à leurs enfants : en six ans, la gent écailleuse n'apparaîtrait que trois mois plus tard. Qu'est-ce qui l'en empêcherait ? Pas d'hiver en ce pays. Mais par cette combinaison, plus de bouilleries sur les berges inondées, plus de parcs à huile que le courant emporterait ! Voilà ce que j'ai dit à un petit poisson resté dans l'eau non écopée d'une pirogue. Mais vous verrez qu'il n'en tiendra pas compte.

18 février.

Cette végétation du Bassak n'a point l'allure de celle du grand fleuve. Non qu'elle soit laide, mais elle joue à l'octave au-dessous et varie peu. Le faux cotonnier domine, souvent en plantations serrées. Les arbres précoces, dépouillés de leurs feuilles, ne portent que leurs gousses, suspendues comme des chauves-souris. Leurs branches horizontales forment avec leurs troncs un quadrillage monotone, un fond de papier millimétrique au-dessus des rives. Touffes de bambous, quelques beaux arbres, leurs racines décharnées à l'air. Pas de grosses jonques : les eaux trop basses les empêchent de passer pendant deux mois, dès l'île d'Anlong Chèn, à 20 kilomètres de Phnom Penh. La population est dense mais inactive en cette saison : les riz sont récoltés, le tabac sort de terre et ce n'est pas ici la région des pêcheries. Nous les trouverons, celles-ci, dans l'autre bras, au-delà de Kompong Luong.

Encore quelques bouilleries d'huile de poisson : elles sont un des charmes des basses eaux. Nous en verrons beaucoup. Dans le Tonlé Sap, l'espèce de poisson employée étant plus grosse que dans le Sud, on n'utilise que les têtes, les entrailles et les vessies natatoires. Les Cambodgiens de l'intérieur viennent en caravanes de charrettes apporter du paddy qu'ils échangent contre les corps de ces poissons dont la décomposition commence. Ce mois durant, les pistes, les routes sont empoisonnées par une odeur puissante et tiède de pourriture laissée par les charrettes, à la traîne. Certains villages deviennent inabordables. Cette chair déjà vermineuse est pilée avec du sel, macère quelques jours encore, jute et fermente, fromage verdâtre mis en réserve dans des jarres. Il servira de Liebig pour les soupes jusqu'à la saison prochaine.

J'aime mieux le poisson frais ! Il est abondant, aussi j'en mange matin et soir et me rattrape sur ma précédente tournée où je dus m'en priver. À l'aube, les pêcheurs s'assemblent par groupes de six ou sept pirogues. Les femmes pagayent à l'arrière. De l'avant, les hommes jettent leurs éperviers, à un signal, tous ensemble, et autant de cercles crépitants sectionnent l'eau. Ah ! les beaux gestes, une seconde balancés au centre d'amples auréoles qui sortent de bras ouverts et retombent en coupoles ! Puis les pirogues tournent et l'homme accroupi retire sa corderie où s'enchevêtrent des feuilles d'argent. Rarement une belle pièce et des filets sortent souvent vides. Néanmoins, dix ou quinze lancers suffisent à la nourriture journalière du village.

Ma chaloupe s'arrête près de ces groupes et je trouve toujours à me réapprovisionner, ainsi que l'équipage. Dans le panier rond qu'on me tend et d'où l'eau s'égoutte, je vois un poisson plat d'un jaune de cuivre, barré de trois traits obliques, noirs ; une crevette grosse comme une langouste d'un vert décomposé et à longues pinces avortées ; d'autres corps gris transparents, étonnamment fourbis, dont le dos tombe brusquement sur la nuque, ce qui les fait ressembler à des bœufs à bosse, sous le joug. La chair en est blanche et fondante comme de la neige et découvre une colonne vertébrale aussi nacrée que les écailles. Si j'étais naturaliste et avais à baptiser ce poisson sans parure, mais si ravissant, je l'appellerais « lumière de l'eau ».

❦

Nous n'avons visité qu'une quinzaine de pagodes, peu intéressantes, sauf celle de Chruï Kéo, construite il y a une vingtaine d'années par S. M. Sisowath, de bonne tradition, et couverte intérieurement des plus belles peintures murales que je connaisse au Cambodge. Point de soldats français caricaturés aux portes, mais de bons gardiens au masque démoniaque, en costume princier, les mains posées sur de solides massues, raides, bien proportionnés.

L'aspect de ces pagodes serait, aux hautes eaux, celui que nous connaissons. On y accéderait en pirogue et leurs cours les entoureraient d'un cloaque. Aujourd'hui, elles se dressent en couronnes sur le front relevé du rivage et regardent le fleuve venir de loin. Remplaçant leurs reflets dans les eaux par un socle, elles se sont élevées, déroulant à leur suite des escaliers creusés à vif dans le sol soulevé.

Les chiens ont engraissé et trouvent une poussière tiède pour dormir. Une couche épaisse de feuilles sèches est tendue sous les arbres. Devant les monastères, les hibiscus éclatent en fleurs d'un rouge aigu. Les ombres que les eaux ne reflètent plus ont perdu leurs violets, ce qui les rend substantielles et de l'épaisseur d'une étoffe déployée. Il semble qu'on les déchire en y passant et qu'elles laissent alors s'évader la fraîcheur de la terre.

Aucune mousson ne balayant l'atmosphère, les lointains les plus proches, estompés par un air trop dense, paraissent plus éloignés qu'ils ne le sont, ce que prouvent leur masse et les détails qu'on y distingue. Ainsi, au-delà de premiers plans trop accusés par contraste, le paysage se désarticule dans une lumière qu'on croit intense et qui n'est que rompue. Ce qui est terre se vaporise. L'impondérable agit comme un prisme. L'air a un aspect de gelée. Je compare trois plans d'arbres : le premier est d'un vert acide, le second à cent mètres à peine prend une tonalité d'olive, le dernier qui se dessine encore et où l'on voit luire des troncs blancs est imprégné d'un soleil qui n'a déjà plus la force de me revenir.

Autour de cette rutilance factice, le ciel est cylindrique, plat au-dessus, plein d'une vapeur d'eau insuffisante à constituer le moindre nuage, assez diluée pour rester invisible, mais dont la présence permanente épuise toute couleur. Ce ciel baisse avec les eaux, les reflète, et tandis qu'elles s'arrêtent sous les racines des arbres mises à nu, il se pose sur leurs cimes. Entre ces deux disques qui échangent leurs chaleurs dans un silence massif, la vie des hommes le cède à celle des choses. Midi.

ಐ✵ಲ

Des femmes sur la berge. Nous venons d'en dépasser deux qui pagayaient avec quelle aisance et quelle jeunesse ! Des tuniques d'un indigo usé leur moulaient la poitrine. Et je cherche pour la centième fois ce qui peut me suggérer cette notion de perfection humaine que chacune de ces rencontres impose à mon esprit.

ಐ✵ಲ

Ces femmes ne savent pas leur beauté, n'en font rien, ne cherchent pas à la mettre individuellement en valeur. Elles la partagent inconsciemment entre elles dans un costume uniforme depuis des siècles. Dans ces corps assouplis par des travaux nécessaires, les chairs se répartissent mieux qu'avec équilibre : avec bien-être. C'est là une grâce qui dépasse toute définition. Est-ce que je m'imagine que ces femelles rustiques éprouvent dans leur âme la satisfaction qu'elles me donnent, et qu'elles se moulent en elles-mêmes comme dans la lumière où je les saisis ? Évidemment non. Et sans doute cette ignorance d'elles où elles se présentent (sans que rien d'humain que je pourrais comprendre ne les accompagne) contribue-t-elle à les rendre à la fois animales et inaccessibles.

Elles sont brutes et parfaites. Aussi, il n'y a échange qu'entre leur corps et ma pensée, tandis que jamais le désir d'elles ne s'infiltre en ma chair. Je peux donc d'autant mieux les suivre en leur perfection plastique. Comment l'inventerais-je et comment la leur prêterais-je ? Sans elles, je ne l'eusse jamais conçue. Étrangères par leur race, leurs habitudes, leurs sentiments, leurs amours — il suffit d'une minute et tout ce qu'elles m'offrent correspond aux mesures dont je dispose. Peut-être qu'elles bénéficient d'un prestige que je leur ajoute. Mais ce prestige comment l'imaginerais-je avec pertinence, si elles ne me fournissaient pas les moyens de les en doter et si elles n'étaient pas aptes à s'en parer ?

Peu à peu, le fait devient celui-ci : en Occident, l'individualisme et la mode font de chaque femme un type plastique toujours différent, édulcoré, incomplet et souvent méconnaissable de la femme. Ici, au contraire, chacune représente le type pur et complet où tout le sexe se condense et s'exprime d'un seul coup. Elle n'est pas une forme qui se retranche et se compose arbitrairement, soumise au goût d'une intelligence moyenne, selon des conventions provisoires : elle est la somme permanente des besoins féminins de l'homme.

L'homme indigène n'est pas moins beau. Mais par le même jeu des idées auxquelles il s'oppose ou répond, il apparaît incomplet. Bien qu'il soit tout aussi parfait de lignes, grimpeur et nageur agile, souple, astucieux dans son commerce avec la terre et l'eau, je suis plus fort que lui, physiquement et intellectuellement. Cette servilité et cette insuffisance désarmées, qui contribuent à la beauté de sa femme, atteignent la sienne qui ne se pourrait maintenir que si je le sentais mon égal. Par ce désaccord, cet homme féminin me déçoit dans ses formes masculines. Elles mentent !

Il me répugne de le dominer alors qu'il me plaît justement que la belle pagayeuse qui l'accompagne soit une esclave. Je voudrais le voir avec ses beaux muscles, ses membres solides, plus sauvage, dur, dressé contre moi, m'épiant pour me trahir, hostile — je ne le vois que souriant, alangui dans sa médiocrité et portant une écharpe, cet imbécile, au lieu d'un arc !

19 février.

Le soleil décline et je monte sur le toit de la chaloupe peint en blanc, encore brûlant. La cheminée noire est rougie à vif du côté du couchant. À son ombre, Eh! se gratte les orteils. Le pilote, encore ébloui par l'après-midi, assis en tailleur, tient sa roue d'une main molle.

Dans la tache que projette sa petite tente sur le pont, je vois un tas de chiffons. Deux pieds minuscules en sortent : c'est une fillette de quatre ou cinq ans qui dort. Sa tête repose sur un maillot de matelot. Un cordon de coton est noué à chacune des chevilles. Qui est cette passagère clandestine ? C'est la fille de Eh! Elle est là depuis notre départ de Phnom Penh.

Comment ! Je ne la découvre qu'après plusieurs jours de navigation dans cette barque où nous sommes les uns sur les autres ? Il est vrai que je monte ce soir pour la première fois sur ce toit, long de huit mètres, large de deux, encombré du radeau de sauvetage, de la caisse à eau et de la cage aux poules. Depuis plusieurs jours, cette gamine vit là-dessus, sans que je l'entende. La mère est morte, m'a dit Eh! et l'homme voyage avec la fille, et tant pis si elle en crève. De ce toit sans rambarde, ne peut-elle pas tomber à l'eau ? Eh! me dit non, comme si mon hypothèse était folle et avec le souci protecteur de me rassurer.

— Et tu crois qu'elle s'amuse, cette gosse, sur cette plaque chauffée à blanc ?

Eh! ne répond pas.

— Qu'est-ce qu'elle fait toute la journée ?

— Elle regarde le fleuve.

Elle regarde le fleuve, les arbres, les gens. Je ne fais rien de plus, il est vrai. Elle ne fera rien de plus toute sa vie et, en certaines heures, je voudrais que ma destinée se mêle à la sienne. À présent, il dort ce petit être déjà éprouvé par la rudesse du climat ; il mijote au soleil, sa fragilité résiste à ce qui m'accable. Elle existe pourtant si peu que, depuis plusieurs jours, elle vit à quelques mètres de moi, sur ma tête, sans un rire, sans un cri, sans un ébat qui me l'ait révélée. Je ne vois même, la découvrant, qu'un profil écrasé sur le maillot paternel qui lui tord la bouche. Une main renversée tient l'autre. Je n'ai pas une impression d'enfance, d'éclosion, mais une impression brutale et désenchantée : trente livres de chair humaine.

Imaginez ceci : un escalier, taillé dans la berge, monte entre de hautes herbes. Au sommet, un seul arbre qui plafonne. Au pied de cet arbre, une petite chapelle en bambou, sur pilotis, à l'image d'une case et de proportions exquises, se découpe sur le ciel, entre la coupole de verdure et la crête de la berge. Ce lieu est maudit : il y a soixante ans, un bonze fornicateur y fut tué par le mari de sa maîtresse et l'assassin se pendit à une branche de cet arbre.

L'eau clapote. Un oiseau blanc et noir à silhouette courte de martin-pêcheur s'immobilise, surveille une proie, se laisse tomber verticalement sur l'eau et repart. Le soleil se couche sans fards, dans un ciel immédiatement gris. Et je vois arriver lentement, au fil de l'eau, une embarcation merveilleuse.

Elle est pavoisée d'oriflammes. À l'arrière flotte un long pavillon denticulé. Silhouette de jonque et de caravelle, château de poupe recouvert de papier doré. Est-ce la nef de Jaufré Rudel ?

Non. À peine deux mètres de long. Elle passe à mes pieds et je distingue la carcasse ingénieuse de bambou dont elle est faite. Au centre, un petit tas de riz, des bananes, des fleurs à moitié fanées, reposent sur un plateau de feuilles tressées. Ses flancs sont de papier huilé et badigeonné de vermillon. Elle tourne sur elle-même, en se dandinant, sous une voile rose vif déchirée. C'est un ex-voto lancé par un village pour apaiser les génies aquatiques du choléra.

Et comme si un pilote familier de la berge guidait cette embarcation, je la vois se prendre dans les herbes, contre l'escalier, et suspendre au malheur du lieu le malheur des eaux.

20 février.

La pagode de Samphan est la cent vingt-troisième que je visite et la première où je trouve une statue ancienne, conservée dans un coin, couverte de poussière, transportée là on ne sait d'où. La région est pourtant pauvre en ruines de monuments des grandes époques. La carte archéologique en signale une dizaine : tours en briques, levées de terre, vestiges, dont la plupart remontent avant même la prospérité angkorienne. Hier, dans l'après-midi, nous étions à la hauteur d'une vieille capitale, Vyadhapura, maintenant Angkor Borei, située à quelques kilomètres du Bassak, sur un de ses affluents.

C'est aux environs de cette antique métropole qu'il y a quelques années nous eûmes la chance de découvrir deux Bouddhas extraordinaires, hanchés, d'art gréco-gupta — plus grecs que guptas ; d'un art nouvellement importé au Cambodge vers le V-VIe siècle au plus tard et non encore assimilé par le génie khmer. Ils semblent avoir été les prototypes d'un art second que nous appelons « pré-khmer », d'autres « primitif », d'autres « préangkoriens » : l'archéologie cambodgienne n'est pas encore bien fixée ! L'art qui succéda et dégénérait déjà fut l'art d'Angkor. Nous parvenons avec ce dernier au XIVe siècle. À partir du XVe siècle, l'influence siamoise imprègne et maintient debout le vieillard, fils de tous ces vieillards.

La statuette trouvée ce matin est un exemple pré-khmer passable : un dieu au gros cou. Un bras manque. La main qui reste tenait un attribut disparu. Sous un chignon cylindrique, le visage est à type vaguement sémite, d'une indécision de facture qui le métisse. Le corps, sans un bijou, est nu, sauf un court sarong noué devant. En le faisant laver pour le photographier, je voyais au fond du sanctuaire le Bouddha actuel en ciment doré, les yeux baissés sur ce minuscule ancêtre en grès, de qui il se recommandait et de qui quatorze siècles le séparaient.

Le pays paraît primitif, la vie des hommes, élémentaire, et, sauf sur les bords du fleuve, ces régions sont à peu près désertes. Charrues de bois, fourneaux d'argile, pirogues faites d'un tronc d'arbre, costumes drapés depuis mille ans, peuple misérable, quelques chansons, presque pas de littérature, cases de paillote et de bambou, sans meubles ; il semble qu'on traverse des populations adolescentes, tâtonnantes, dont l'évolution est à son premier stade et qui se dégageraient à peine de leur pauvreté originelle.

Et puis, pour peu qu'on se penche et regarde mieux, on voit que l'enfant porte le fardeau d'un vieil homme, qu'il a construit des villes fortifiées et des temples immenses, éprouvé plusieurs civilisations successives. Sa langue comme une cendre garde des tisons sanscrits, palis, malais, chinois, thaïs. Ces bonzes que voici précédèrent des Brahmanes qui couvrirent le pays et disparurent. Des générations de philosophes épiloguèrent dans ces monastères. Et l'on reconnaît bientôt que rien ne naît, ne peut plus naître en ce tuf humain épuisé qui n'a même plus de mémoire.

La fille de Eh!, ce petit bourgeon obscur à peine dégagé du plasma, barbare fillette, — c'est une prodigieuse matrone métisse, fille de métisses. Elle a été princesse et esclave, marchande, danseuse royale et danseuse sacrée. Elle a traîné dans d'autres pays d'où elle est revenue bonzesse. On la vit, au XIIe siècle, secrétaire du roi et s'occuper d'astronomie ; chanteuse d'un prince, puis épouse de Chinois, régente de l'empire, concubine de mandarin, brodeuse, pileuse de paddy, sampanière, mère d'ascète et de grands généraux. Elle prit part à des combats et fit des fondations pieuses. Elle a eu toutes les vertus humaines et tous les vices. Elle a vécu couverte d'or, de brocart et de vermine. Eh!, sa brute de père, depuis sa sortie des cavernes, depuis qu'il a quitté les colliers de coquillages qu'on retrouve à cent kilomètres d'ici, dans le sous-sol de Samrong Tong, si j'essayais de refaire sa généalogie jusqu'à sa nomination de premier matelot à bord de cette chaloupe, j'aurais le vertige.

Je reviens à Eh! et à sa fille après un détour fantasque de ma méditation, car ce matin même, à mon réveil, ils répondirent aux idées mêmes que je viens d'exprimer. J'entendis un clapotement d'eau, levai mon volet et vis Eh! qui lavait sa fille. Elle flottait devant lui et il la tenait par un bras. De sa main ouverte, elle essuyait l'eau qui huilait son visage et l'aveuglait. Elle ne riait pas, elle ne pleurait pas, ne disait rien. Il l'enfonçait dans le fleuve tout entière et la ressortait. Je crus qu'il allait la tordre comme une serviette. Elle est rasée, sauf sur le dessus de la tête, et les cheveux qu'on a laissé pousser là, en friche, sont noués en un chignon serré en forme d'escargot.

Enfin Eh! vint à la rive, sortant peu à peu de l'eau, sa fille à cheval sur sa hanche. Elle était claire et minuscule à côté de cet homme massif. Ils apparurent liés l'un à l'autre par le soleil levant et l'eau dont ils ruisselaient. Le petit corps sortait de l'homme, de sa hanche — fait de sa côte. J'eus une vision fulgurante de création devant la terre d'une berge où aucune végétation jamais n'a germé et issue de la même eau que le couple.

J'appelai la première femme. Elle tomba de l'homme comme un fruit et je vis un instant son ventre étroit et fendu. Elle enfila un sarong grisâtre et déchiré. Son petit pas précis la porta sur la planche-passerelle qui ne plia pas. Et la voilà debout, devant moi.

— *Sampéah louk* ! lui crie son père.

Elle s'agenouille et me tend ses mains jointes. Des gouttelettes roulent de l'escargot sur son front, puis sur ses joues, larmes. Un nez large, une bouche menue en croissant, des traits déjà dépouillés du flou de l'enfance, que l'âge n'accentuera plus, qu'il agrandira seulement — sauf les yeux déjà à leur largeur définitive. Un petit cou maigre sur un thorax bombé et pourtant trop serré. Et je mets cette petite bête sur mes genoux.

Moi, père, qui depuis douze ans serre des enfants contre moi, les caresse, j'attendais de la mollesse, cet abandon hardi des petits, je croyais prendre de la pulpe — et je tiens un petit corps dur qui se raidit, et frais de l'eau qui s'en évapore. Elle a peur, mais me regarde bien en face. Elle ne cherche pas à s'en aller, mais ne s'abandonne pas. Cette passivité est affreuse.

— Comment t'appelles-tu ?

Elle me répond en vibrant l'*r* :

— *Trâp*.

Ce qui veut dire: aubergine.

— N'aie pas peur ! Ris ! Ris !

Elle rit de la bouche et je vois qu'elle a perdu en haut ses dents de lait.

Je demande encore :

— Tu es contente de te promener sur le fleuve, hein ?

Elle ne répond pas. Elle ne répondra plus. Je la repose sur la planche. Elle me tourne le dos, cherche son père des yeux, mais ne part pas, n'ose partir, avant que je le lui dise.

Elle s'en alla en tenant à hauteur de son épaule, dans son petit poing serré et renversé, la pièce de vingt cents que je lui avais donnée. Puis, quand elle fut près de Eh!, elle la lui montra dans sa main entr'ouverte, et l'inséra avec soin dans son chignon.

21 février.

Revenus à Phnom Penh pour prendre le quatrième bras du Mékong, le Tonlé Sap — nous débouchons dans l'étonnant carrefour fluvial à cinq heures. Je m'étais arrangé pour l'observer à ce moment qui est le plus beau, celui d'une cérémonie journalière où les eaux et la lumière officient.

Derrière nous, le Bassak rejoint presque le soleil déjà bas et comme s'il en était aspiré, dans une réverbération insoutenable aux regards.

Le bras du Sud-Est éclairé de biais, à notre droite, se couvre de reflets sans éclats, devant une rive rendue si mince par l'éloignement qu'elle se tend et vibre comme une lame de scie.

Au-devant de nous, dans un déploiement impérial, le haut fleuve, coulant du Nord-Est sous des moires lilas tracées au pastel, lève des voiles qu'il ne semble pas porter. Le soleil les illumine et elles plongent des traits de feu jaune jusqu'au ciel qui forme le fond des eaux. La presqu'île de Chruï Changvar reçoit le couchant en plein flanc sans un trou d'ombre.

Enfin le bras Nord-Ouest, devant la presqu'île, éclairé comme elle, couvert de batellerie, se dore, se beurre de safran au pied de Phnom Penh étalée à contre-jour et pointant ses flèches sacrées au-dessus de sa verdure.

Ainsi, quatre fleuves s'ouvrent autour de nous vers les quatre points cardinaux: l'un de mercure, le second ardoise, le troisième céleste et nacré, le dernier de miel. Ils se mêlent entre deux rives si éloignées que de l'une, l'autre à peine s'aperçoit, et deux presqu'îles pointe à pointe. Quatre ciels sont tendus sur ces quatre chemins auxquels une seule voûte ne suffirait pas et où elle ne poserait qu'en porte-à-faux.

Tandis que nous naviguons au centre de cet écartèlement qui se perd dans quatre horizons, j'essaye d'ouvrir mon esprit. Il oscille comme l'aiguille aimantée sur la rose des vents. Je sens sur moi le passage des aigles pêcheurs roux, à tête blanche. Ils dominent des terres qui semblent flotter, s'articulent mollement, tendues en franges lointaines ; une ville de cent cinquante mille âmes étirée sur dix kilomètres de longueur, moins épaisse que mon doigt et bleuissant. Et je crois découvrir une architecture liquide, une cathédrale couchée. Si j'y criais, mon cri se ferait quadruple. Au-dessus d'elles, l'immensité est un nœud qui se dénoue.

Basses eaux. Cette majesté n'est qu'un apaisement. Les courants du grand fleuve et du Tonlé Sap s'accolent, presque épuisés, au fond d'un lit ensablé et repartent divergeant à peine. Mais dans quelques mois, le carrefour haussera son niveau de huit mètres. Les eaux venues du Tibet, de la Chine et du Laos y tourbillonneront massives et véloces. Elles chercheront une voie, brisant un instant leur élan. Les unes, frôlant à l'Est cette arène, fuiront aussitôt. Les autres, l'ayant traversée et soulevant de nouveaux limons, dévieront dans le Bassak. Les autres enfin, s'arrêtant brusquement, bavant sur leurs mors, tourneront court et, la crinière retroussée, repartiront vers le Nord-Ouest, presque dans la direction d'où elles viennent, remplir le Grand Lac, d'où elles déborderont…

Puis il y aura un instant d'équilibre solennel durant lequel cette réserve d'eau exténuée s'immobilisera, maintenue prisonnière par les trois autres fleuves, eux-mêmes installés sur le reste du pays. Mais un jour, le fleuve originel baissant le dos, reculant, le Grand Lac relâchera ses eaux aussitôt vers le Sud, se videra. Après s'être gonflé six mois durant de sang veineux épaissi par le frai de poisson, ce cœur près de rompre exprimera pendant six autres mois un sang artériel miroitant d'écailles. Phnom Penh voit donc à ses pieds un fleuve passer en sens inverse deux fois par an ; un autre venir s'y perdre et deux autres la quitter comme s'ils naissaient d'elle.

Lorsqu'on connaît ce phénomène de bascule, cette pulsation du lac, ce va-et-vient du Tonlé Sap, cette oscillation grandiose entre deux moments immobiles, l'un où les forces des eaux s'équilibrent en s'affrontant ; l'autre qui reçoit celles-ci, plates et nonchalantes, telles que nous les voyons aujourd'hui ; lorsque l'on sait cela, l'aspect de ce lieu unique acquiert plus de signification encore.

Par-dessus les basses eaux, je vois, ce soir, monter leurs plus hauts efforts. En une minute, les courants se renversent, s'épuisent et se reforment. Dans cet épanchement horizontal, agit un rythme vertical. Hautes eaux, basses eaux. Si bien que, sans rien perdre de son immensité, ni de son expression géologique, transformant tout à son échelle, ce paysage auguste, vu à travers le temps, respire.

ಲ☙಼ಃ

Chaque année, à la pleine lune de novembre, au moment où le courant du Tonlé Sap se renverse, on tend une corde à travers. Et au cours d'une fête, le roi arrive en grand cortège dans sa maison flottante d'où part cette corde et la sectionne. Par ce geste symbolique, supprimant la barrière qui les retenait captives, il libère les eaux et leur permet de s'élancer vers la mer. Trois nuits durant, les chanteuses de la cour font entendre les chants Sakrava qui sont des salutations à la lune; et les trois jours enclos dans ces nuits sacrées, des courses de pirogues ont lieu. Tel est le thème de cette fête, l'une des plus belles du royaume: la fête des eaux.

À cette occasion, elles reprennent le fleuve, les fines pirogues que nous vîmes en cale sèche, dans l'enclos des pagodes, sous les arbres. Écopées les feuilles mortes qui s'y étaient accumulées et l'or de leur décor rallumé, on les pousse à l'eau où, tout de suite, elles se meuvent telles de longs sauriens ressuscités.

Creusées dans un seul tronc d'arbre, quelques-unes de ces pirogues de course atteignent quarante mètres de longueur, sur un seul de largeur maîtresse. Touchant à peine l'eau, elles s'effilent presque invisibles dans l'air. Plus de quarante pagayeurs assis deux à deux, trois pilotes, un bouffon glapissant au centre et un patron accroché à l'avant, garnissent les plus grandes ou alors une vingtaine d'hommes, ramant debout. Un panneau de soie de deux coudées pend de leur pointe avant, qu'encadrent des floches de crins. À l'arrière flotte un pendentif de fleurs.

À l'heure de la course, le soleil tombe derrière la berge où la foule s'étage. En face, les grands nuages de la saison réverbèrent sa lumière déjà rouge. L'eau roule de l'amarante et des violettes. Chaque pirogue remonte lentement le courant et passe devant l'estrade flottante du roi, très près. Quarante petites pagaies plongent en même temps. L'eau jaillissante ruisselle sur les pagayeurs. Au centre, le bouffon se contorsionne et chante, en donnant le rythme, des phrases satiriques et légères que les piroguiers ponctuent d'un cri régulier. Cri joyeux, à deux temps : « Ha » au moment où les pagaies se lèvent, « Ya » alors qu'elles replongent. Ha...

Ya !... Le son mâle et joyeux roule, appuyant la pirogue qui, soulevée de l'avant à l'arrière, avance par bonds réguliers, passe, en présentant un à un ses couples d'hommes, puis ses barreurs. Ha... Ya !... Elle est passée. Et maintenant qu'elle s'éloigne, vue par l'arrière entre la levée régulière des pagaies et leur superposition perspective, elle semble un cloporte aux pattes luisantes. Une trentaine vont ainsi prendre le départ, à deux kilomètres en amont.

Elles réapparaissent tout à coup, grandissant de seconde en seconde, avec une vélocité incroyable, luttant trois à trois, l'eau hachée, blanchie, volatilisée le long d'elles. Les bras des piroguiers, dans une cadence folle, font à chacune des flancs haletants. À l'avant, un rameur agrippé par les jambes comme sur l'encolure d'un cheval emporté, brandit une rame dorée de laquelle il fend d'imaginaires obstacles. Tout se confond. Voilà le but. Des hurlements grondent et accourent à la berge avec les grandes vagues soulevées par cet assaut, tandis que les pirogues, rames, levées et courant sur leur erre, décrivent un vaste cercle.

Or, tout à coup, après cette ruée, il semble qu'elles soient mélancoliques et se souviennent les grands arbres qu'elles furent naguère, sur le bord de ce même fleuve, en cette heure crépusculaire où leur feuillage frissonnait d'aériennes caresses.

22 février.

Phnom Penh est une fille qui atteint l'âge de la puberté. Une crise de croissance la disgracie. Sur un plan qui pourrait être grandiose, on édifie par tranches une villote et le long de boulevards de vingt mètres de large s'alignent des villas de Viroflay, entourées de jardins riquiquis fleuris de linge familial au séchage. Autour d'une butte, le Phnom dressé comme un sein, couronné d'un stoupa trois fois centenaire et d'une pagode, on avait tracé un petit parc. Mais la pagode étant vieille, on l'a refaite en béton. On a flanqué la butte d'escaliers couverts de moulages. Et comme le parc était exquis, on y a mis une usine électrique. Pour faire les boulevards, on a pris de la terre le long d'eux, de sorte que pendant trente ans, les boulevards devinrent des digues, tandis que la ville s'enfonçait de chaque côté. Maintenant on bouche tous ces trous. Les maisons ayant été construites au niveau futur, elles attendent leur remblai sur des pilotis échasses : on voit le jour sous les murs des clôtures.

Un ancien canal, élargi pour fournir de la terre aux deux boulevards qui le longent, coupe la ville en deux. Aux basses eaux, il est à sec. Ses ponts enjambent de la verdure et les égouts y débouchent à ciel ouvert. Aux hautes eaux, ces mêmes ponts atteints par la crue emprisonnent ceux mois durant toute la batellerie. Alors, on va combler le canal. Paris ne s'est pas fait en un jour.

Le long du fleuve, on n'a pas encore pu trouver la place du port, il est donc partout. Dix kilomètres de berges étirées devant un des panoramas les plus beaux du monde servent d'avenue, de quais, de docks, de chantiers, d'entrepôts, d'appontements, de rue, d'esplanade où cent chaloupes chinoises embarquent et débarquent leurs voyageurs du matin au soir entre mille jonques ventrues. On charge et décharge des peaux, des barils de ciment, du bois, du charbon et des pierres ; des tonneaux et de la ferraille : tout ce qu'un port peut avaler et vomir, en pleine ville, devant les principaux magasins, le cercle, les pagodes, le collège et l'hôpital ; le long de l'avenue magistrale qui conduit de l'hôtel du Protectorat français au Palais royal. Ainsi les pompes officielles se déroulent parmi les coulis qui, pour les voir passer, laissent un temps, en épongeant leurs torses nus, sacs de riz et paniers de charbon de bois. Et à cela d'ailleurs tout gagne en pittoresque.

D'un côté, ville chinoise, de l'autre européenne — les Cambodgiens sont au Sud, en dehors, et peuplent les faubourgs. Malgré ces divisions, une pagode chinoise occupe la ville européenne avec des épiceries entre les deux banques ; par contre, les grands garages et une partie des services administratifs français sont installés en plein quartier chinois.

En 1863, Phnom Penh n'était qu'une bourgade de trois cents paillotes semblables à celles que nous venons de voir tout le long du fleuve. Elle n'était pas encore redevenue capitale après l'avoir été à plusieurs reprises, au cours des derniers siècles. Depuis, ses édiles tentent d'en suivre le développement, ajoutent comme ils peuvent des pièces à un vêtement toujours trop court. Aussi cette ville toute jeunette semble avoir tout manqué, depuis son port ensablé aux basses eaux, jusqu'à son aspect européen, type 1900, qui ne parvient pas à s'affirmer. Sauf quelques pagodes dont l'allure ne l'emporte que de peu sur celles que nous visitons du nord au sud du pays, aucun édifice d'art indigène authentique n'apparaît et les riches Cambodgiens, les opulents Chinois retirés des affaires, se rallient avec un enthousiasme enfantin au style comprador.

Il y avait, en 1903, trois cent cinquante Européens et on en comptait mille quatre cent cinquante l'année dernière, sans la troupe. En trente ans, les commerçants français, d'une vingtaine, ont passé à cent soixante. Ils ne vendaient que mille huit cents bicyclettes en 1921, en 1929 ils en ont écoulé cinq mille quatre cent cinquante. En 1910, la première automobile apparut ; la veille de la guerre, il en circulait trente-cinq ; en 1929, les cinq garages de la ville en placèrent deux mille neuf cent trente. Il fallut faire des routes pour ces automobiles. Cinquante kilomètres existaient en 1900 ; aujourd'hui, Phnom Penh est au centre d'une étoile routière empierrée et en partie macadamisée de deux mille quatre cents kilomètres de développement. Et dans cette jeune cité, circulent vingt-cinq mille Chinois, vingt-deux mille Annamites, trois cent cinquante Malais et Hindous. Quant aux Cambodgiens qu'on voit peu hors de leurs quartiers, ils sont trente-six mille.

Ces chiffres et ces dates suffisent à définir la ville, à expliquer son destin et en partie sa disgrâce et ses mérites. Comment aurait-elle de l'unité ? Son passé n'a pas laissé de trace, son avenir est indéfinissable. C'est une ville administrative et marchande, surtout chinoise et boutiquière. Son quartier royal et son palais où l'on s'attendrait à entendre une rumeur de monastère et à voir des dorures vénérables, se déploient battant neuf au soleil et entièrement reconstruits en béton armé, jusqu'aux écuries de l'éléphante blanche, princesse sacrée, toute jeune aussi.

೮⊛ʊ

Laissons donc cette ville qui sort du fleuve et des marais, effaçons-la dans un fondu de cinéma et courant à rebours du temps, sur ce fond récent qui, par notre artifice, va devenir brumeux comme du passé, superposons en gros plan la première Phnom Penh historique, telle que l'impeccable George Cœdès l'a sortie des chroniques.

Notre voyage sur le fleuve nous a mieux préparé d'ailleurs que la ville de nos architectes officiels à reconnaître en elle l'ancien village. Nous y abordons ce soir, tels ces deux mandarins versés dans la connaissance des emplacements favorables que le roi Ponhéa Yât y envoya au XVe siècle. La capitale de paillote et de bois que va projeter désormais notre appareil, à mesure que l'historien en ouvrira le diaphragme, prit le nom de « Capitale des Quatre Bras, heureuse maîtresse du Cambodge, nouvelle Indraprastha, noble, fortunée et frontière du Royaume ». Simplement.

Le roi ordonna une levée en masse des hommes corvéables et fit remblayer les berges afin d'empêcher le fleuve d'inonder la ville, préparant ainsi le port-boulevard de 1930. Il prit la terre à l'ouest, laissant un vaste marécage que nous venons de combler en aspirant le sable du fleuve à l'aide d'un matériel perfectionné venu d'Amsterdam.

Le palais de Ponhéa Yât se trouvait à la place du marché actuel, de la Banque de l'Indochine et de la Résidence-Mairie. Pour alimenter le palais en eau, les constructeurs du XVe siècle creusèrent un canal qu'ils recouvrirent de dalles et de remblais : c'est celui que les édiles de 1880 agrandirent et que ceux de 1931 vont reboucher.

Au Nord, pour fortifier la ville, on creusa un fossé qui prit le nom de « ruisseau des forgerons chinois », parce que là, Sa Majesté avait installé des fabricants d'armes. Ce canal porte toujours ce nom et même un pont étonnant construit il y a quarante ans : il est fait de quatre tours carrées destinées aux chaînes d'un tablier qu'on devait lever, afin de laisser passer les jonques — mais jamais ce pont ne fonctionna. Alors on enleva les chaînes, on laissa les tours et ce pont-levis immobile sert aujourd'hui de porte septentrionale à la ville.

Au Sud, « la Capitale, heureuse maîtresse du Cambodge », fut aussi défendue par un autre ruisseau qui n'a point disparu, ni son nom : le ruisseau du vieillard Kév. Ainsi la ville d'aujourd'hui s'encadre exactement entre ses limites de jadis où fonctionnaires et habitants construisirent leurs demeures à leur gré. Deux fils du roi y établirent aussi leurs palais, le premier, au sud-est de celui qu'habite le roi Sisowath Monivong ; le second, là où nous trouvons aujourd'hui le dépotoir de la ville. Évolution.

Déjà s'était élevée, quelque soixante ans plus tôt, la colline qui devait donner à la ville son nom d'aujourd'hui, Phnom Penh : la colline de la dame Penh. Cette dame avait fait grossir avec de la terre rapportée une butte qui se trouvait devant sa maison, afin d'y déposer quatre statues de bronze et une de pierre, trouvées miraculeusement dans un tronc d'arbre flottant. De ce tronc, on fit la charpente de la chapelle qui abrita les idoles. Comme elle tombait en ruine à son arrivée, Ponhéa Yât restaura cette chapelle, empierra le sommet du Phnom et y éleva un grand stoupa, peut-être celui que nous voyons encore.

ဢ❈ɷ

Moins de cent ans après la fondation de Phnom Penh, les premiers Européens y apparaissent qui appellent la ville Churdumuco, de son nom pâli Catummukha : les Quatre Faces. C'étaient des Portugais, prêtres et aventuriers venus de Malacca. Mais afin de courir l'aventure à leurs trousses, changeons de savant et feuilletons un petit in-4°, relié en veau plein à nerfs, fleurdelisé d'or, édité à Valladolid en 1604, retrouvé et traduit avec enthousiasme par M. Cabaton.

J'imagine, quant à moi, qu'on ne portait pas à cette époque de casques, ni de costumes coloniaux, et je vois nos Castillans débarquer aux Quatre Bras sous le béret plat, avec emmanchures ornées d'épaulettes en bourrelets, braguette en forme de coquillage, haut-de-chausses à lanières et peut-être guêtrés de cuir souple. Cheveux courts et barbe en pointe à cause de la fraise dont on ne devait pourtant pas s'encombrer par cette chaleur... Sûrement, enfin, une longue épée au ceinturon, le poignard à droite suspendu à une cordelière, le pistolet bien assujetti et la poire à poudre en scapulaire — oui, bien armés, nous le verrons, et la moustache retroussée.

De beaux noms, au surplus : Diego Belloso, originaire d'Amarante, Pantaléon Cornero, de Lisbonne, Francisco Machado et Blas Ruiz, Chul de Diaz et Col de Monteiro. Et ces conquérants ne se firent pas faute aussitôt d'engrosser de belles Khmères dont les arrière-petits-fils, dans la Phnom Penh d'aujourd'hui, rappellent, lorsqu'ils se nomment et comme s'ils portaient une fleur rouge à la bouche, les sonores patronymes.

Le rideau fermé devant les monuments de la scène angkorienne ondulait encore de sa chute récente. Il se releva sur des hommes nouveaux, la rondache au poing et l'arquebuse sous le coude. À travers les fumées des feux sacrés et les chants sanscrits murmurés dans les monastères, le roman castillan vient traîner sa plume. La jonque chinoise croise la flûte portugaise. Le Kshatrya, descendant de son éléphant de combat badigeonné de fiel humain, voit débarquer des condottières. La dernière inscription est à peine gravée que le roi qu'elle célèbre a pour amis et conseillers deux bretteurs : Blas Ruiz et Diego Belloso.

Comment se trouvent-ils sur la colline de la dame Penh vers 1590 ? On ne sait. Belloso est marié à une princesse, parente du monarque. Blas Ruiz avait été déjà esclave au Champa et n'avait guère plus de vingt ans. Le roi l'envoie à Manille demander du secours au Gouvernement espagnol. En cours de route, il est pris par les Siamois avec deux compagnons et on les ligote sur une jonque. Ces singuliers prisonniers se débrouillent pourtant, tuent les Siamois et s'emparent de la jonque.

Qu'y avait-il dans cette embarcation à tête de monstre, longue et basse sur l'eau et qui semblait sortir des bas-reliefs ? Des brûle-parfums, des clochettes, des moustiquaires en soie de Chine pour les divinités ? Était-elle épicière comme celle que nous visitâmes, il y a quatre jours sur le Bassak ? Non. Blas Ruiz y trouve cinq cents arquebuses, cent couleuvrines, cinquante faucons, cent jarres de poudre, des masques de fer (?), des lances et des morions, dix mille chausse-trapes. Satisfait de son inventaire, il continue tout bonnement son chemin sur Manille et y arrive en même temps que Belloso qui, croyant mort son compère, était parti de son côté afin de le remplacer dans sa mission.

Ils obtiennent l'aide sollicitée par le roi khmer et repartent pour le Cambodge avec deux jonques, une frégate, un amiral, cent vingt Espagnols — je vous laisse imaginer les trognes de ces volontaires ! Il y avait, en plus, des religieux. Ils arrivèrent aux Quatre Bras pour apprendre que le roi, peu avant, avait fui au Laos avec sa famille et qu'un usurpateur occupait le trône. Se seraient-ils dérangés pour rien ?

Ils commencent par se battre à la tête de soixante hommes contre trois mille Chinois, en tuent trois cents, leur prennent, après ce discours, leurs biens et leurs jonques, y ajoutant les jonques et les biens des autres Chinois qui avaient fui. Ah ! les Chinchoes d'alors commerçaient moins tranquillement qu'aujourd'hui !

Blas Ruiz et Belloso, ainsi mis en goût, investissent le Palais royal, font sauter la poudrière et tuent l'usurpateur d'un coup d'arquebuse, ni plus, ni moins. Alors des milliers de Cambodgiens les attaquent et les poursuivent. Il pleut à torrent. On passe les rivières à la nage et, ajoute ingénument le bon père dominicain qui raconte ces faits : « Avec les rondaches, on couvre les bassinets des arquebuses afin que la poudre ne se mouille ». Le chef khmer se risque un peu trop et le voilà, malgré ses amulettes, ouvert en deux d'un coup de hallebarde. Vlan ! Les Castillans regagnent leurs bateaux et s'en vont, « regrettant de n'avoir pu faire mieux et davantage ».

Ruiz et Belloso sont avec eux, mais pour faire le tour de l'Indochine sur la frégate de l'amiral. Ils débarquent sur la côte d'Annam et se mettent à marcher vers l'Ouest, traversent la chaîne annamitique, les savanes immenses de l'Interland, des embûches de toutes sortes, se rendant simplement au Laos rechercher le roi khmer dépossédé, car ils avaient de la suite dans les idées.

Comme leurs hauts-de-chausses devaient être usés et leurs manches bouffantes dégonflées, ils arrivèrent à poil, comme des Moïs — sauf une ceinture où passer leurs épées. Ils retrouvent leur roi, réveillent son courage, jettent du poivre sur son ambition et du piment dans ses souvenirs, le ravigotent, le rajeunissent, l'empoignent par les épaules, le ramènent au Cambodge, le remettent sur son trône. Il y eut de la bousculade. Et les voilà chacun gouverneur de province et comblés de faveurs.

Ah ! Je vois d'ici ce repos ! Quelles cuites, mes amis ! Et des orchestres forcenés toutes les nuits, et de fins sampots de soie autour des cuisses, et des pièces de brocart importées de Bombay qui servaient de jupes aux danseuses et où les rois taillent leurs costumes de couronnement ; et des douches avec l'eau du fleuve bien rafraîchie où macéraient des fleurs de jasmin, et des massages à l'huile de coco, par d'autres mains que celles de ma vieille sorcière de Viléa, et des cigares gros comme des manguiers, et des bijoux bien pesés et l'épée à coquille ajourée sous la main !

Mais nos deux gouverneurs apprennent que deux frégates espagnoles ont été attaquées et capturées par des Japonais et des Cambodgiens conduits par un chef malais. Ils laissent là cigares, danseuses, soies molles, eau fraîche, tout — sauf les flamberges ; volent au secours de leurs compatriotes, tombent dans un guet-apens et sont massacrés. On emporta leurs têtes dans une cage comme deux tourterelles...

Entre Phnom Penh et Kompong Luong où nous passerons demain, le XVIIe siècle continua les drames commencés au XVIe. Des missionnaires évangélisent après le Père de La Bastide, tué. Les Hollandais viennent à la rescousse, ouvrent un comptoir en 1643 ; Regesmortes, le gérant, est tué à l'instigation des Portugais. La cour passe d'une rive à l'autre, monte et descend le courant au fil des intrigues, des usurpations et des assassinats. Un beau matin, un nouvel aventurier portugais débarque, arrivant du Brésil : Melchior Diaz. Il acquiert, on ne sait comment, un titre princier, se marie avec une Cambodgienne, et ses enfants reçoivent du roi une province en apanage.

Entre temps, ou se greffant sur la guerre de partisans, il y a les incursions siamoises et annamites. Tantôt on fortifie Phnom Penh ou la capitale du moment ; tantôt on plie bagage pour filer vers le Nord si ce sont les Annamites qui attaquent, ou vers le Sud quand les Siamois dévalent du Nord. Dès qu'il se croit tranquille, le roi fait construire un palais dans la région où il se trouve, signe une ordonnance accordant à une classe de mandarins le droit d'avoir un sceau orné d'un cercle de feuillage et un parasol à deux volants. Sur ce, un usurpateur le tue et l'on se bat entre soi jusqu'à ce que la branche légitime ou un ministre adroit, sous forme de régence, reprenne le pouvoir.

L'un de ces rois se convertit à l'islamisme et voilà les Malais en faveur. Un autre se marie avec une princesse Annamite dont les compatriotes entrent dans la place. Les Siamois reviennent alors mettre de l'ordre, brûlent les villages et repartent avec une armée d'otages. Après cette saignée, on allait respirer, mais un gouverneur de province se révolte sous la pression d'un bonze illuminé et marche sur la capitale. Il fut arrêté par des inondations si violentes que tout le bas pays fut dévasté. Les fauves se réfugiaient sur les hauteurs que les habitants leur disputaient.

En 1816, on retrouve un Monteiro, métis portugais, ministre prévaricateur, « qui forniquait en outre avec les femmes et les concubines d'autrui qu'il attirait chez lui et qu'il s'appropriait ». On le prend, il s'échappe, on le rattrape : décapité. Son fils, qui avait aidé à cette fuite, fut arrêté aussi, mais le roi le gracia « parce qu'il avait agi par piété filiale comme il le devait ».

Puis on vit une femme recevoir la couronne sous la domination Annamite. On l'accusa bientôt d'être la maîtresse de l'ambassadeur ennemi. Cette accusation la rendit folle. Phnom Penh perdit son nom et prit celui de Nam Vian, annamite. Trois envoyés de l'empereur Ming Mang administraient le Cambodge avec une telle discrétion qu'ils imposèrent le costume et le chignon annamites aux fonctionnaires cambodgiens. Alors le peuple se révolta, appela le Siam à l'aide qui arriva et après quatre années de guerre, expulsa les Annamites. Nouveau roi khmer sur le trône à Phnom Penh (1845). On démolit les forteresses et, avec les briques, on bâtit des pagodes, mais on était de nouveau vassal du Siam.

En 1855, un Français, le premier je crois, que les chroniques connaissent, M. de Montigny, porteur d'un ordre de Napoléon III, fut accrédité pour passer un traité d'alliance avec le roi cambodgien. Il arriva à Kampot, sur le golfe de Siam, trouva qu'il faisait trop chaud et que Phnom Penh était trop loin. Il se déclara fatigué et s'en retourna sans avoir vu le monarque qui l'attendait avec impatience. Ah ! si ce singulier diplomate avait été Blas Ruiz...

En 1859, survient Mouhot, naturaliste français, chargé de mission par l'Angleterre. Il traverse le Cambodge, découvre Angkor qu'avaient découvert avant lui le Révérend Père Bouillevaux et, trois cents ans avant Bouillevaux, les Pères Dorta et Luis de Fonseca, dominicains. En passant, notre naturaliste, qui cherchait des petites herbes et des papillons mais ne faisait pas de politique, est reçu par le roi khmer à Oudong, dans son palais, à trente kilomètres au nord de Phnom Penh. Après cette audience, il continue sa route et va mourir d'épuisement à Luang Prabang.

Le roi d'Oudong meurt peu après, laissant trois fils. L'un est couronné, un des deux autres proteste et voilà de nouveau le pays à feu et à sang, tandis que le nouveau roi se sauve à Battambang (encore au Siam) avec les attributs de la royauté. On vit un cul-de-jatte à la tête d'une troupe livrer bataille aux royaux. On le tua et on le pendit tête en bas et poitrine ouverte. Il se balancerait encore à son arbre sans le soleil et les rapaces.

À ce moment, arrive sur une petite canonnière un lieutenant de vaisseau français. C'était en avril 1862, en cette saison-ci, aux basses eaux. Il s'appelait Doudart de Lagrée et fut notre premier représentant au Cambodge. Sa seule présence pacifia ce pays en ébullition depuis des siècles. Qui connaît ce nom en France ? La hardiesse de l'aventurier, mais sans épée dégainée. Une main de fer qu'il ne ferma jamais : il suffisait qu'il la levât. Il ne fit que passer, cueillit le pays comme un fruit, mit sur le trône les rois qui règnent depuis, dissipa les factions sans délacer la housse de ses canons, et après avoir hissé nos couleurs sur Phnom Penh fumante, il poursuivit sa mission d'études jusqu'en Chine — où il mourut.

Peu après, un autre Français survint, petit de taille, ancien postier : Auguste Pavie. Il avait fait le tracé de la ligne télégraphique Phnom Penh-Bangkok, et montré de telles qualités qu'on le chargea ensuite de missions. Il passe, recrute des Cambodgiens, se met en route sous un chapeau de feutre à larges bords et marchant sur sa grande barbe, ce qui n'avait pas d'importance, parce que cet explorateur conquérant allait pieds nus. Après avoir parcouru le Cambodge, il monte au Laos comme Blas Ruiz et Diego Belloso, le traverse du sud au nord, faisant la carte, sans une arme dans ses bagages, racontant le soir, à l'étape, des histoires, et plantant de temps en temps un petit drapeau à trois couleurs. Après quelques années de cette promenade, il se trouve que toute la terre du Laos a collé aux pieds déchaux de cet évêque laïc et est devenue française.

En dix ans, ces pays volcaniques où depuis quatre siècles des aventuriers de tous poils taillaient des croupières dans un désordre politique invraisemblable, deux Français ignorés alors et qui, depuis, le sont restés presque autant, ces pays, ils les ont conquis, délivrés de leurs cauchemars ; l'un en y promenant ses regards, l'autre sa barbe, à petits pas, à petits moyens, mais à grandes idées ; sans avoir heurté une conscience, laissé un mort, un seul petit mort indigène derrière eux — seulement mille et mille villages aux bords des eaux, au cœur des terres et qui, depuis, chaque soir, regardent au loin s'ils ne voient pas revenir ces voyageurs...

24 février.

En quittant Phnom Penh sur le Tonlé Sap, on navigue entre deux rives où, sur une trentaine de kilomètres, on ne rencontre presque pas de Cambodgiens, mais une population annamite catholique et malaise mahométane. Après les pagodes cambodgiennes et chinoises de la capitale, voici dans son faubourg la cathédrale, la chapelle d'un séminaire, un carmel. Les portes des cases et les faîtes des toitures en tuiles sont surmontés de croix. Et voici une mosquée.

Puis tandis que la rive gauche s'aplatit et devient déserte et inculte, la rive droite dresse un étroit rideau d'arbres et de maisons malaises, jusqu'à Kompong Luong, la « Rive Royale », dernière capitale où la cour était installée au moment où le Protectorat français déploya son pavillon sur le royaume. À l'ouest, de molles collines d'une centaine de mètres dressent dans un ciel pâle et dense les fines silhouettes des sépultures royales.

La belle pagode de Kompong Luong date de cette époque historique si récente et dont on ne sait déjà plus grand-chose. Elle est fortement métissée, mais vénérable et vétuste. Sa porte et ses abords sont chinois et ses fenêtres s'encadrent de stucages vaguement inspirés de ces glaces et fauteuils Louis XIV et Louis XV importés autrefois au Siam par la Compagnie des Indes. Ce qui reste est du bel art cambodgien du milieu du XIXe siècle. Il subsiste quelques tuiles de chéneau à about décoré d'une femme en prière et, à l'intérieur, un exquis autel secondaire à l'image d'une tour élancée, formant vitrine et finement sculpté. On voit aussi un coffre-fort avec une fente pour recevoir les offrandes.

L'ancien palais se trouvait à quelque cinq cents mètres au sud-ouest. Plus rien n'en reste que des ondulations de terre imperceptibles, recouvertes de touffes de bambou, entre des rizières à perte de vue. Un vieil architecte m'a retracé de mémoire et d'après les on-dit le plan de ce caravansérail que j'ai donné ailleurs.[1]

Il ne correspond pas à l'idée que nous nous faisons en France d'un palais royal asiatique. C'était une sorte de village couvert en paillote et un petit lac entouré de palissades. La demeure du monarque était en bois, la salle du trône en pisé. Les archives, les tapis et le trésor étaient renfermés dans un pavillon construit sur pilotis, au milieu d'un étang qui le préservait de l'incendie et des termites. Le naturaliste Mouhot a donné une bonne description de ce palais, lorsqu'il y passa en 1859. Depuis, la vie des berges n'a que peu changé. La même lumière flamboyante les recouvre. Et peut-être y vibre encore la dernière des intrigues que le palais disparu distillait et que les nuits mystérieuses y déposaient comme la rosée.

C'est là que se déroule en trois journées mon roman, *Monsieur de Lagarde, roi*, nourri d'événements choisis dans trois siècles d'histoire d'où j'ai sorti les personnages qui répondaient à mes desseins : roi, princesses et frères de la côte. J'ai copié les chroniques en y prenant ce qui me frappait comme, dans ce journal de route, je copie ce que je vois. Il est regrettable que trop d'héroïsme en pousse l'aventure et qu'au lieu de choisir un héros médiocre et mince, je m'y sois épris d'un individu passionné dont les gestes se déploient comme une queue de paon, d'un aventurier qui s'arc-boute à de grands événements comme Belloso et tire à boulets rouges sur son destin. C'est regrettable, dis-je, car cet héroïsme ne satisfait pas le goût d'aujourd'hui et les éditeurs me retournent l'un après l'autre mon manuscrit, poliment.

Eh!, premier matelot, mon ami, qui porte tatoué sur le côté un des singes du Ramayana ; noir Cambodgien en qui je vois ce chef couvert d'amulettes que Blas Ruiz fendit en deux d'un coup de hallebarde — laissons, je te prie, ces rives mauvaises inspiratrices.

25 février.

Au-delà de Kompong Luong, les pêcheries commencent. Elles viennent de s'installer et se multiplieront jusqu'au Grand Lac. Je renonce à les compter depuis hier. Qu'est-ce qu'une pêcherie au Cambodge, en cette

---

[1] *Recherches sur les Cambodgiens*. Challamel, éd., Paris.

saison, sur le Tonlé Sap ? J'y fais serpenter la chaloupe, les examine et j'ai peine à croire à ce que je viens de voir. J'ai encore les yeux brûlés par les eaux réverbérant le soleil, éblouis par d'étranges visions, je ne sais quel chaos de mercure, de nacre et d'acier où piochent des corps humains à gestes désordonnés.

D'abord un endroit reconnu favorable : estuaire, sortie d'île, tournant ; endroit repéré depuis des générations par des hommes aquatiques qui connaissent jusqu'à son goût chaque filet d'eau. Ensuite, à certains signes saisonniers, à des présages secrets, un hectare de fleuve est isolé par une claie de rotin, muraille mobile et verticale, plantée dans la vase, ouverte avec astuce en amont, hermétique partout ailleurs. Dans ce parc, des branches, des troncs morts sont immergés pour servir de gîtes. Et l'on attend quinze jours, un mois. Le courant redescend du Grand Lac et fait le rabatteur. Enfin, un jour jugé propice, le patron de pêcherie dispose sur la rive des offrandes aux génies. On ferme l'immense piège et une vingtaine d'hommes sautent à l'eau.

Par des manœuvres prudentes, d'une lenteur mesurée, la muraille peu à peu se resserre. Les claies en trop sont à mesure roulées et emportées par des sampans. Un chenal d'environ trois mètres de largeur sur une cinquantaine de long subsiste enfin du périmètre initial, sans qu'à un seul moment de cette longue et pénible réduction un seul espace de la grosseur du bras reste ouvert. Déjà l'eau ainsi « comprimée » se plisse de singuliers frissons. Partout et incessamment, des nageoires la déchirent, les unes aiguës, les autres longues et ondulant comme des franges, d'autres ouvertes, pareilles à des ailes de chauve-souris.

À ce moment, une claie transversale part du fond du couloir et avance comme un piston dans son cylindre, poussée par des hommes épaule à épaule. Tous les mètres, il faut la lier aux murailles du corridor et se reposer. Derrière cette cloison, une seconde suit dans le cas où la première laisserait passer du poisson, puis derrière cette deuxième claie, un filet traîne à tout hasard. Peu à peu, le couloir est réduit de moitié, puis de deux tiers...

Nous tombons sur une pêcherie à ce moment extraordinaire. Il est midi et demie. Deux grands sampans sont amarrés à l'extrémité, en aval du couloir, de cette poche de soixante-dix mètres carrés sur un mètre vingt de profondeur, impasse terrible dans lequel depuis la veille, à l'aube, le poisson est poussé ; où le conduisent irrésistiblement ses fuites désespérées et les plus véloces ; ce poisson qui, depuis un mois, s'accumulait et grouillait dans un parc d'un hectare !

L'eau bout, fulgure, crève sous des bondissements insensés. Cent bêtes s'élancent en l'air à la fois, jusqu'à deux mètres de hauteur, se tordent et retombent ou se heurtent par des sauts obliques et dans des claquements contre les claies qui les pressent. D'énormes corps s'affalent avec fracas après avoir mêlé au soleil des formes rendues floues par la vitesse et le rutilement ; ou bien de fines fusées, aiguës comme un grincement, tracent des paraboles de projectiles. Trois hommes restés emprisonnés dans cette chaudière, titubent, s'agrippent à des piquets, parmi ces corps écailleux, sous les coups de ces mufles mous qui butent contre eux, égratignés par des nageoires, fouettés par des queues nerveuses, environnés de cette multitude inconcevable de coups de sabres entrecroisés.

Je saute sur le premier sampan qui va recevoir cette chair, sorte de bachot recouvert d'une claie, et dont j'évalue la capacité à cinq mètres cubes environ. D'autres sont amenés en réserve. Autour, on a immergé à demi des casiers de rotin, trappe bâillante, destinés à conserver vivants les poissons de choix. Tout est prêt. Des femmes, des enfants arrivent en renfort sur des pirogues, tout ce monde annamite né dans le poisson, vivant de lui, jusqu'à la mort.

On jette un fort panier cylindrique aux hommes restés dans le vivier. Ils l'attrapent par les anses, le plongent et le ressortent d'un monstrueux effort. Il vibre et flamboie dans le temps que d'autres hommes le saisissent et, d'un seul coup, trente kilos de poissons roulent dans le bachot. En une demi-heure, celui-ci est plein, enfoncé dans l'eau jusqu'à son bord, sous une masse vivante qui agonise. Un autre le remplace... Et tandis que ce décharnement du fleuve se poursuit, je songe que cent pêcheries pareilles à celle-ci, en cette même heure et jusque dans les lacs à cent kilomètres d'ici, et depuis un mois, et durant trois mois encore... Je songe au bord de la Seine, au pêcheur à la ligne du pont Mirabeau... Et je considère ces cinq mètres cubes de poissons, écrasés à mes pieds, là, sous le soleil, deux tonnes, trois tonnes peut-être, ce magma...

Les uns ont le corps reptilien. D'autres, plats comme des soles. Une femme en tire un par la queue : il a un mètre de long. Je revois ma « lumière de l'eau », mais ils pèsent vingt livres et sont truffés de six lunules noires de chaque côté du ventre. Beaucoup bavent de longs barbillons cassés et qui saignent. D'autres sont tuilés d'écailles que leur colère décolle comme la colère hérisse les poils des chiens. Des corps à section triangulaire comme un toit, le ventre plat, la tête plate. Il y en a de cylindriques ou en forme de serpettes, de massues, de fruits, de feuilles charnues qu'on dirait déchirées. Les poissons encore vivants nagent dans du poisson qui meurt. Des morts, à ce contact, ressuscitent et fouettent l'air avec un crépitement électrique. Une agitation atroce, éperdue. Le soleil allume des yeux sanglants. Oh ces bouches molles, mouvantes, suceuses ! Le blanc des ventres est glacial, gluant le gris vert des dos. Des rampements. L'immense fleuve opaque, le paysage vide, le ciel morne et toute cette vie insoupçonnée, secrète, mise à nue, révélée en quelques instants, si lourde, toute en spasmes innombrables ! Du sang rouge sort de cette chair blanche et métallique.

Les caïlocs, rois des poissons, mouchetés, à nageoires vertes, sont mis de côté ainsi que d'autres espèces savoureuses, par des fillettes. Des poissons de mer enfin, adaptés au fleuve, surgissent : des soles, de petits maquereaux et une raie monstrueuse qui n'entrait pas dans le panier et que le couli leva, ses dix doigts enfoncés dans elle, tandis qu'une queue fine comme une lanière cinglait l'air.

Et tout à coup, je me penche, tends l'oreille. Qu'est-ce ? Le froissement mouillé de ces corps ? Non. Des heurts de nageoires ? Mais non. Un dégorgement de bouches squameuses, les déchirements de branchies qui se dessèchent ? Non plus. C'est une rumeur de petits cris graves, grêles, imperceptibles, un grelottement d'une affreuse tristesse. Je suppute le comique d'une méprise possible. Mais il faut me convaincre ; j'entends un murmure d'agonie surprenant et pathétique. En dépit des dictons, ces poissons sanglotent. Les savants sans doute savent cela, mais moi, je le découvre. Chaque sanglot est bref. Son timbre est celui d'une corde tendue qui se casse. Isolé, il serait insaisissable, mais mille poissons meurent à la fois, à cinquante centimètres de mon oreille.

Cette pêcherie, d'importance moyenne, emploie une quinzaine de coulis permanents. Une centaine de femmes ouvrent, vident le poisson et le font sécher au soleil. On sort du fleuve, chaque année en trois mois, quatre-vingts tonnes de poissons dont les têtes et les vessies fournissent dix mille litres d'huile. Le matériel de rotin et de bambou, les nasses, la batellerie, sont évalués dix mille piastres. Le patron en fait cinq mille de bénéfice net. Voilà ce qu'il m'apprend en m'offrant du thé dans sa jonque.

Elle est luxueuse et vernie. L'autel des ancêtres rutile au fond, entre deux arbres nains et séculaires, plantés dans des pots de faïence. Deux panneaux de bois précieux portent, incrustés en nacre, les nom et profession du maître de céans. En haut, un bandeau de soie rouge, brodé de caractères de bon augure en fils d'or, couronne cette chapelle. Une guitare, plate, ronde et de bois clair est suspendue à une cloison, parmi des photographies de famille. Le plancher, encore humide d'un lavage, reflète le ciel qui tombe d'une fenêtre. Un poisson-lune à bec de perroquet, évidé et séché dans sa forme sphérique, pend en lanterne au-dessus d'un lit de camp si luisant qu'il semble liquide.

Sur la terrasse où s'ouvre ce salon de jonque, un couli, à l'ordre du maître, m'apporte une dizaine de poissons disposés en étoile, sur un panier plat, d'aspect moitié velours et moitié fer étamé. Voilà, me dit-on, les meilleurs poissons qu'on puisse manger.

— Et le caïloc ?

À ma question, l'Annamite répond par une mine dégoûtée et je comprends qu'à côté de ces losanges, le caïloc est un poisson pour guenilleux. Je demande alors pourquoi on ne trouve pas le premier sur le marché de Phnom Penh, puisque ç'en est la saison. L'expression dégoûtée de mon hôte se change en moue suffisante : cette espèce de poisson est très rare, les riches Chinois se la disputent à n'importe quel prix, retiennent d'avance les envois des pêcheries. Aussi les Européens (y compris les gros pontes) ne l'ont jamais vue sur leurs tables, parce qu'ils n'y entendent rien en poissonnerie, que leurs cuisiniers se lèvent trop tard ; et d'ailleurs, si ces cuisiniers trouvaient par hasard un de ces poissons au marché, ils commenceraient par le garder pour eux...

Ah ! qu'il est difficile de connaître un pays ! Depuis plus de trois lustres, je fais profession d'étudier celui-ci, j'y voyage en toutes les saisons et ce n'est qu'aujourd'hui que je découvre que les poissons y chantent comme les cygnes et que ceux qui parent nos tables les plus réputées et qui me semblaient excellents sont ceux dont les Chinois ne veulent pas ! Qu'on imagine, si l'on peut, avec quelle effusion j'ai remercié mon riche pêcheur, et quelles recommandations j'ai faites à Eh! quand je le vis se charger du fastueux présent.

D'ailleurs, j'aurais dû le laisser faire. Pris d'un zèle trop stimulé, n'enveloppa-t-il pas ce poisson dans le voile noir de l'appareil photographique !

26 février.

De Kompong Chhnang, « la rive des marmites », jusqu'au Grand Lac, le fleuve n'est plus qu'une vaste pêcherie. Il se ramifie en plusieurs petits bras par où l'eau redescend du lac et qui font sur la carte une image de la circulation du sang.

Presque pas de végétation sur les berges basses que les crues inondent. Les villages de pêcheurs et de poissonniers se succèdent, sans ombrages. Peu de pagodes : la population, surtout annamite, n'apparaît qu'à la saison de la pêche. On voit des échafaudages de bambous hauts de quatre ou cinq mètres et longs d'une centaine où des sennes au séchage tendent une brume marron que glace le soleil.

Trois bambous couchés sur l'eau desquels se détourne la chaloupe. Remarquez qu'ils ne bougent pas et que des liens de rotin y sont noués. Ce sont les flotteurs de filets dormants qui cloisonnent le fleuve. Les mailles sont calculées pour que certaines espèces de poissons s'y engagent jusqu'aux ouïes et restent cloués à ces murailles invisibles. Et, à tout moment, nous rencontrons ces bambous. Point de pirogue qui ne porte des pêcheurs au carrelet, au haveneau. Partout déposées sur les berges, suspendues aux cases, des nasses compliquées, merveilles de rotinage, compartimentées avec une astuce déconcertante, furent retirées de l'eau ce matin, et, ce soir, y seront replongées. L'une d'elles, accrochée à l'arrière d'une jonque, sert de cage à un couple de merles mandarins.

Une mousse ignoble de détritus de poisson en décomposition descend le courant sur une eau moirée d'huile et dégage une odeur immonde. Elle s'écoule d'un village entièrement pavoisé de petits cerfs-volants pendus à des cordes tendues, couleur de paille et d'ambre, maintenus par des T de bambou : autant de poissons ouverts qui sèchent. Des groupes de femmes, les bras ensanglantés et couverts d'écailles, les préparent à coups de tranchet, inlassablement. Il faut aller vite, apprêter dans l'heure la manne déversée par chaque sampan pour éviter qu'elle ne pourrisse — et le flot qui apporta la bête vivante en emporte les déchets. Les oiseaux ichtyophages ne guettent pas, ne cherchent plus, et d'un vol lassé choisissent dans les tas. En trois mois, tout le poisson que deux millions d'hommes mangeront le reste de l'année, que des centaines de jonques emporteront à Singapore et sur les côtes malaises, ce poisson est pêché, ouvert, séché dans cette région, ses boyaux pourrissent là, son huile bout là, et là scintillent ses écailles.[2]

Voilà donc un lieu mortel, probablement unique au monde, où, chaque matinée, le plus de bêtes vivantes se réunissent et crèvent à la fois sans combattre, sans autre défense qu'une fuite inutile, sans que l'homme les tue, en somme !

Et comme il reste encore quelques arpents de berge déserte et trop d'eau qu'un filet ne filtrerait pas et trop de poisson vivant, nous croisons de tardives compagnies de pêcheurs qui montent s'installer. En grappe à la suite d'une chaloupe haletante, une trentaine de jonques et de sampans sont remorqués flanc à flanc et proue à poupe, sans voiles, gouvernail abandonné, chargés de filets neufs, de claies roulées, de pièges, de pieux, de cordes — et de personnel couché parmi des vivres accumulés, sous des tentes de paillote.

14-15 mars.

Au Nord-Ouest du Cambodge, dans un cirque de collines et de montagnes dont l'une atteint près de mille mètres d'altitude, à quelques kilomètres de la frontière du Siam, un chasseur birman arriva il y a un demi-siècle. Comment ce chasseur, traversant le Siam de l'Ouest à l'Est, parvint il jusque-là ? On ne sait.

Il trouva sur le sol des pierres d'un noir bleuâtre semblables à des caillots de laque. Les Cambodgiens de la région s'en servaient avec indifférence pour tirer des étincelles de leurs briquets. Le voyageur en serra quelques-unes dans sa ceinture et retourna dans son pays où il apprit que ces pierres à briquet étaient des saphirs. Il revint aussitôt avec une centaine de ses compatriotes laveurs de sable et tailleurs de gemmes, quelques tours de lapidaires, et cette colonie birmane s'installa dans ce creux de terre cambodgienne qui prit le nom de Païlin (prononcez Païline).

Elle ne devint pas khmère pour deux raisons. La première parce que l'exportation des saphirs sur Bangkok, puis sur l'Europe payant bientôt et largement les expatriés, ils firent venir parents, femmes et amis. La deuxième, parce que les premiers colons moururent rapidement : il n'en reste que quelques-uns aujourd'hui. Mais, en cinquante ans, un deuxième village se construisit à quelques kilomètres du premier. Cinq ou six pagodes furent fondées, de style birman. Et maintenant cette petite Birmanie est peuplée de trois mille âmes qui vivent comme dans la mère-patrie et où chaque maison, ou presque, abrite un mineur, un tailleur ou un marchand de saphirs.

---

[2] L'année dernière, 120.000 tonnes dont 24.000 ont été exportées (statistiques officielles).

Un millier de Cambodgiens leur servent de coulis et de cultivateurs. Les épiceries sont, bien entendu, chinoises. Nous sommes au Cambodge, Protectorat français, mais les papiers d'affaires, factures et reçus de ces Birmans sont rédigés en anglais. Enfin, une partie des marchandises que vendent les Chinois sont siamoises, et anglaises aussi. Mais cet étonnant mélange auquel quiconque est vite habitué qui voyage en Extrême-Orient, s'étant dosé petit à petit selon les besoins, donne un tout homogène où domine nettement la couleur birmane.

Ces jours-ci sont fériés : hier, pleine lune de mars, celle de l'année que les Birmans célèbrent avec le plus de faste. Ma tournée sur le fleuve était terminée. Mong Phothy, Birman, représentant des lapidaires de Pailin et qui tient boutique à Phnom Penh où il vend des étoffes, des réveille-matin, des pierres fausses, un peu de tout, sauf des saphirs, entra dans mon bureau. Il est ventripotent, avec un masque de Vitellius. Il s'inclina et m'invita à aller assister aux fêtes. Païlin est à 400 kilomètres de Phnom Penh. Nous sommes partis le lendemain avant l'aurore, mon Birman me laissant tout juste le temps de prendre ma brosse à dents, m'assurant que je trouverais tout ce qu'il me faudrait chez sa sœur où il comptait que je descendrais avec lui. Nous brûlâmes Kompong Chhnang que j'avais touché en chaloupe huit jours plus tôt, déjeunâmes à Pursat d'une soupe chinoise brûlante. Entre ce poste et Battambang, nous eûmes les loisirs, en dépassant une charrette qui transportait un madrier de huit mètres de long, de recevoir ce madrier dans notre garde-boue arrière, car la charrette tourna à notre passage. Et, à midi, nous entrions à Païlin, dans un autre monde.

❦

C'est un village entouré de montagnes et de collines, ai-je dit. Il commence au pied de l'une de ces dernières et s'allonge jusqu'au centre du cirque en compagnie d'une rivière. Un sanctuaire couronne la colline autour de quoi le paysage s'ouvre comme une corolle. Au lieu d'étamines, une forêt de cocotiers. De gros insectes y sont nichés qui se gorgent de pollen : les pagodes. Quel contraste avec le fleuve et ses berges plates ! La terre est d'une richesse inouïe, ocre rouge, et je songe sans cesse qu'en nourrissant cette végétation épaisse et rapide, elle sue du saphir.

Il est partout. Les hommes, jusque dans le village même, grattent à peine le sol, le lavent dans de petits cours d'eau vermiculaires et les gemmes restent dans leurs paniers. Ce saphir n'est pas de très belle qualité, présente souvent des défauts et des nuages, mais il a cours sur le marché européen. Peu importe ces considérations de lapidaires : ici la terre a des caillots de sang bleu. On y trouve aussi, mais plus rarement, des topazes qui, brutes, surgissent gonflées et humides comme des larmes.

Jour de fête — mais n'est-ce pas toujours fête en ce village fortuné, isolé, avec sa race, son âme, ses traditions étrangères, par ce cirque éloigné du Cambodge ? Une longue rue déclive y serpente entre de grandes maisons en planches, bien menuisées, couvertes de chaume, dont quelques-unes à étage et balcon, pourvues de frises ajourées par des décors sculptés. Chacune est entièrement ouverte sur la rue comme une boutique. On y voit un petit autel fleuri honorant une image du Bouddha encadrée ou sa statuette dans une vitrine, des balancements de berceaux, des hommes paisibles, les cuisses gainées dans un caleçon de tatouages, assis le dos à la rue, devant des tours horizontaux qu'ils actionnent d'un pied. La pierre fait un léger crissement de papier qu'on déchire et, de maison en maison, ce susurrement se prolonge. Les jeunes femmes, qui ne se cachent point comme les Cambodgiennes, font leurs petits ménages, c'est-à-dire rien, parées de tous leurs bijoux, enveloppées de sarongs à grands dessins, nonchalantes, gaies et le chignon piqué de fleurettes. Les parquets luisent sous l'entretien incessant des pieds nus.

Devant ces maisons, entre elles et la rue, sans discontinuer, des jardinets de deux coudées de large sont fleuris comme des reposoirs. Leurs arbustes : rosiers, gardénias, jasmins, champas, hibiscus aux fleurs suspendues comme des petits lustres, sont corsetés de bambou afin que les chèvres ne les ravagent pas. Au-delà des toits s'élèvent des cocotiers magnifiques, plus grands, me semble-t-il, que dans le reste du Cambodge.

❦

Mon Birman courtois avait eu le temps de télégraphier, la veille, à sa famille, de sorte que, lorsque j'arrivai, la maison était prête à me recevoir. Une salle unique de dix mètres de long, huit de large, et autant du parquet à la poutre faîtière. Une chambre haute y avance comme un balcon, encadrée de sculpture et où l'on accède par un escalier intérieur. C'est cette chambre qu'on m'a réservée, d'où je domine, tel un oiseau dans sa cage, la vaste pièce et, au-delà, la rue.

Je n'y suis pas seul : un Bouddha assis sur un lotus est installé dans son autel comme moi dans la chambre ; autel dominant ma chambre comme ma chambre domine la maison. Le Dieu est entouré de bouquets en papier, derrière trois veilleuses. Ce matin, il y avait devant cet autel, sur un guéridon, l'offrande journalière : une assiette de riz, un verre d'eau, une banane et des fleurs tombées d'un frangipanier invisible autour des aliments. Lit de camp, moustiquaire très blanche, des nattes neuves partout où je devais poser les pieds. Comment dire mieux l'urbanité de ces Birmans ?

La sœur de Mong Phothy, veuve, courtière en pierres précieuses, vit là, entourée de famille et de serviteurs, solide matrone d'une quarantaine d'années. Je n'ai encore vu d'elle, tant il m'a ébloui, qu'un étonnant sarong décoré de guitares, de bandes géométriques et de fleurs extravagantes, le tout colorié et jeté au hasard sur un fond topaze brûlée. Tissu anglais fait spécialement pour les colonies, dans le goût indigène d'après des modèles locaux (ce que nous ne savons pas faire en France). Et puis, près de la matrone, sa dernière fille — elle en a eu je ne sais combien — âgée de huit ans, dont je reste ébloui plus encore que par le sarong de la mère. Son nom ? On me le dit en birman, que l'oncle traduisit en cambodgien, ce qui donna, en français : « Émeraude ».

Émeraude, Aubergine, l'aristocrate et la roturière, la fillette de riches bourgeois et celle d'un premier matelot, la lapidaire et la potagère. Entre elles deux races, deux civilisations, deux castes, et le hasard des noms marquant les différences. Je retrouve en Émeraude la synthèse exquise de toutes ces mignonnes fillettes que je vois passer depuis ce matin, déjà pareilles à des femmes, sauf par la coiffure.

Cheveux d'un noir tel qu'ils en sont alourdis et minéralisés. L'huile de coco les glace. D'abord une frange fait le tour de la tête, bien lissée, trois doigts de large, coupée net. Au-dessus de cette frange et de la ligne bleue qui la sépare du reste des cheveux, le chignon est noué — pas l'escargot minable d'Aubergine — un chignon en cône, où une grosse rose sinon une fleur d'or est piquée. À sa base, une couronne d'orchidées d'un jaune perdu et analogues aux boutons d'or de nos prés. Un caraco très court s'évase, boutonné sous le bras, blanc ou de couleur très tendre, jamais passée : une couleur qui naît. Enfin, les hanches grêles entourées d'un sarong sans pli. Ainsi vont ces petites Birmanes, silhouettes de femmes vues de loin.

Leurs aînées portent le chignon en turban, la frange a disparu, mais point la couronne de fleurs. Leurs jupes sont à grands ramages. Leurs socques traînent deux notes, cloc, clôc, cloc, clôc, sur le sol. Quant aux hommes, le port fier et le masque grave, ils nouent un mouchoir sur l'oreille, comme des bandits corses.

❧❦☙

Je bois un soda tiède importé du Siam, d'un vert de menthe et qui a un goût de rouge à lèvre. Et ce fut pendant qu'elle préparait et allumait la lampe qu'elle avait posée sur le plancher, et dans la lumière soudain jaillissant de ses mains, que j'ai observé Émeraude, son chignon, ses fleurettes. Nous eûmes fini ensemble. Et elle me tendit la lampe comme une offrande.

Ma table est recouverte d'une nappe à jour. Au centre, dans un verre, un bouquet de roses jaunes et dans un autre verre un bouquet de cigares : ils ont vingt-cinq centimètres de long, le tabac est dans un tube de papier épais. Ils ressemblent à des mirlitons. Une coupe d'argent fortement repoussée de personnages mitrés, rocailleuse d'aspect, contient des cigarettes.

Émeraude me verse du thé. Elle me guette et, dès que je repose ma tasse, elle la remplit derechef. Je n'ai pas soif, n'aime pas beaucoup le thé, mais je bois, je bois pour ne pas ennuyer cette petite. Chaque fois que je mets de la cendre dans le cendrier, elle va la jeter dehors, essuie la coupe et la rapporte. Elle ne comprend ni le français, ni le cambodgien. Mais entendrais-je le birman, elle ne me parlerait pas davantage, parce que je suis infiniment grand et puissant, elle, infiniment humble et petite. Si je faisais des grâces, je l'épouvanterais. Je ne dois pas m'apercevoir qu'elle est là, déléguée par sa mère pour me surveiller, faire le vide de mon cendrier et le plein de ma tasse à thé, à pas muets sur le parquet. Elle porte un saphir pâle à chaque oreille, de menus cercles d'or aux poignets et, en pendentif, une pièce de cinq livres, frappée du profil de la reine Victoria, impératrice des Indes.

La mère trône au fond de la salle, sur une natte, entourée d'accessoires. En fumant un mirliton, elle donne des ordres comme si elle parlait toute seule, mais que ses gens entendent à travers les cloisons. On pile quelque chose dans la cuisine. Et dans la rue, sous un ciel couvert, entre la double rangée des reposoirs, comme une procession, la population va à la fête, par groupes.

Les hommes, de leur côté, les jeunes, dégingandés, vêtus moitié à l'européenne, ce qui leur donne l'allure de voyous, et moitié d'étoffes drapées qui suffisent à les faire ressembler à des princes. L'un d'eux passe à bicyclette et freine avec son gros orteil appuyé sur le pneumatique. Un imbécile fait du genre avec un passe-montagne : où a-t-il pu le trouver ? Les hommes mûrs sont moins occidentalisés, vieux brigands aux joues trouées sous des foulards ponceau ou vert jade, serrés autour de la tête qui conserve le chignon. Ce sont ceux-là dont on dit que, jadis, aux temps troublés, ils transportaient leurs pierres précieuses en se les glissant sous la peau par des incisions qu'ils laissaient cicatriser avant de se mettre en route, et qu'ils rouvraient, parvenus à destination dans la lointaine Rangoun. Ces groupes alternent avec ceux des femmes, sans se mêler.

Celles-ci vont, pareilles de ligne, de style, de démarche — mais différentes de couleurs. Comme le chemin descend, elles se reçoivent à chaque pas, le torse un peu en arrière, sur la jambe pliée. Elles portent des ombrelles plates à nervures de bambou, roues par transparence qu'elles font pivoter incessamment, du bout des doigts, et à peine ombrées par ces auréoles tournoyantes de papier peint. Je ne retrouve pas ces faces fermées, cette démarche altière des Cambodgiennes, mais une douceur nonchalante, je ne sais quelle gaieté secrète qui s'épancherait à leur insu et que les fleurs des chignons et le soin des coiffures font précieuses et intouchables. Les mères, les vieilles, les servantes vont derrière cette jeunesse ravissante comme une bonne brise qui pousserait des feuilles.

☙✻☙

Elles étaient plus belles, hier soir, sous la pleine lune. La rutilance des soies se décomposait en couleurs inconnues. Les conversations se taisaient à ma présence et le cortège ne passait plus que sur le cloc clôc des socques. Les fleurs jaunes étaient blanches ; blanches les petites vestes que je voyais, au jour, rose-pâle, vert de jeune pousse. Car il y avait une lanterne près de moi et, dans sa lumière, ces couleurs originelles réapparaissaient sur une longueur de quelques pas. Un gris argent fut vert-amande et, repris par la lune, redevint gris-argent. D'invisibles bijoux luisaient et je les perdais aussitôt. Des femmes passaient qui n'étaient pas celles que je voyais approcher, mais que je reconnaissais pourtant lorsqu'elles s'éloignaient. Les bavardages reprenaient vie au moment où les couleurs se redécomposaient. Plus d'une heure, j'ai regardé déambuler ces filles du saphir, alternativement lunaires et charnelles.

Or, peu à peu, par une analogie nullement fortuite qui m'obséda dès que je l'eus perçue et qui, de minute en minute, devint de plus en plus saisissante, je trouvais un rythme baudelairien à ce cortège. Il coulait mystérieux et confié. L'abandon de ces passantes n'avait d'égal que leur apprêt. Des bijoux révélés qui fondaient ! Ces chignons émaillés ! Ces marches glissées et ces bras balancés ! La lune et la lanterne, ces deux lumières artificielles ! Oui ! C'était bien l'heure où, vibrant sur sa tige, chaque fleur, chacune de ces femmes, s'évaporait ainsi qu'un encensoir ! L'heure du charbon, de l'argent. Le saphir sous ces pas et des palmes sur ces têtes…

Ce que le génie du poète sut créer par un artifice plein de sang et de recherche passionnée — ah ! comment une telle chose peut-elle être possible ! — se recréait dans la même cadence devant moi, en ce coin perdu de la terre. Et ces bouches prudentes, ces groupes alternés comme des strophes, ces silhouettes de soie, ces filles sous leurs chevelures en fleurs, les vieilles qui avaient enfanté ces êtres chatoyants — murmuraient :

« Entends, ma chère, entends la douce nuit qui marche. »

༄ ❀ ༄

Une heure après, je suis allé à la fête, sur la grande place qui domine Païlin, où le village commence, au pied de sa colline. Celle-ci, je ne la voyais plus, mais seulement en plein ciel la pagode de son sommet, illuminée. Lorsque je quittais des yeux la foule, les boutiques, le théâtre en plein air éclairés par des lampes perfectionnées à vapeur d'essence, j'éprouvais la même surprise à retrouver chaque fois, là-haut, dans la nuit et symétrique à la lune, cette grosse étoile rapprochée. Et ce n'était qu'après en avoir ainsi repéré le sommet, que je retrouvais la colline devenue impondérable comme une buée.

Je me mêlai au peuple en liesse distillé par la nuit. Les hommes s'agrégeaient autour des lampes et des tableaux de jeux parmi lesquels celui des trente-six bêtes dominait. Une ligne de petits cafés bornait la place, au-delà d'un étroit canal d'eau courante. Dans ces échoppes minuscules, faites de bambous et de paillotes, pavoisées de drapeaux, on ne consommait que du thé, du café et de la limonade. En vis-à-vis, la foule longeait une autre ligne d'éventaires illuminés, leurs vendeuses souriantes et mignardes, accroupies derrière des tranches de canne à sucre en brochettes, des mangues vertes, des gâteaux aux fruits ambrés des palmiers sucre, des carrés d'ananas et des pompons de fleurs. Une déambulation silencieuse : les Orientaux se réjouissent dans leurs yeux et dans leur cœur, sans cris ni gambades ; pas un pétale ne tombe d'un chignon.

Une troupe foraine de danseuses cambodgiennes donnait la comédie. Dans ce milieu étranger, le Khmer semblait mafflu et vulgaire. Les cheveux en brosse des femmes se dressaient, élémentaires et rudes, près de ces chignons birmans tordus avec soin et langueur. Sous la paillote bien éclairée où les baladins évoluaient, les Birmanes de Païlin se déployaient en gradins, immobiles, contemplantes. Tout d'un coup, leurs rires s'assemblaient aux farces des bouffons et aussitôt leur sagesse redevenait attentive et silencieuse.

Quelle mosaïque ! Je ne retrouvais plus les couleurs puissantes vues le jour sur les étoffes. Plus gaies, plus claires encore, elles s'unifiaient entre le bleu céleste, un lilas aigu et un vert que je n'ai vu que là : le vert du cœur du concombre, entre les graines. Je crus découvrir que presque toutes ces couleurs du soir non seulement étaient claires, vives dans leur clarté — mais encore froides. Oui ! Offrir instinctivement au jour brûlant, sous le soleil enragé, des jupes qui ressemblent à des forêts et à des jardins, tissées dans l'or, le sang et le cuivre ; mais la nuit n'enrouler sous la lune que des étoffes à luisances froides pour tout ornement — quelle leçon et quelle discipline dans cette collaboration populaire avec l'activité céleste !

༻༶༺

J'avais assisté à la toilette d'Émeraude. Dans son sarong rose raidi par quelques fils d'argent, elle s'était assise sur la natte devant sa mère. Celle-ci avait préparé d'avance de la poudre dans un papier de journal et sur un carré de feuille de bananier encore humide un petit tas de fleurs. Un mouchoir dénoué contenait les bijoux de la fillette.

Elle ne bougeait pas. La matrone la modelait, muette, choisissant chaque fleur et la place de chaque fleur. La frange de cheveux fut égalisée minutieusement par un peigne qui ressemblait à un ébauchoir. À chaque coup de doigt maternel, la petite plus ornée sortait de l'ombre, brillait d'une facette de plus sous la meule centenaire. La poudre appliquée du plat de la main se mêla à l'ambre de son visage repétri. Ses chaînettes sautoirs furent passées autour de son cou, par longueur croissante et dans un ordre que deux heures de promenade ne devaient pas modifier. L'obéissance de l'enfant était faite de certitude. Elle savait ce qu'elle devenait aussi sûrement que si un miroir le lui eût montré. Elle vérifia seulement la fermeture de ses bracelets. Et quand la mère eut fini son œuvre traditionnelle et sans retouche, l'enfant se leva, idole. Je lui pris la main et nous partîmes à la fête.

Mon pas, près d'elle, faisait trembler la terre. Je me sentais une carrure d'aurochs, à peine équarri, et de forme barbare. Jadis, alors que je n'étais qu'un métis de Huns et de Francs, d'autres hommes déjà ornaient cette mignonne telle que je la tenais et le Bouddha souriait pour elle depuis dix siècles. Il y a, malgré la marche rapide de certaines races, quelque chose que leur progrès et leur intelligence ne rattrapent pas et qu'emportent les civilisations lentes. Je le tenais à la main et ça flottait à mes côtés.

FIN

Quelques chapitres d'*Eaux et Lumières* ont été publiés,
de septembre à novembre 1931, dans la revue
TERRE AIR MER - LA GÉOGRAPHIE.

Exotic Visions of French Indochina

Unknown Temples of Ancient Cambodia.
ISBN: 978-1-934431-90-0

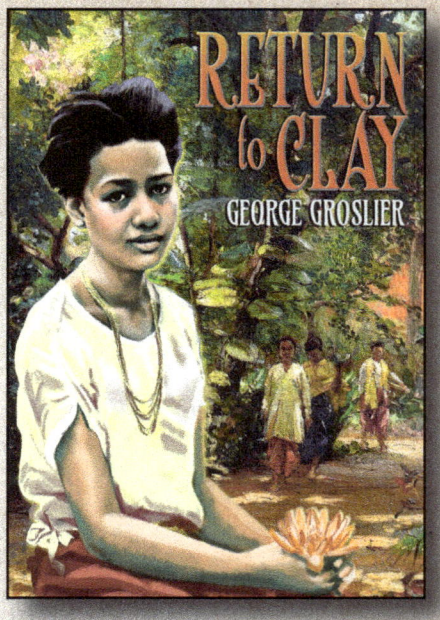

A Romance of Colonial Cambodia.
ISBN 978-1-934431-94-8

Paintings of 1920s Indochina.
ISBN: 978-1934431917

A Romance of Colonial Cambodia.
ISBN: 978-1-934431-16-0

Exotic Visions of French Indochina

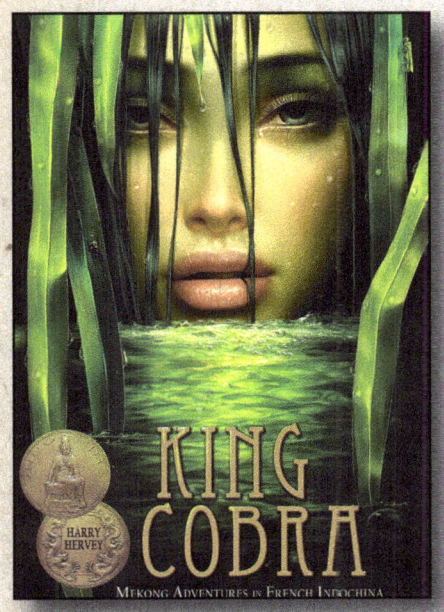

An American in 1920s Indochina.
www.HarryHervey.org

A sensual novel of East and West.
www.HarryHervey.org

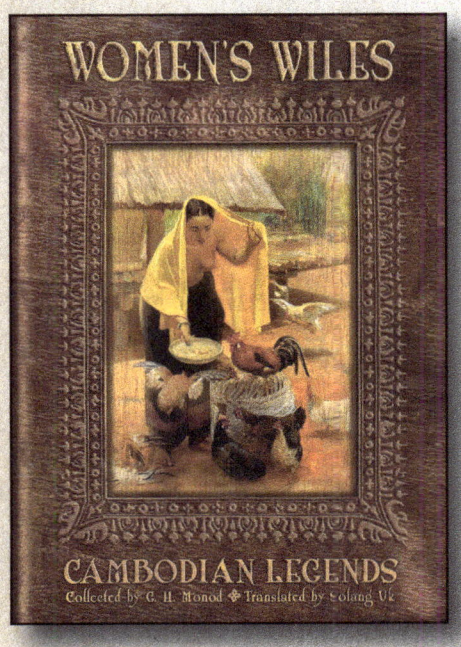

Fantastic folktales from ages past.
ISBN 978-1-934431-21-4

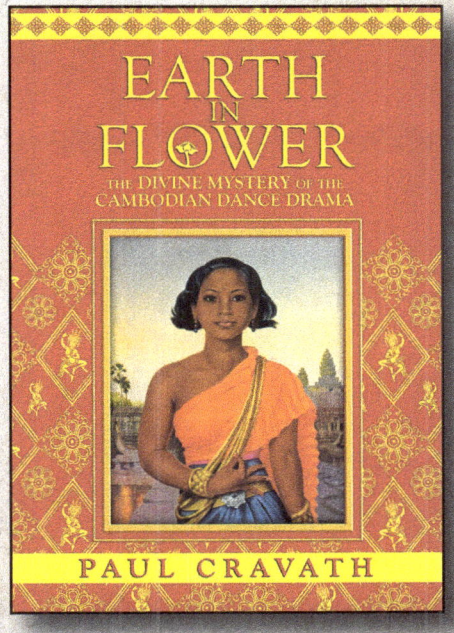

Analysis of Cambodian dance
www.EarthInFlower.com

CAMBODIAN DANCERS

ANCIENT & MODERN

George Groslier

An Artistic Record of Cambodia's Ancient Dance Tradition

With a foreword by Princess Buppha Devi of Cambodia, this modern English translation includes the complete contents of the rare original 1913 publication, more than 250 illustrations, extensive background materials, a bibliography, index and an original biography of the author by historian Kent Davis: *Le Khmérophile: The Art and Life of George Groslier*.

www.CambodianDancers.com

www.ingramcontent.com/pod-product-compliance
Lightning Source LLC
Chambersburg PA
CBHW051252110526
44588CB00025B/2966